MORE PRAISE FOR *THE ETHICAL SLUT*

"*The Ethical Slut*, in this new and expanded edition, is the definitive guide for creating and sustaining all conscious relationships—polyamorous, open, alternative, *and* monogamous. Don't enter into another relationship without it!"

—Barbara Carrellas, author of *Urban Tantra*

"Dossie and Janet's blend of good humor and forthright honesty makes for some of the best writing I have found on sexually complicated relationships and blended family options. Engaging, disarming, forthright—this is the book for those of us still brave enough to make the ethically complex choices."

—Dorothy Allison, author of *Bastard Out of Carolina*

PRAISE FOR THE FIRST EDITION

"I couldn't stop reading it, and I for one identify as an ethical slut. This is a book for anyone interested in creating more pleasure in their lives . . . a complete guide to improving any style of relating, from going steady to having an extended family of sexual friends."

—Betty Dodson, PhD, author of *Sex for One*

"A useful guidebook for radical relationship travelers . . . experienced counsel to those on the polysexual frontier."

—Ryam Nearing, *Loving More* magazine

"A postgraduate course in ethical relationships of every stripe. The authors pull no punches and are totally outrageous. . . . You'll never be bored."

—Stan Dale, DHS,
founder of the Human Awareness Institute

"Frank, funny, and full of practical advice . . . life-saving validation, empathy, and plenty of insider tips from the experienced big sisters you probably weren't fortunate enough to have."

—Deborah Anapol, PhD, author of
Polyamory: The New Love without Limits

THE
ETHICAL
SLUT

A PRACTICAL GUIDE TO POLYAMORY, OPEN RELATIONSHIPS & OTHER ADVENTURES

2ND EDITION
UPDATED & EXPANDED

DOSSIE EASTON AND JANET W. HARDY

CELESTIAL ARTS
Berkeley

Published in the United States by Celestial Arts, an imprint of the Crown
Publishing Group, a division of Random House LLC, a Penguin Random House
Company, New York.
www.crownpublishing.com
www.tenspeed.com

Celestial Arts and the Celestial Arts colophon are registered trademarks of
Random House LLC.

Previous edition published as *The Ethical Slut: A Guide to Infinite Sexual
Possibilities*, by Dossie Easton and Catherine A. Liszt (Greenery Press, 1997).

LIBRARY OF CONGRESS CATALOGING-IN-PUBLICATION DATA
Easton, Dossie.
  The ethical slut : a practical guide to polyamory, open relationships, and other
adventures. — 2nd ed., updated & expanded / Dossie Easton and Janet W. Hardy.
     p. cm.
  Includes index.
  Summary: "A practical guide to practicing polyamory and open relationships in
ways that are ethically and emotionally sustainable"—Provided by publisher.
  1. Non-monogamous relationships—United States. 2. Free love—United States.
3. Sexual ethics—United States. 4. Sex—United States. I. Hardy, Janet W. II. Title.

  HQ980.5.U5E27 2009
  306.84'230973—dc22

                                        2008043651

ISBN-13: 9781587613371

Printed in the United States of America

Cover design by *The* Book Designers
Interior design by Chris Hall, Ampersand Visual Communications

15 14 13 12 11 10 9

Second Edition

Contents

Acknowledgments

We'd like to thank: Amy, Kay, and Bo; Barbara Carrellas; Cecelia & Corwin; Jennifer Collins; Betty Dodson; "E"; Jaymes Easton; "Finn"; Rae Goldman; Francesca Guido; Kai Harper; Lizzard Henry; Sybil Holiday; Ron Hoffman; Richard Karpinski; J Kimball; Laurie and Chris; Deirdre McGrath; Sunny Knight; Adric Petrucelli; Carol Queen; Reid & Marsha; Paul Romano; Maggi Rubenstein; Ruth and Edward; "Sockermom"; Doug Stinson; Susan S.; "Snow White"; Ben Taber; Miles Taber; Tom and Katy; Jay Wiseman; Lolita Wolf; and Joi Wolfwomyn.

With special thanks to our editor, Brie Mazurek, and all our dear lovers, friends, clients, colleagues, families, and advisors.

Acknowledgments

PART ONE

Welcome

CHAPTER ONE

Who Is an Ethical Slut?

MANY PEOPLE DREAM of having an abundance of love and sex and friendship. Some believe that such a life is impossible and settle for less than they want, feeling always a little lonely, a little frustrated. Others try to achieve their dream, but are thwarted by outside social pressures or by their own emotions, and decide that such dreams must stay in the realm of fantasy. A few, though, persist and discover that being openly loving, intimate, and sexual with many people is not only possible but can be more rewarding than they ever imagined.

People have been succeeding at free love for many centuries—often quietly, without much fanfare. In this book, we will share the techniques, the skills, the ideals that have made it work for them.

So who is an ethical slut? We are. Many, many others are. Maybe you are too. If you dream of freedom, if you dream of intimacy both hot and profound, if you dream of an abundance of friends and flirtation and affection, of following your desires and seeing where they take you, you've already taken the first step.

Why We Chose This Title

From the moment you saw or heard about this book, you probably guessed that some of the terms here may not have the same meanings you're accustomed to.

3

What kind of people would revel in calling themselves sluts? And why would they insist on being recognized for their ethics?

In most of the world, "slut" is a highly offensive term, used to describe a woman whose sexuality is voracious, indiscriminate, and shameful. It's interesting to note that the analogous word "stud," used to describe a highly sexual man, is often a term of approval and envy. If you ask about a man's morals, you will probably hear about his honesty, loyalty, integrity, and high principles. When you ask about a woman's morals, you are more likely to hear about whom she shares sex with, and under what conditions. We have a problem with this.

So we are proud to reclaim the word "slut" as a term of approval, even endearment. To us, a slut is a person of any gender who celebrates sexuality according to the radical proposition that sex is nice and pleasure is good for you. Sluts may choose to have solo sex or to get cozy with the Fifth Fleet. They may be heterosexual, homosexual, or bisexual, radical activists or peaceful suburbanites.

As proud sluts, we believe that sex and sexual love are fundamental forces for good, activities with the potential to strengthen intimate bonds, enhance lives, open spiritual awareness, even change the world. Furthermore, we believe that every consensual sexual relationship has these potentials and that any erotic pathway, consciously chosen and mindfully followed, can be a positive, creative force in the lives of individuals and their communities.

Sluts share their sexuality the way philanthropists share their money: because they have a lot of it to share, because it makes them happy to share it, because sharing makes the world a better place. Sluts often find that the more love and sex they give away, the more they have: a loaves-and-fishes miracle in which greed and generosity go hand in hand to provide more for everybody. Imagine living in sexual abundance!

Your Authors

Between us, we represent a fairly large slice of the pie that is sexual diversity.

Dossie is a therapist in private practice in San Francisco, specializing in relationship issues and alternative sexualities. She has identified as lesbian for the past twenty-five years and still values her experience as both bisexual and heterosexual before that. She has always been a slut. She committed to an open sexual lifestyle in 1969 when her daughter was newborn, and taught her first workshop on unlearning jealousy in 1973. She has spent about half of her adult life living single, sort of, with families of housemates, lovers, and other intimates. She currently makes her home with her partner in the mountains north of San Francisco.

Many of you may remember Janet from the last edition of this book as Catherine A. Liszt, a pen name she used back then when her sons were still minors. Now that they're grown and independent, she has gone back to using her real name. Janet lived as a teenaged slut in college but then essayed monogamy in a traditional heterosexual marriage for well over a decade. Since the end of that marriage, she has not considered monogamy an option for her. While most people would call her "bisexual," she thinks of herself as gender-bent and can't quite figure out how sexual orientation is supposed to work when you're sometimes male and sometimes female. She's married to a bio-guy whose gender is as flexible as hers, which is less complicated than it sounds. She makes her living as a writer, publisher, and teacher.

Together, we have been lovers, dear friends, coauthors, and co-conspirators for a decade and a half, in and out of various other relationships, homes, and projects. We are both mothers of grown children, both active in the BDSM/leather/kink communities, and both creative writers (Dossie of poetry, Janet of personal essays). We think we're an excellent example of what can happen if you don't try to force all your relationships into the monogamous till-death-do-us-part model.

Sexual Adventurers

The world generally views sluts as debased, degraded, promiscuous, indiscriminate, jaded, immoral adventurers—destructive, out of control, and driven by some form of psychopathology that prevents them from entering into a healthy monogamous relationship.

Oh, yes—and definitely not ethical.

We see ourselves as people who are committed to finding a place of sanity with sex and relationships, and to freeing ourselves to enjoy sex and sexual love in as many ways as may fit for each of us. We may not always know what fits without trying it on, so we tend to be curious and adventurous. When we see someone who intrigues us, we like to feel free to respond, and, as we explore our response, to discover whatever is special about this new, fascinating person. We like relating to people and are quite gregarious, enjoying the company of different kinds of people and reveling in how our differences expand our horizons and offer us new ways to be ourselves.

Sluts tend to want a lot of things: different forms of sexual expression, different people, perhaps men, or women, or people in between, or some of each. We are curious: what would it be like to combine the energies of four or five people in one incandescent sexual encounter? What would it be like to share erotic energy with that person who has been our best friend for years and years? What would it be like to share a household with multiple friends and lovers? What would it be like to be intimate with someone who is very different from us?

Of course, each slut is unique, with virtues and faults and diverse needs and values. Some of us express different parts of ourselves with different people. Some of us love flirtation for its own sake. Some of us make an art form out of sex. Some of us find these parts of our lives so important that sluttiness is a basic part of our identity, one of the ways we define ourselves, while others drift in and out of sluttiness according to desire and circumstance.

Sluts are not necessarily sexual athletes—although many of us do train more than most. We value sex, not as a way to set records, but for the pleasure it brings us and the good times we get to share with however many wonderful people.

We love adventure. The word "adventurer" is sometimes used pejoratively, suggesting that the adventurous person is immature or inauthentic, not really willing to "grow up" and "settle down" into a presumably monogamous lifestyle. We wonder: what's wrong with having adventures? Can't we have adventures and still raise children, buy houses, and do the work that's important to us? Of course we can; sluts qualify for mortgages just like everybody else. We tend to like our lives complicated, and the challenge of maintaining stable work and home lives while discovering new people and ideas is just what we need to keep us interested and engaged.

One of the most valuable things we learn from open sexual lifestyles is that our programming about love, intimacy, and sex can be rewritten. When we begin to question all the ways we have been told we ought to be, we can begin to edit and rewrite our old tapes. By breaking the rules, we both free and empower ourselves.

We hate boredom. We are people who are greedy to experience all that life has to offer and are also generous in sharing what we have to offer. We love to be the good time had by all.

What's New Here

In the decade-plus since we wrote the first edition of *The Ethical Slut,* we've learned a lot. Dossie, in her therapy practice, has worked with hundreds of singles, couples, and moresomes who are trying to navigate the uncharted pathways of nontraditional relationships, and she has developed new concepts and tools that have proven very helpful to them. Janet has moved out of the relationship she was in at the last time you saw her, has spent several years as a single slut, and has negotiated a relationship with a new lover who went on to become her legal spouse. We've also become (if we say so ourselves) better writers, both individually and together.

If you read the first edition of this book, you'll see a lot of new material in here, and you'll notice that the old material has been substantially rewritten and reorganized. You'll also notice one major change—this book contains many exercises that you can use to explore your feelings and chart your progress as you read the book, either on your own or together with a partner or partners.

So, whether you're an old friend or a new acquaintance, we're happy to welcome you into our book, and into our slutty, happy lives.

The Language in This Book

When you sit down to write a book about sex, as we hope you one day will, you will discover that centuries of censorship have left us with very little adequate language with which to discuss the joys and occasional worries of sex. The language that we do have often carries implicit judgments: If the only polite way to talk about sexuality is in medical Latin—vulvas and pudendas, penes and testes—are only doctors allowed to talk about sex? Is sex all about disease? Meanwhile, most of the originally English words—cock and cunt, fucking, and, oh yes, slut—have been used as insults to degrade people and their sexuality and often have a hostile or coarse feel to them. Euphemisms—peepees and pussies, jade gates and mighty towers—sound as if we are embarrassed. Maybe we are.

Our approach to a sex-positive language is to reclaim the original English words and, by using them as positive descriptors, wash them clean. Hence our adoption of the word "slut." You will also find in this book words like "fuck" and "cock" and "cunt" used, not as insults, but to mean what they actually mean.

Furthermore, cultural blind spots can show up as centrisms such as couple-centrism, heterocentrism, and eurocentrism. Nonmonogamy, extramarital sex, open relationships, all define themselves by what they *aren't*, thus implying that they're some exception to the "normal" relationships that "normal" people have.

"Polyamory" is a brave new word, coined by Morning Glory Ravenheart Zell around 1990 and currently, we are thrilled to report, included in the *Oxford English Dictionary*. Formed from Latin and Greek roots that translate as "loving many," this word has been adopted by many sluts to describe their lifestyles, often abbreviated as "poly," as in "I am a poly person." Some use it to mean multiple committed live-in relationships, forms of group marriage; others use it as an umbrella word to cover all forms of sex and love and domesticity outside conventional monogamy. *Polyamory* has moved into the language so rapidly that we think maybe the language has been waiting for it for a very long time.

In this new world of sex and relationships, new terms get coined all the time to describe, or attempt to describe, the ever-changing spectrum of ways in which people arrange their lives. If, as you're reading, you encounter a term you don't understand, please check the Glossary in the back, where we've defined these terms for you.

Finally, we are doing our best to make the language in this book as pansexual and gender neutral as we can: we are writing this book for everybody. Pansexual means including everyone as a sexual being: straight, bi, lesbian, gay, transgendered, queer, old, young, disabled, perverts, male, female, questioning, in transition. The examples and quotes in this book have been drawn from throughout the huge array of lifestyles we have encountered in our combined seven decades of sluthood: there are infinite "right" ways to be sexual, and we want to affirm all of them.

8

CHAPTER TWO

Myths and Realities

THOSE WHO SET OFF down the path of exploring new kinds of relationships and new lifestyles often find themselves blocked by beliefs—about the way society should be, the way relationships should be, the way people should be—that are both deeply rooted and unexamined.

We have all been taught that one way of relating—lifelong monogamous heterosexual marriage—is the only right way. We are told that monogamy is "normal" and "natural"; if our desires do not fit into that constraint, we are morally deficient, psychologically disturbed, and going against nature.

Many of us feel instinctively that something is wrong with this picture. But how can you dig up and examine a belief that you don't even know you hold? The ideal of lifelong monogamy as the only proper goal for relationships is so deeply buried in our culture that it's almost invisible: we operate on these beliefs without even knowing we believe them. They're under our feet all the time, the foundation for our assumptions, our values, our desires, our myths, our expectations. We don't notice them until we trip over them.

Where did these beliefs get started? Often, they evolved to meet conditions that no longer exist.

Our beliefs about traditional marriage date from agrarian cultures, where you made everything you ate or wore or used, where large extended families helped get this huge amount of work done so nobody starved, and where marriage was a working proposition. When we talk about "traditional family values," this is the family we are talking about: an extended family of grandparents and aunts and cousins, an organization to accomplish the work of staying alive. We see large families functioning in traditional ways in America today, often in cultures recently transplanted from other countries, or as a basic support system among economically vulnerable urban or rural populations.

Curiously, controlling sexual behavior didn't seem to be that important outside the propertied classes until the Industrial Revolution, which launched a whole new era of sex-negativity, perhaps because of the rising middle class and the limited space for children in urban cultures. Doctors and ministers in the late eighteenth century began to claim that masturbation was unhealthy and sinful, that this most innocent of sexual outlets was dangerous to society—nineteenth-century childrearing manuals show devices to prevent babies from touching their genitals in their sleep. So any desire for sex, even with yourself, became a shameful secret.

But human nature will win out. We are horny creatures, and the more sexually repressive a culture becomes, the more outrageous its covert sexual thoughts and behaviors will become, as any fan of Victorian porn can attest.

In his lectures to young communists in Germany during the rise of Hitler and the Nazis, psychologist Wilhelm Reich theorized that the suppression of sexuality was essential to an authoritarian government. Without the imposition of antisexual morality, he believed, people would be free from shame and would trust their own sense of right and wrong. They would be unlikely to march to war against their wishes, or to operate death camps. Perhaps if we were raised without shame and guilt about our desires, we might be freer people in more ways than simply the sexual.

The nuclear family, which consists of parents and children relatively isolated from the extended family, is a relic of the twentieth-century middle class. Children no longer work on the farm or in the family business; they are raised almost like pets. Modern marriage is no longer essential for survival. Now we marry in pursuit of comfort, security, sex, intimacy, and emotional connection. The increase in divorce, so deplored by today's religious right, may simply reflect the economic reality that today most of us can afford to leave relationships in which we are not happy; nobody will starve.

And still modern puritans, perhaps not yet ready to deal with the frightening prospect of truly free sexual and romantic choice, attempt to enforce the nuclear family and monogamous marriage by teaching sexual shame.

We believe that the current set of "oughta-be's," and any other set, are cultural artifacts. We believe that Nature is wondrously diverse, offering us infinite possibilities. We would like to live in a culture that respects the choices made by sluts as highly as we respect the couple celebrating their fiftieth anniversary. (And, come to think of it, what makes us assume that such a couple is monogamous anyway?)

We are paving new roads across new territory. We have no culturally approved scripts for open sexual lifestyles; we need to write our own. To write your own script requires a lot of effort, and a lot of honesty, and is the kind of hard work that brings many rewards. You may find the right way for you, and three years from now decide you want to live a different way—and that's fine. You write the script, you get to make the choices, and you get to change your mind, too.

EXERCISE *Sluts We Know and Love*

Make a list of all the people you can think of who are not monoga-mous, including characters from TV, movies, books, and so on. How do you feel about each of them? What can you learn (positive or negative) from him or her?

Judgments about Sluts

As you try to figure out your own path, you may encounter a lot of harsh judgments about the ways different people live. We're sure you don't need us to tell you that the world does not, for the most part, honor sluthood, or think well of those of us who are sexually explorative.

You will probably find some of these judgments in your own brain, burrowed in deeper than you ever realized. We believe that they say a lot more about the culture that promotes them than they do about any actual person, including you.

"PROMISCUOUS"

This means we enjoy too many sexual partners. We've also been called "indiscriminate" in our sexuality, which we resent: we can always tell our lovers apart.

We do not believe that there is such a thing as too much sex, except perhaps on certain happy occasions when our options exceed our abilities. Nor do we believe that the ethics we are talking about here have anything to do with moderation or abstinence. Kinsey once defined a "nymphomaniac" as "someone who has more sex than you" and, scientist that he was, demonstrated his point with statistics.

Is having less sex somehow more virtuous than having more? We think not. We measure the ethics of good sluts not by the number of their partners, but by the respect and care with which they treat them.

"AMORAL"

Our culture also tells us that sluts are evil, uncaring, amoral, and destructive: Jezebel, Casanova, Don Juan. The mythological evil slut is grasping and manipulative, seeking to steal something—virtue, money, self-esteem—from his partners. In some ways, this archetype is based on the idea that sex is a commodity, a coin you trade for something else—stability, children, a wedding ring—and that any other transaction constitutes being cheated and betrayed.

We have rarely observed any Jezebels or Casanovas in our community, but perhaps it is not very satisfying for a thief to steal what is freely given. We do not worry about being robbed of our sexual value by the people we share pleasure with.

"SINFUL"

Some people base their sense of ethics on what they've been told that God, or their church, or their parents, or their culture, believes to be okay or not okay. They believe that being good consists of obedience to laws set down by a power greater than themselves.

Religion, we think, has a great deal to offer to many people—the comfort of faith and the security of community among them. But believing that God doesn't like sex, as many religions seem to, is like believing that God doesn't like you. Because of this belief, a tremendous number of people carry great shame for their own perfectly natural sexual desires and activities.

We prefer the beliefs of a woman we met, a devoted churchgoer in a fundamentalist faith. She told us that when she was about five years old, she discovered the joys of masturbation in the back seat of the family car, tucked under a warm blanket on a long trip. It felt so wonderful that she concluded that the existence of her clitoris was proof positive that God loved her.

"PATHOLOGICAL"

When psychological studies of human behavior came into vogue in the late nineteenth century, Krafft-Ebing and Freud attempted to create more tolerance by theorizing that sluts are not bad but sick, suffering from psychopathology that is not their fault, since their neurosis derives from having their sexuality warped by their parents during their toilet training. So, they said, we should no longer burn sluts at the stake but instead send them to mental hospitals to be cured, in an environment that permits no sexual expression at all, healthy or otherwise.

During your authors' childhood and adolescence in the early 1960s, it was common practice to certify and incarcerate adolescents for "treatment" of the "illness" of being sexual, especially if they were gay or lesbian, or female and in danger of damaging their market value as virgins. This sort of thing still takes place more often than you might think. More recently we hear about sex addicts, avoidance of intimacy, commitment-phobia, and attachment disorders. These terms were created to describe genuine problems, but they are far too often used as weapons in a moral war against all sexual freedom.

The whole idea of sex addiction is a controversial one: many people feel that the word "addiction" is not well suited to discussing behavioral issues like sex. However, everybody seems to agree that substituting sex for fulfillment of other needs—to allay anxiety, for instance, or bolster sagging self-esteem—represents a problem.

Only you can decide whether your sexual behaviors have become compulsive and whether you wish to change them. Some people try to validate their sexual attractiveness over and over, using sex as constant reassurance because they do not see themselves as inherently attractive or lovable. Sex can be used as a substitute for connection. Sex can be the only coin valuable enough to attract attention and approval.

Some twelve-step groups and therapists who subscribe to the addiction model may try to tell you that anything but the most conservative of sexual behaviors is wrong, or unhealthy, or "into your addiction"; we encourage you to trust your own beliefs and find yourself a supportive environment. Sexual Compulsives Anonymous and Sex Addicts Anonymous encourage you to define the healthy sex life you want for yourself. If your goal is monogamy, that's fine, and if your goal is to stop seeking sex in the place of friendship, or any other behavior pattern that you wish to resculpt, that's fine too. We do not believe that successfully recovering sex addicts have to be monogamous unless they want to be.

"EASY"

Is there, we wonder, some virtue in being difficult?

Myths about Sluts

One of the challenges facing the ethical slut is our culture's insistence that, simply because "everybody knows" something, it must obviously be true. We urge you to regard with great skepticism any sentence that begins "Everybody knows that . . ." or "Common sense tells us that . . ." or "It's common knowledge that . . ." Often, these phrases are signposts for cultural belief systems that may be antisexual, monogamy-centrist, and/or codependent. Questioning "what everybody does" can be difficult and disorienting, but we have found it to be rewarding: questioning is the first step toward generating a new paradigm, your own paradigm of how you ought to be.

Cultural belief systems can be very deeply rooted in literature, law, and archetypes, which means that shaking them from your own personal ethos can be difficult. But the first step in exploring them is, of course, recognizing them. Here, then, are some of the pervasive myths that we have heard all our lives and have come to understand are most often untrue and destructive to our relationships and our lives.

MYTH #1: LONG-TERM MONOGAMOUS RELATIONSHIPS ARE THE ONLY REAL RELATIONSHIPS

Lifetime monogamy as an ideal is a relatively new concept in human history and makes us unique among primates. There is nothing that can be achieved within a long-term monogamous relationship that cannot be achieved without one. Business partnership, deep attachment, stable parenting, personal growth, care and companionship in old age are all well within the abilities of the slut.

People who believe this myth may feel that something is wrong with them if they aren't in a committed twosome—if they prefer to remain free agents, if they discover themselves loving more than one person at a time, if they have tried one or more traditional relationships that didn't work out. Instead of questioning the myth, they question themselves: Am I incomplete? Where is my other half? The myth teaches them that they are not good enough in and of themselves. Often people develop a very unrealistic view of couplehood—Mr. or Ms. Right will automatically solve all their problems, fill all the gaps, make their lives complete.

A subset of this myth is the belief that if you're really in love, you will automatically lose all interest in others; thus, if you're having sexual or romantic feelings toward anyone but your partner, you're not really in love. This belief has cost many people a great deal of happiness through the centuries yet is untrue to the point of absurdity: a ring around the finger does not cause a nerve block to the genitals.

And, we must ask, if monogamy is the only acceptable option, the only true form of love, than are these agreements genuinely consensual? We have many friends who have chosen to be monogamous, and we applaud them. But how many people in our society consciously make that choice?

MYTH #2: ROMANTIC LOVE IS THE ONLY REAL LOVE

Look at the lyrics of popular songs, or read some classical poetry: the phrases we choose to describe romantic love don't really sound all that

15

pleasant. Crazy in love, love hurts, obsession, heartbreak . . . these are all descriptions of mental or physical illness.

The thing that gets called romantic love in this culture seems to be a heady cocktail of lust and adrenaline, sparked by uncertainty, insecurity, perhaps even anger or danger. The chills up the spine that we recognize as passion are, in fact, the same physical phenomenon as hair rising up on a cat's back and are caused by the fight-or-flight response.

This kind of love can be thrilling and overwhelming and sometimes a hell of a lot of fun, but it is not the only "real" kind of love, nor is it always a good basis for an ongoing relationship. Yet as George Bernard Shaw famously remarked, "When two people are under the influence of the most violent, most insane, most delusive, and most transient of passions, they are required to swear that they will remain in that excited, abnormal, and exhausting condition continuously until death do them part."

MYTH #3: SEXUAL DESIRE IS A DESTRUCTIVE FORCE

This one goes all the way back to the Garden of Eden and leads to a lot of crazy-making double standards. Some religions appear to believe that women's sexuality is evil and dangerous, and exists only to lure men to their doom. From the Victorian era, we get the idea that men are hopelessly voracious and predatory when it comes to sex, and women are supposed to control and civilize them by being pure, asexual, and withholding—men are the gas pedal and women the brakes, which is, we think, pretty hard on the engine. Neither of these works for us.

Many people also believe that unashamed sexual desire, particularly desire for more than one person, inevitably destroys the family—yet we suspect that far more families have been destroyed by bitter divorces over adultery than have ever been disturbed by ethical consensual nonmonogamy.

MYTH #4: LOVING SOMEONE MAKES IT OKAY TO CONTROL HIS OR HER BEHAVIOR

This kind of territorial reasoning is designed, we guess, to make people feel secure, but we don't believe that anybody has the right, much less the obligation, to control the behavior of another functioning adult.

Being treated according to this myth doesn't make us feel secure, it makes us feel furious. The old "awww, she's jealous—she must really care about me" reasoning, or the scene in which the girl falls in love with the boy when he punches out a rival suitor, are symptomatic of a very disturbed set of personal boundaries that can lead to a great deal of unhappiness.

This myth also leads to the belief, so often promulgated in Hollywood films and popular literature, that sleeping with someone else is something you do *to* your partner, not *for* yourself, and is, moreover, the very worst thing you can do to someone. For many years, in New York State, adultery was the only legally acceptable grounds for divorce, leaving those who had unfortunately married batterers or drunks in a very difficult position. And the legal punishment for "cheating" could be to lose one's job, home, money, and kids, because of the wounding to the "betrayed" partner—that is, if you got caught. So one was supposed to cheat in secrecy to protect one's partner's dignity and keep the family together.

MYTH #5: JEALOUSY IS INEVITABLE AND IMPOSSIBLE TO OVERCOME

Jealousy is, without a doubt, a very common experience, so much so that a person who doesn't experience jealousy is looked at as a bit odd, or in denial. But often a situation that would cause intense jealousy for one person can be no big deal for another. Some people get jealous when their honey takes a sip out of someone else's Coke, others happily watch their beloved wave bye-bye for a month of amorous sporting with a friend at the far end of the country.

Some people also believe that jealousy is such a shattering emotion that they have no choice but to succumb to it. People who believe this often believe that any form of nonmonogamy *should* be nonconsensual and completely secret, in order to protect the "betrayed" partner from having to feel such an impossibly difficult emotion.

On the contrary, we have found that jealousy is an emotion like any other: it feels bad (sometimes very bad), but it is not intolerable. We have also found that many of the "oughta-be's" that lead to jealousy can be unlearned and that unlearning them is often a useful process. Later in this book, we will spend a lot more time talking about jealousy and the strategies many people have successfully employed to cope with it.

MYTH #6: OUTSIDE INVOLVEMENTS REDUCE INTIMACY IN THE PRIMARY RELATIONSHIP

Most marriage counselors, and certain popular TV psychologists, believe when a member of an otherwise happy couple has an "affair," this must be a symptom of unresolved conflict or unfulfilled needs that should be dealt with in the primary relationship. Of course, this is occasionally true, but not nearly as often as many "relationship gurus" would like us to believe. Moreover, this myth leaves no room for the possibility of growthful and constructive open sexual lifestyles.

It is cruel and insensitive to interpret an affair as a symptom of sickness in the relationship, as it leaves "cheated-on" partners—who may already be feeling insecure—to wonder what is wrong with them. Meanwhile, "cheating" partners get told that they are only trying to get back at their primary partners and don't really want, need, or even like their lovers.

Many people have sex outside their primary relationships for reasons that have nothing to do with any inadequacy in their partner or in the relationship. The new relationship may simply be a natural extension of an emotional and/or physical attraction to someone besides the primary partner. Or perhaps this outside relationship allows a particular kind of intimacy that the primary partner doesn't even want (such as kinky sex or going to football games) and thus constitutes a solution for an otherwise insoluble conflict. Or perhaps it meets other needs—like a need for uncomplicated physical sex without the trappings of relationship, or for sex with someone of a gender other than one's partner's, or for sex at a time when it is otherwise not available (during travel or a partner's illness, for example).

An outside involvement does not have to subtract in any way from the intimacy you share with your partner unless you let it. And we sincerely hope you won't.

MYTH #7: LOVE CONQUERS ALL

Hollywood tells us that "love means never having to say you're sorry," and we, fools that we are, believe it. This myth has it that if you're really in love with someone, you never have to argue, disagree, communicate, negotiate, or do any other kind of work. It also tells us that love means we automatically get turned on by our beloved and that we never have to lift a finger or make any effort to deliberately kindle passion. Those who believe this myth may find themselves feeling that their love has failed every time they need to schedule a discussion or to have a courteous (or not-so-courteous) disagreement. They may also believe that any sexual behavior that doesn't fit their criteria for "normal" sex—from fantasies to vibrators—is "artificial" and indicates that something is lacking in the quality of their love.

EXERCISE *Why Sluthood? Why Not?*

Write a list of every reason you can think of that any person anywhere might want to be a slut. You can do this on your own, or with a friend or a lover. Which of these tell you what kind of slut you don't want to be? Which of these are your very good and valid reasons?

Steps to a Freer Paradigm

So in this slightly disorienting world of sluthood, in which everything your mom, your minister, your spouse, and your television ever told you is probably wrong, how do you find new beliefs that support your new lifestyle? Letting go of old paradigms can leave you in a scary emptiness, your stomach churning as if you were in free fall. You don't need the old myths, but what will you have instead? We encourage you to seek your own truths on your way to slutty bliss, but just in case you could use a hint or two, here are some of the ones that have worked well for us.

CHAPTER THREE

Our Beliefs

WE ARE ETHICAL PEOPLE, ethical sluts. It is very important to us to treat people well and to do our best not to hurt anyone. Our ethics come from our own sense of rightness, and from the empathy and love we hold for those around us. It is not okay to hurt another person because then we hurt too, and we don't feel good about ourselves.

Ethical slutdom can be a challenging path: we don't have a polyamorous Miss Manners telling us how to do our thing courteously and respectfully, so we have to make it up as we go along. However, we're sure you've figured out by now that to us, being a slut doesn't mean simply doing whatever you want, whenever you want, with whomever you want.

Most of our criteria for ethics are quite pragmatic. Is anyone being harmed? Is there any way to avoid causing that harm? Are there any risks? Is everybody involved aware of those risks and doing what can be done to minimize them?

On the positive side: How much fun is this? What is everybody learning from it? Is it helping someone to grow? Is it helping make the world a better place?

First and foremost, ethical sluts value *consent*. When we use this word—and we will, often, throughout this book—we mean an active collaboration for the benefit, well-being, and pleasure of all persons concerned. If someone is being coerced, bullied, blackmailed, manipulated, lied to, or ignored, what is happening is not consensual. And sex that is not consensual is not ethical—period.

Ethical sluts are *honest*—with ourselves and others. We take time with ourselves, to figure out our own emotions and motivations and to untangle them for greater clarity when necessary. Then we openly share that information with those who need it. We do our best not to let our fears and bashfulness be an obstacle to our honesty—we trust that our partners will go on respecting and loving us, warts and all.

Ethical sluts *recognize the ramifications* of our sexual choices. We see that our emotions, our upbringing, and the standards of our culture often conflict with our sexual desires. And we make a conscious commitment to supporting ourselves and our partners as we deal with those conflicts honestly and honorably.

We do not allow our sexual choices to have an unnecessary impact on those who have not consented to participate. We are *respectful* of others' feelings, and when we aren't sure how someone feels, we ask.

Ethical sluts recognize the difference between things they can and should control, and things they can't. While we sometimes may feel jealous or territorial, we *own those feelings*, doing our best not to blame or control, but asking for the support we need to help ourselves feel safe and cared for.

Don't panic—the rest of this book is about *how* you can learn to be such a fine sexy grown-up. Your authors are here to help. We wrote this book to help you become an ethical slut. Here are a few of the ideas and beliefs that have helped us get here and might help you too.

Rethinking Sex

Are you having sex right now? Yes, you are, and so are we.

Perhaps you're looking around you in bewilderment: You still have your clothing on, and maybe you're sitting in a restaurant or a crowded bus. How could you be having sex?

We think that the question of when you're having sex is actually sort of meaningless. Sexual energy pervades everything all the time; we inhale it into our lungs and exude it from our pores. While it's pretty easy to determine whether or not you're engaging in a particular sexual activity at any given time—neither you nor we are probably having intercourse at this moment—the idea of sex as something set aside, a discrete, definable activity like driving a car, just doesn't hold up very well.

You can compare this idea to the idea of eating, if you like. Most people would define "eating" as the actual activity of placing food in the mouth. But gourmets might spend a long time savoring the aroma and appearance of their food before actually taking a bite, so that smell and vision have become part of eating. For those who open themselves to the possibilities, every stray aroma that floats under our nostrils, the ocean breeze with its tang of oysters and seaweed, the peaty whiskey-like whiff of woodsmoke, becomes a kind of eating. And our eyes take in colors and shapes, apple red and creamy custard yellow, while our busy brains, remembering yesterday's wonderful meal, plan another for tomorrow, and the whole world becomes our food.

Similarly, we think erotic energy is everywhere—in the deep breath that fills our lungs as we step out into a warm spring morning, in the cold water spilling over the rocks in a brook, in the creativity that drives us to paint pictures and tell stories and make music and write books, in the loving tenderness we feel toward our friends and relatives and children. In our combined half century of work as sex writers and educators, we've found that the more we learn about sex, the less we know about how to define it, so now we just say the truth as we know it: sex is part of everything.

Right now, we're writing about sex, and you're reading what we have to say about it. You're having sex with us! Was it good for you? It sure has been for us.

More pragmatically, we have had long, intense intimate conversations that felt deeply sexual to us. And we have had intercourse that didn't feel terribly sexual. Our best definition here is that sex is whatever the people engaging in it think it is. For some people, spanking is sex. For others, wearing a garter belt and stockings is sex. If you and anybody else involved feel sexual when you eat ice cream sundaes together, that's sex—for you. While this may sound silly now, it's a concept that will come in handy later in this book when we discuss making agreements about our sexual behaviors.

Denial vs. Fulfillment

Dossie's bachelor's thesis was called "Sex Is Nice and Pleasure Is Good for You." That idea is as radical now, in the twenty-first century, as it was back in the 1970s when Dossie first wrote it.

Our culture places a very high value on self-denial, which is fine when there is hard work to be done. But all too often, those who unapologetically satisfy their desire for pleasure in their utterly free time are seen as immature, disgusting, even sinful. Since we all have desires, puritanical values lead inevitably to self-loathing, hatred of our bodies and our turn-ons, and fear and guilt over our sexual urges.

We see ourselves surrounded by the walking wounded—by people who have been deeply injured by fear, shame, and hatred of their own sexual selves. We believe that happy, free, guiltless connection is the cure for these wounds; we believe that sexuality is vital to people's sense of self-worth, to their belief that life is good. We have never met anyone who had low self-esteem at the moment of orgasm.

You Don't Need a Reason

If you walk up to a randomly selected individual and propose that sex is nice and pleasure is good for you, you will probably hear a lot of spluttering, argument, and "yahbuts"—STDs, unwanted pregnancies, rape, the commodification of sexual desire, and so on. None of which changes the core idea.

There is nothing in the world so terrific that it can't be abused if you're determined to do so: Familial connections can be violated, sexual desire can be manipulated. Even chocolate can be abused. Abuse doesn't change the basic wonderfulness of any of these things: the danger lies in the motivation of the abuser, not the nature of the item.

If there were no such thing as sexually transmitted disease, if nobody got pregnant unless she wanted to, if all sex were consensual and pleasurable, how would the world feel about it then? How would *you* feel? If you look deep inside yourself, you may find bits and pieces of sexnegativism, often hiding behind judgmental words like "promiscuous," "hedonistic," "decadent," and "nonproductive."

Even people who consider themselves sex positive and sexually liberated often fall into a different trap—the trap of rationalizing sex.

Releasing physical tension, relieving menstrual cramps, maintaining mental health, preventing prostate problems, making babies, cementing relationships, and so on are all admirable goals, and wonderful side benefits of sex. But they are not what sex is *for*. Sex is for pleasure, a complete and worthwhile goal in and of itself. People have sex because it feels very good, and then they feel good about themselves. The worthiness of pleasure is one of the core values of ethical sluthood.

Love and Sex Are the End, Not the Means

Our monogamy-centrist culture tends to assume that the purpose and ultimate goal of all relationships—and all sex—is lifelong pair bonding, and that any relationship that falls short of that goal has failed.

We, on the other hand, think sexual pleasure can certainly contribute to love, commitment, and long-term stability, if that's what you want. But those are hardly the only good reasons for having sex. We believe in valuing relationships for what we value in them, a seeming tautology that is wiser than it sounds.

A relationship may be valuable simply because it affords sexual pleasure to those involved; there is nothing wrong with sex for sex's sake. Or it might involve sex as a pathway to other lovely things—intimacy, connection, companionship, even romantic love—which in no way changes the basic goodness of the pleasurable sex.

A sexual relationship may last for an hour or two. It's still a relationship: the participants have related to one another—as sex partners, companions, lovers—for the duration of their interaction. Longevity is not a good criterion by which to judge the success or failure of a relationship.

One-night stands can be intense, life-enhancing, and fulfilling; so can lifetime love affairs. While ethical sluts may choose to have some kinds of relationships and not others, we believe that all relationships have the potential to teach us, move us, and above all give us pleasure.

Dossie remembers an interview with a young flower child back in 1967 who made the most succinct statement of ethical sluthood we've ever seen: "We believe it's okay to have sex with anybody you love, and we believe in loving everybody."

You Are Already Whole

Jane Austen wrote, "It is a truth universally acknowledged that a single man in possession of a good fortune must be in want of a wife." While we think Jane probably had her tongue firmly planted in her cheek, a great many people do believe that to be single is to be somehow incomplete and that they need to find their "other half." A lot of the myths we mentioned in the previous section are based on that belief.

We believe, on the other hand, that the fundamental sexual unit is one person; adding more people to that unit may be intimate, fun, and companionable but does not complete anybody. The only thing in this world that you can control is yourself—your own reactions, desires, and behaviors. Thus, a fundamental step in ethical sluthood is to bring your locus of control into yourself, to recognize the difference between your "stuff" and other people's; when you do this, you become able to complete yourself—that's why we call this "integrity."

When you have built a satisfying relationship with yourself, then you have something of great worth to share with others.

Abundance Is Entirely Available

Many people believe, explicitly or implicitly, that our capacities for romantic love, intimacy, and connection are finite, that there is never enough to go around, and that if you give some to one person, you must be taking some away from another.

We call this belief a "starvation economy"; we'll talk much more about it later. Many of us learned to think this way in childhood, from parents who had little affection or attention for us, so we learned that there is only a limited amount of love in the world and we have to fight for whatever we get, often in cutthroat competition with our brothers and sisters.

People who operate from starvation economies can become very possessive about the people, things, and ideas that matter to them. They see the whole world in that limited light, so that anything they get comes from a small pool of not-enough and must thus be taken from someone else—and, similarly, anything anyone else gets must be subtracted from them.

It is important to distinguish between starvation economies and real-world limits. Time, for example, is a real-world limit: even the most dedicated slut has only twenty-four hours every day. Love is not a real-world limit: the mother of nine children can love each of them as much as the mother of an only child.

Our belief is that the human capacity for sex and love and intimacy is far greater than most people think—possibly infinite—and that having a lot of satisfying connections simply makes it possible for you to have a lot more. Imagine what it would feel like to live in an abundance of sex and love, to feel that you had all of both that you could possibly want, free of any feelings of deprivation or neediness. Imagine how strong you would feel if you got to exercise your "love muscles" that much, and how much love you would have to give!

Openness Can Be the Solution, Not the Problem

Is sexual adventurousness simply a way to avoid intimacy? Not ordinarily, in our experience. While it is certainly possible to misuse your outside relationships to avoid problems or intimacy with your life partner, we do not agree that this pattern is inevitable or even common. Many people, in fact, find that their outside relationships can increase their intimacy with their primary partner by reducing the pressures on that relationship and by giving them a safe place to discuss issues that may have them feeling "stuck" in the primary relationship.

This chapter contains some of our beliefs. You get to have beliefs of your own. What matters to us is not that you agree with us, but that you question the prevailing paradigm and decide for yourself what you believe. Exercise your judgment—isn't exercise supposed to make you stronger? Thousands and thousands of ethical sluts are proving every day that the old "everybody knows" myths don't have to be true.

We encourage you to explore your own realities and create your own legend, one that spurs you onward in your evolution, supports you as you grow, and reflects your pride and happiness in your new-found relationships.

CHAPTER FOUR

Slut Styles

ETHICAL SLUTHOOD is a house with a lot of rooms: it shelters everyone from happy celibates to ecstatic orgiasts and beyond. In this chapter, we'll talk about the many styles of sluthood that have worked for us, for the people we know, and for happy sluts throughout history. Whether or not any of these scenarios fit you, we hope they will offer you some ideas about where to start your exploration, or perhaps the validation of knowing that there are others like you out there.

Relationship Pioneers

Although the phrase "ethical slut" is new—Dossie coined it in 1995—the practice is not. Cultural acceptance of practices outside monogamy has roller-coastered up and down from acceptance to stern rejection, but regardless of the opinions of church and state there have always been those who have found happiness and growth in sexual openness.

ANCIENT CULTURES
You could spend your life as a cultural anthropologist trying to describe the innumerable ways that human beings have chosen to be together sexually, romantically, and domestically—from the temple prostitutes of ancient Babylon to Mormon polygyny and far, far beyond. So, rather

than trying to list them all, we just want to note that the prevailing cultural values that twenty-first-century North America inherited from Europe seem to date back to the Roman empire, and to early Christianity, which recommended monogamous marriage only for those who couldn't manage celibacy, the ideal state. Cultures without those influences have developed all sorts of ways for people to bond— polygyny (many wives), polyandry (many husbands), group marriage, arrangements in which marriage is fundamentally a domestic business relationship and sexual dalliance takes place elsewhere, ritual group sex, and pretty much any other configuration of human hearts and genitals that you can imagine.

UTOPIAN SEXUAL COMMUNITIES

History is dotted with experiments in creating intentional sexual utopias, often with a philosophical or religious basis: if you're curious, read up on the Oneida community of nineteenth-century Ohio; Rajneeshpuram in India from the late 1960s and Oregon in the 1980s; and Kerista in New York, Belize, and San Francisco from the early 1960s through the 1990s . . . to name just a few. Such communities are usually built by one leader and may falter when the leader is no longer available. However, their philosophies live on, adding new visions and practices to the mainstream culture. Many practitioners of Western tantra today, for example, can trace their practice to the teachings of Osho, the guiding spirit behind Rajneeshpuram.

ARTISTS AND FREETHINKERS

It's easy to point to artists and writers who have built their lives around intentional exploration of alternative relationships. If you're curious about the ways in which alternative relationships played out in times when there was even less support than there is now, you can read up on the Bloomsbury group in early twentieth-century England, and freethinkers like George Sand, H. G. Wells, Simone de Beauvoir, Alfred Kinsey, and Edna St. Vincent Millay. What we can't know is how many *non*writers were also building the kind of sexually open lives that worked for them, because there are no records of such lives. We feel safe in supposing, though, that a significant minority of people have always gotten their needs met through ethical multipartner living.

THE LOVE GENERATION

Dossie came of age surrounded by the utopian concepts of the 1960s, and Janet shortly afterward; both of us have been influenced greatly in our thinking and our lives by those days of radical exploration. Many ideals of that era—nonconformity, exploration of altered states of consciousness, equality of race and gender, ecological awareness, political activism, openness about sexuality, and, yes, the possibility of ethical and loving nonmonogamy—have permeated the greater culture. We very much doubt that we could have written this book or published it in the 1950s, so if you're reading and enjoying *The Ethical Slut* today, thank a hippie.

Sluthood Today

Sluts come in all the various forms and styles that humans come in: men and women in all cultures, from all parts of the world, of all religions and lifestyles, rich and poor, with formal and informal education.

Most of us today live in communities of nonsluts, with only occasional or limited contact with other people who share our values: some groups hold conferences and conventions to mitigate isolation and expand their members' intimate circles. These conferences are very important in bringing sexual undergrounds into the view of those who are looking for them and building institutions aboveground that can better support their members. Other sluts drop out of mainstream culture to some extent to live in communities composed of people whose sexuality is like their own. San Francisco's Castro district is a good example of a modern urban "ghetto" for sexual minorities.

A slut living in mainstream, monogamy-centrist culture in the twenty-first century can learn a great deal from studying other cultures, other places, and other times: you're *not* the only one in the world who has ever tried this, it *can* work, others have done it without harming themselves, their lovers, their kids—without, in fact, doing anything except enjoying themselves and each other.

Pioneering sexual subcultures with extensive documented and undocumented histories include communities of gay men and of lesbian women, transgender groups, bisexuals, the leather communities, the swing communities, and some spiritually defined subcultures of pagans, modern primitives, and Radical Faeries. And that's just in the United States. Even if you don't belong to any of these sexually oriented communities, it's worth taking a look at them for what they can teach us about our own options as they develop ways of being sexual, ways of communicating about being sexual, and ways of living in social and family structures that are alternative to sex-negative traditions in America.

Dossie's favorite dance club in 1970 was a remarkable miniculture of polymorphous perversity. She remembers:

> The Omni, short for "omnisexual," was a small North Beach bar whose patrons were men and women, straight, gay, lesbian, bisexual, and often transgendered. The sexual values were very open, from hippie free-love freaks to sex industry professionals, and most of us came there to dance like wild women and cruise like crazy.
>
> Thanks to the large transgender faction, there was no way of pigeonholing the person you were cruising into your categories of desire. You might dance with someone you found very attractive and not know if they were chromosomally male or female. It's difficult to get attached to preferences like lesbian or straight when you don't know the gender of the person you are flirting with.
>
> This may sound crazy, but the results were surprising: I patronized the Omni because it was the safest environment available to me. Because there was no way to make assumptions, people *had* to treat each other with respect. No one could assume what kind of interaction might interest the object of their attention, so there was nothing to do but ask. And if you were, as I was, a young woman in your twenties, to be approached with respect was a most welcome relief from straight social environments where it was customary for men to prove their manhood by coming on too strong, evidently in the belief that women who cruise in singles bars have problems with virginal shyness and don't mean "no" when they say it. The Omni provided my first experiences with true respect.

Since we see some of the problems in attaining a free and open expression of our own individual sexuality as having to do with living in a sex-role-bound culture, we have found it useful to learn from people who have shifted the boundaries of what it means to be male or female, or what it means to choose partners of the same or opposite sex. Thinking about different ways of living and loving can help us as we consider whether we want to change anything about how we go about living as men and women, or somewhere in between.

LESBIAN WOMEN

In the lesbian community, we get to look at what happens in a world consisting almost entirely of women. For women, relationship can get confused with their sense of identity, especially since our culture in its most traditional form hardly allows women any sense of identity at all. Thus, many women act as if they would lose their entire sense of themselves without their relationship. The most common relationship sequence, as we see it magnified in the lesbian community, is the form of nonmonogamy known as serial monogamy. Often the connection to the partner of the future precedes the breakup with the partner of the past, with accompanying drama that presumably feels safer than the vast, empty, unknown, and terrifying identity void of being a woman living as a single human being.

Younger lesbians are questioning these traditions, and often that questioning includes looking into nonmonogamy as a way to form less insular relationships. Lesbian polyamory is characterized by a lot of serious thoughtfulness and attention to consensuality, and thus to tremendous openness about processing feelings, an area in which the women's community excels.

Our lesbian sisters also have a lot to teach us about new ways of developing a woman's role as sexual initiator. In heterosexual culture, men have been assigned the job of initiator, and men are trained to be sexually aggressive, sometimes to a fault. In the world of women who relate sexually to other women, it rapidly becomes apparent that if we all see ourselves as Sleeping Beauties waiting for Princess Charming to come along and wake us up, we also might get to wait a hundred years. Or else we need to learn to do something new—to meet the eye, touch the shoulder, move in a little closer, or just plain blurt out, "I think you're really attractive; would you like to talk?"

Women's style of coming on—when shyness doesn't get in the way—tends to be forthright, with respect for consent, and is unlikely to be intrusive or pushy, as many women have had a little too much experience with being violated to want to go down that road. Women have strong concerns about safety and so tend to move slowly and announce their intentions. They may be shy in the seductive stages, and bolder once welcome has been secured. Women tend to want explicit permission for each specific act, so their communication could serve as an excellent role model for negotiated consensuality.

We would like to draw your attention to another illuminating difference about sex between women. A sexual encounter between two women rarely involves the expectation of simultaneous orgasm, as many people believe penis-vagina intercourse should, so women have become experts at taking turns. Lesbians are world-class experts on sensuality and outercourse, those wonderful forms of sexuality that do not rely on penile penetration. When penetration is desired, the focus is on what works for the recipient: we have yet to meet a dildo that got hung up on its own needs.

For those of you, female or male or gay or straight, who haven't considered these options, think of all the fun you could have with never a worry about pregnancy and sexually transmitted diseases!

GAY MEN

The gay male community reflects some of the traditional images of male sexuality in intensified form. While some gay men are indeed interested in long-term relationships and settling down, many have set records as world-class sluts. The gay baths are the ultimate role model of friendly group sex environments and easy sexual connection for its own sake.

Dossie learned her group sex etiquette from gay men and is glad she did. We both, in fact, have always identified strongly with gay men: Dossie sees herself as a drag queen trapped in a woman's body, and Janet calls herself a "girlfag," a gay man who happens to have breasts and a vagina. This may not really be too surprising, since the gay male community has always modeled sluttery for the rest of us to admire and, perhaps, emulate.

Gay male sex, as a rule, starts from a presumption of equal power, without the dynamic of overpowerment and withholding that often pervades male/female interactions. Thus, men do not generally try to get consent from each other by manipulation and pressuring: connection is more commonly made by a gentle approach, meeting a gentle response, and no need to ask three times. Gay men give each other a lot of credit for being able to say no, and for meaning it when they say it—this makes coming on very simple, since you are never trying to sneak up on anybody and you are not required to be subtle. It is always okay to ask as long as it is okay for the other person to say no. This straightforward and admirably simple approach to consensuality cannot be recommended too highly.

Men in general have had less reason to fear sexual violation than their sisters. Although it is true, and terrible, that boys do get molested and men do get raped, men seem to have more confidence than women in their power to protect themselves. Men also tend to get a lot of cultural support for being sexual. So although the forbiddenness of homosexuality may give many gay men a lot of questions about being okay, or having something wrong with them, or other forms of internalized homophobia, this is most often not reflected in sexual dysfunction. Gay men as a group are really good at exploring, and finding out, what feels good to them.

And it is gay men who have established most of our understanding of safer sex. In the face of the AIDS epidemic, where many people might have retreated into sex-negativism, the gay community held its ground and continued to create environments where hot, creative, safer sex could be learned and practiced.

BISEXUALS

Often stigmatized as "gays unwilling to relinquish heterosexual privilege" or "hets taking a walk on the wild side," bisexuals have recently begun developing their own forceful voice and their own communities.

Looking at the theory and practice of bisexual lifestyles offers opportunities to explore our assumptions about the nature of sexual and romantic attraction and behaviors. Some folks have had sex only with members of one gender, but know that they have within themselves the ability to connect erotically or emotionally with both genders, and thus consider themselves bisexual—while others may be actively having sex with the gender opposite their usual choice, and still consider themselves heterosexual or gay. Some bisexuals prefer one type of interaction with men and another with women, while others consider themselves gender-blind. Some can be sexual with either sex but romantic with only one, or vice versa. And so on, through all the spectrums of bisexual attractions and choices. Bisexuals challenge a lot of our assumptions about gender, and many bi's can tell you what is different for them between sex with a woman and sex with a man. This interesting and privileged information can provide all of us with new stories about sex and gender.

The increasing visibility of bisexuality has led to some challenges to traditional definitions of sexual identity. Specifically, we are having to look at the fact that our sexual attractions may say one thing about us, while our sexual behaviors say another, and our sexual identity says yet a third. Questions like these are eating away at some of the traditional boundaries we place around sexual identity, much to the dismay of purists of all orientations. Your authors, sluts that we are, enjoy this kind of fluidity and appreciate the opportunity to play as we like with whoever looks good to us without relinquishing our fundamental sexual identities.

Janet's path toward her current identity as a bisexual has been a confusing one: it was nearly a decade after she began having sex with women before she began to feel comfortable using the term to describe herself.

> I felt turned off by the trendiness of "bisexual chic," and under some pressure to claim an identity that didn't feel right to me. And at the same time, I was hearing some genuinely cruel judgments from both heterosexuals and homosexuals about bi's.
>
> Add to that the difficulty I was having sorting out my own feelings—I knew my feelings toward women were different from those toward men, and I wasn't sure what *that* meant—and things just got very confusing. As a result, it wasn't until I knew for sure that I was capable of having both sexual and romantic feelings toward both men and women—and until I felt strong enough to claim the identity in the face of all those negative judgments—that I finally began calling myself "bisexual."
>
> I look back on my life now and see that I've generally expressed my domestic urges toward men but that my romantic and sexual feelings are about equally likely to be inspired by a man, a woman, or some-

one in between. The bisexual community also offers more support than either straight-land or gay-land for my rather ambiguous gender presentation: some days I like to wear red lipstick and heels and other days men's trousers and oxfords. So "bisexual" is the identity that fits me best, and where I expect to stay.

HETEROSEXUALS

In bygone decades, there were relatively few role models for heterosexual interaction in mainstream culture: an Ozzie and Harriet household, monogamous, patriarchal, and focused on conformity and child rearing, was presented to us all as our sexual and romantic ideal. Your authors are very glad to have outlived this era.

Modern heterosexuality offers a plethora of options for happy sluthood, from long-term "vee" triads, where two partners are both sexual with one "hub" partner but not with each other, to orgiastic recreational sex, with lots of possibilities in between, including open relationships, secondary partners, poly pods, and intimately extended families we sometimes call "constellations."

In the past, nonmonogamous heterosexual interactions were called "wife-swapping," a term with a built-in sexist bias that we find offensive. Today, heterosexuals seeking no-strings sex outside a primary relationship often seek out the swing community. These groups are well worth looking at for what they have to teach us about how heterosexual men and women can interact outside the confines of the "shoulds" of mainstream, monogamous culture.

Swinging is a broad term that gets used to define a wide variety of interactions, ranging from long-term two-couple sexual pairings through the wildest of Saturday-night puppy-pile orgies. Swingers tend to be heterosexual; although female bisexuality is relatively common, male bisexuality is often frowned upon. They are most often coupled, and are often more mainstream in their politics, lifestyles, and personal values than other kinds of sluts. Some swing communities confine themselves explicitly to sexual interactions and discourage emotional connections outside primary couples, while others encourage all forms of romantic and sexual partnering.

Swinging has offered many a heterosexual woman her first opportunity to explore greedy and guilt-free sexuality—in fact, we often hear of women who attend their first swing party very reluctantly, their second one hesitantly, and their subsequent ones avidly. We also like the sophistication with which many swing communities have evolved patterns of symbols and behavior to communicate sexual interest without intrusiveness (one now-defunct local swing club used to have a fascinating code of opening doors and windows to communicate, variously, "Keep away," "Look but don't touch," or "Come on in and join us").

TRANSGENDER AND GENDERQUEER FOLKS

Transgendered people form a variety of communities, all of which have much to teach to those who are interested in transcending their gender-role programming. Dossie, in the early years of her feminism, found friends and lovers among male-to-female transsexuals who became her wonderful role models for how to be female, indeed often ultra-feminine, and still be assertive and powerful.

What we can all learn from transgendered people is that gender is malleable. From people who take hormones to express male or female gender, we learn about how some behaviors and emotional states may be hormone related. People who have lived parts of their lives in both gender modes, physiologically and culturally, have a great deal to teach us about what changes according to hormones, and what does not, and what gender characteristics remain a matter of choice no matter what your endocrine system says. Genderqueer people—those who choose to live their lives somewhere between the usual gender roles—are softening the boundaries of gender and demonstrating what life without binary gender might look like.

If you think this doesn't apply to you, that you are certain of your gender and that it's immutable, please consider that a great many people are born with characteristics of both genders: depending on whose definition you use, anywhere from two to seventeen babies out of a thousand are born with chromosomes and/or genitalia that place them somewhere between the extremes of the gender continuum. We're not generally aware of these people in our midst because their appearance is usually surgically altered early in life, but it appears that Mother (Father?) Nature doesn't believe in only two genders, and neither do your authors. And a great many people whose genitals and chromosomes are all lined up with biological norms nonetheless feel strongly that they would live more happily and appropriately when presenting as a different gender than the one the doctor assigned to them at birth; you may have such people among your friends and family without knowing it unless they choose to tell you.

Transsexuals can tell us a lot about how differently other people treat you when they see you as a man, or as a woman. Perforce, transgendered people become experts at living in a very hostile world. It takes a strong-minded person to stand up to our culture's rigidity about "real men" and "real women." No other sexual minority is more likely to suffer direct physical oppression in the form of queer-bashing. It was mostly transgendered people, butch women and drag queens, who rebelled against police brutality in the famous Stonewall riots of 1969 that initiated the Gay Liberation movement. Transgendered people can teach us a lot about the determination to be free.

TANTRA AND SPIRITUAL SEX PRACTITIONERS

Celibacy is not the only sexual practice of the spiritually inclined. Early examples of religious communities based on nonmonogamy included the Mormon church, the Oneida community, the practices of *maithuna* and *karezza* in tantric yoga, and the temple whores of the early Mediterranean goddess worshipers. Tantra as we know it today is actually a Westernized form of classical tantric practice taught in workshops in most major cities and in many excellent books and videos. Other classical spiritual/sexual traditions have been updated for Western consumption in practices like Healing Tao and Quodoushka. Pagans and Radical Faeries come together for festivals and gatherings to celebrate ancient sexual rites such as Beltane, or make up their own rituals that are appropriate to current lifestyles, like the open sexuality of Faerie gatherings or the more subtle eroticism of sacred dance and drumming.

These practitioners understand that sex is connected to the spiritual. As we said in an earlier book, "Every orgasm is a spiritual experience. Think of a moment of perfect wholeness, of yourself in perfect unity, of expanded awareness that transcends the split between mind and body and integrates all the parts of you in ecstatic consciousness. . . . When you bring spiritual awareness to your sexual practice, you can become directly conscious of—connected to—that divinity that always flows through you. . . . For us, sex is already an opportunity to see god."

SEX WORKERS

Despite what you might have learned from the TV or the tabloids, sex workers really are not all desperate drug addicts, debased women, or predatory gold diggers. Many healthy and happy women and men work in the sex industry, doing essential and positive work healing the wounds inflicted by our sex-negative culture. We know them as friends, lovers, colleagues, writers, therapists, and educators, as well as performers and artists. These folks have a great deal to teach us about boundaries, limit-setting, communication, sexual negotiation, and ways to achieve growth, connection, and fulfillment outside a traditional monogamous relationship. Do not imagine that connections between sex workers and clients are necessarily cold, impersonal, or degrading, or that only losers frequent prostitutes. Many client/prostitute relationships become a source of tremendous connection, warmth, and affection for both parties, and last many years. Practitioners of the world's oldest profession offer all of us the wisdom of the ages about understanding, accepting, and fulfilling our desires: these are the real sex experts.

Cultural Diversity

While we are looking at sexual diversity, let's remember that we live in a multicultural society, and that every culture in our world, every subculture, every ethnic culture, has its own ways of creating relationship, connecting in sex, and building families. All of those ways are valid and valuable.

One of the great joys of living as a slut is the opportunity to make intimate connections with people whose background is very different from your own. When you do that, you will find yourself tripping, with some embarrassment, over a lot of differences, the way Dossie and her friends from Japan used to trip over each other in doorways: in Japan, men go through the door first. Getting used to differences can feel awkward, but every time it happens you've learned something new about how people go about being human.

Maybe something that you learn will be just the thing you've been looking for that was lacking in your own culture. Dossie came from a small town in New England that had tried, with little success, to pound her into the form of a nice, respectable young lady. When she got to New York City, she discovered cultures in which strong women were accepted and respected: she got to have chutzpah. Talk about opening up a whole realm of possibilities!

Boundaries in communication, connection, and relationship vary from culture to culture. Personal distance differs enormously—they say you can recognize the European-American at a Latin American cock-tail party: he's the one who is frantically backing away from everyone who wants to talk to him because they keep stepping too close. Volume varies too: some cultures value being subdued and quiet, others are dramatically expressive and, well, loud.

We recommend that you look for these differences and suspend your judgments. Is that person who seems too loud actually able to be more expressive than you? Does that quiet person notice more? What's the intelligence of a person who hasn't read a lot of books but understands how your car, or your computer, works? Who are these unbelievably self-confident people who make sexual propositions openly and enthu-siastically and get really confused when you accuse them of coming on too strong? Maybe they have some ways of making connection that you could learn from.

It is sad, indeed tragic, that so many of our sexual communities fail to welcome people from the whole world of cultures, of races, of genders, of sexualities. When you look at the people around you and dismiss them—or, worse yet, assume you know all there is to know about them—because of their skin color, gender, way of speaking, mode of dress, religion, or country of origin, you'll never get to hear any of the new and fascinating things that those people might have to say. Our friend Jaymes says, "I believe that every person you connect with on this planet has some sort of a message to give you. If you cut yourself off from whatever kind of relationship wants to form with that person, you're failing to pick up your messages" . . . and what a shame that would be!

When we are attracted to someone who comes from a background different from our own, and we fail to take that difference into account, then we will mess up what could have been a great connection. We think learning about cultures different from our own helps us to learn to think outside of our boxes and that celebrating diversity can hugely expand our range of choices about our own lives.

We recommend, when you are in the company of the unfamiliar, that you look for unfamiliar wisdom. You'll find lots of it, and it will make you richer.

What Can You Learn?

If thinking about all this makes you kind of nervous, we are not surprised. What you are experiencing is how threatening it feels when the customary boundaries you take for granted, and believe apply to all social and sexual situations, are very different from what you are used to. There are no universally accepted boundaries of gender or attraction among consenting adults, and the limits of sexual exploration are not handed down on stone tablets by some higher authority.

When you look at people who meet your standards of happiness and success without buying into the world's standards of lifetime heterosexual monogamous pair-bonding, you begin to see how such things can be possible for you too—even if these people aren't doing it the same way you want to. Recognizing other sexual cultures offers an opportunity to become aware of your own preconceptions and uncertainties. Listen to your fears: they have a lot to teach you about yourself.

Think of Dossie's old dance club, The Omni. Not knowing what's what can feel scary—but think of it as a chance to scrap all your preconceptions and start from scratch. It's only by recognizing all the possibilities out there that you can truly choose the ones that work for you. Then you can be free to figure where you want the boundaries in your life, what your personal limits are, and if you ever want to expand those limits.

Learning and establishing your own boundaries is a great opportunity and a serious responsibility. Accomplishing this amazing task will set you free to explore beyond your wildest dreams.

CHAPTER FIVE

Battling Sex Negativity

FROM THE SLUT'S point of view, the world is sometimes a dangerous place. Lots of people seem to think it is okay to go to any lengths to stop us from being sexual.

Some antisex crusaders try to make loving dangerous for women by outlawing birth control and abortion, leading to unwanted pregnancies and back-alley medical care. Others would outlaw access to sex information, in schools or on the Internet, so that our children cannot learn to care for their health and well-being and have no access to safer-sex training that would teach them how to avoid spreading AIDS. In an appalling development since the first edition of this book, a vaccine that helps prevent cervical cancer in women is being met with resistance from puritans who believe that inoculating a young woman against cancer somehow encourages her to have sex. Some people purporting to have the word from God preach on the public airwaves that AIDS is divine punishment for any sexuality that deviates from what they believe to be normal. We find such preaching far more obscene than any possible form of sex.

There are places where some people believe that being a slut makes you fair game for violence. Why were you walking down that street at night in a short dress or tight pants? No wonder you got raped or assaulted. It must be the victim's fault. And you look so queer—no wonder that gang decided to beat you up.

We are also considered fair game for other forms of oppression. Multiple sexual partners can be seen as a good reason to take all your property, your children, and your future income in a punitive divorce settlement. You could lose your job, or your promise for advancement, or your professional reputation, if the wrong people find out about your personal life.

Judging Ourselves

We hope this examination of the dangers of sluttery will lead you to ask yourself some questions. What is my experience of oppression and how does it affect me? Who do I have to lie to in my life? What are my closets? As you look deeper, you might ask yourself: what assumptions have I made about how my sexuality should be? Do I hold judgments about what "good" and "nice" people do that I wind up turning against myself?

When we judge ourselves by cultural values imposed from the outside, when women believe they ought to be small and quiet, when gay people believe that their sexual choice is a neurosis, or when we all believe we would be better people if we were able to be monogamous, this is internalized oppression. When we apply these unfair judgments to other people who are like us, when we see our friends as *too* slutty or *too* free, this is called horizontal hostility. We suggest you look through chapter 2, "Myths and Realities," as a checklist, to see where the beliefs that you learned in our sex-negative culture might be getting in your way.

It's a Harsh World out There

Those of us who choose to run our lives and loves in an unconventional manner should probably be prepared for the fact that many parts of the world will not welcome us with open arms. While there are certainly ways to protect yourself against some social, logistical, and financial consequences, we can't guarantee that there never will be consequences. It's not easy being easy.

Ex-spouses, parents, in-laws, and others who don't share your values about the potential for inclusive relationships may be hostile. Your friendly neighborhood pastor may not be sympathetic, either. Bringing both of your partners to the company picnic is not a good way to ensure your continued ascent through the corporate hierarchy. We recommend extreme caution in choosing who to come out to: yes, we know you're blissfully happy and want to share your joy with the world, but remember, you can't un-tell. We know people who have lost jobs, child custody, and more because the wrong people have become aware of their sexual choices.

Some landlords are reluctant to rent to groups that don't conform to the traditional family structure; although this may be technically illegal, in our experience it's common, and we suggest that you be prepared to tell a teeny white lie when necessary. ("Why, yes, he's my adopted brother.") Some leases contain clauses that allow landlords to terminate rental agreements on the basis of "immoral behavior" or "association with undesirable people" and most allow them to kick you out for illegal behavior—which in some states includes nonmarital sex.

Similarly, your personal love and sex arrangements are best kept out of the workplace: both of us have lost jobs and clients for being who we are. While some cities and states offer some protection to people who are gay, lesbian, or transgender, we are not aware of any that guarantee equal rights for sluts. Unless you are absolutely certain that your employer or your coworker is slut-positive—not just gay, or a swell person with a great fund of dirty jokes, or someone who used to sleep around in college—we recommend a capacious and well-insulated closet.

For information about protecting your legal and political rights as a practitioner of a nontraditional sexual lifestyle, check out the Resource Guide at the end of the book.

Legal Agreements

If you and your partner(s) are living in a somewhat marriage-like structure, with the expectation of sharing property, providing for one another in the event of illness or death, raising children, or running a business together, we strongly recommend official legal documentation of your status and intentions. Terrifying stories of lover kept from lover when one of them is hospitalized, a longtime partner left penniless and homeless after someone's unexpected death, individuals who have been parents in all ways but blood losing an orphaned child to a partner's parents or ex-spouse, and so on should be enough to convince you that it's time to get official about all this.

You do not legally own your children, and the legal agreements you can make about them are limited by that fact. You can use your will to express your desires about who will care for your children after your death, but the court may not be obliged to follow your wishes. In some cases a nonbiological parent can adopt a lover's children as a stepparent. But your children are not property, and you cannot give them to anyone you choose. States that don't allow same-sex couples to adopt also resist second-parent adoption, meaning if you are a child's third parent from birth, you have fewer rights than any parent from a second, third, or fifteenth marriage.

Aside from that, it is possible, and not difficult, to make fully legal contracts to document your agreements on relationship issues. A publishing company called Nolo Press specializes in do-it-yourself legal books, complete with forms and step-by-step instructions. Janet and her previous partner chose not to engage in legal marriage although, since they were an opposite-sex couple, they could have done so; instead, they used a Nolo Press book to outline their legal agreements with powers of attorney and wills.

Pay special attention to durable powers of attorney for finance and health care, and to wills. While the law will not support everything an eager slut might want to do with his money and property, your chances of having your desires upheld by the law will be greatly improved if you express them in a formal and legal manner.

If your agreements are particularly complicated, or if things of great value (such as a lot of money or a successful business) are involved, you may want to go beyond the do-it-yourself level and contact an attorney. If you have that kind of money, you probably know more about this than we do. Do try to find an attorney who is open to nontraditional relationships; you can find referral lists in the Resource Guide at the end of the book.

We have neither the space nor the expertise to tell you all the ways that people with nontraditional sexualities can go about setting up their lives—options range all the way from adopting your partner to setting up a business trust, and beyond. But please, don't assume that your good intentions, heartfelt love, and general wonderfulness will protect you. Sluts don't have that luxury. Do your homework and get the law on your side.

CHAPTER SIX

Infinite Possibilities

THE FIRST EDITION of this book was subtitled "A Guide to Infinite Sexual Possibilities." Now that we're older and a little bit wiser, even that sweeping statement seems a bit limiting: sluthood means infinite possibilities of all kinds, not just the sexual. If you think a "celibate slut" is a contradiction in terms, we have a few surprises in store for you: sluthood lives in the brain, not between the legs, and can fit comfortably and joyously into whatever consensual sexual and relationship pattern you choose.

Asexuality and Celibacy

Folks who say no thanks to sex are becoming an increasingly visible minority. Asexuality refers to people who simply don't experience sexual attraction, and celibacy to those who feel attraction but prefer, for whatever reason, not to act on it. We think that any kind of sexual freedom must include the freedom to *not* have sex, without being pestered or pathologized.

Traditionally, celibacy has offered a way for people to focus on intellectual or spiritual concerns, without the distraction of fleshly lusts. If you're on a religious quest, or working on your doctoral dissertation, or undergoing a major life change, celibacy—short-term or long-term—may offer a valid means of narrowing your focus for a while.

Similarly, people for whom sex or relationships have caused problems may choose a period of celibacy as a pathway toward self-examination: "What kind of person am I when I'm being me just for myself?" Dossie was celibate for this reason for five months after she left an abusive partner, after which she burst forth into feminism and conscious sluttery.

Some people are celibate, but not by choice: people who are incarcerated, ill or disabled, geographically isolated, socially unskilled, or underage may have trouble finding partners for consensual sex. Others are celibate simply because they do not, for whatever reason, feel like being sociable or sexual for a while, or perhaps for good.

We do not see "celibate slut" or "asexual slut" as in any way a contradiction in terms. There are infinite ways of relating to other people—romantically, intimately, domestically, and more—and if you've opened your life and heart to as many of those ways as possible, you're one of us.

Platonic Relationships, aka Friendships

One friend of ours drives us nuts by moaning, "I don't have a relationship . . . just all these *friends*!" We have news for him, and for you: friendship *is* a relationship, an important one that offers tremendous opportunities for the things we need most out of our relationships: intimacy, companionship, support in times of trouble, and more.

We are amused by sluthood-skeptics, often straight women, who are appalled by the idea of loving more than one person . . . and who nonetheless have a best friend, someone with whom they share their deepest secrets, who may in fact be as important a part of their lives as their spouse or lover. If you have a lover and a best friend who are not the same person, you're already practicing many of the skills of sluthood as you manage each of their needs for intimacy, time, and affection.

Friendly Sex

If one of those good, intimate friends becomes your lover . . . what then? Will it ruin the friendship? Will it lead to something more, something that threatens another part of your life? These are the concerns of many people encountering the possibilities of friendly sex for the first time.

47

The cultural ban on having sex with your friends is an inevitable offshoot of a societal belief that the only acceptable reason to have sex is to lead to a monogamous marriagelike relationship. We believe, on the other hand, that friendship is an excellent reason to have sex and that sex is an excellent way to maintain a friendship.

But monogamy-centrist culture affects us all. In single life, we can observe the Land of One-Night Stands, in which you go home with a pick-up and share some hot sex, then the next morning you look at each other and decide if the relationship has life-partner potential. If not, you leave, with much embarrassment, and the unspoken rule is that you will never be comfortable with that weighed-in-the-balance-and-found-wanting person again. Sex as audition is detrimental to people and to relationships. It happens because most people have no script for sexual intimacy in the midrange between complete stranger and total commitment.

How do you learn to share intimacy without falling in love? We would propose that we *do* love our friends, and particularly those we share sex with: these individuals are our family, often more permanent in our lives than marriages. With practice, we can develop an intimacy based on warmth and mutual respect, much freer than desperation, neediness, or the blind insanity of falling in love—that's why the relationships between "friends with benefits" are so immensely valuable. When we acknowledge the love and respect and appreciation that we share with lovers we would never marry, sexual friendships can become not only possible but preferred. So while you're worrying that your sexual desire could cost you your best friend, the more experienced slut could be wondering why you are the only friend she has never fucked.

Dossie, when she was first a feminist, vowed to remain unpartnered for five years to find out who she might be when she was not trying to be somebody's "old lady." She had many wonderful relationships during those years, a rainbow of intimacies, including the sharing of childrearing and households and fixing cars and, of course, lots of lovely sex and affection. She decided that if she made sure to be affectionate, to let people know what she loved about them, that most would find a way to be comfortable with her without needing to be territorial, and it worked. Her quest helped her discover new ways of being in the world as a woman, and as a sexual human being—the foundation of who she is and what she teaches today.

Each relationship seeks its own level, or will if you let it. Like water, you and whatever person has caught your fancy can flow together as long as you let it happen in the way that is fitting to you both.

Living Single

For some sluts, being single may be a temporary condition between partners, a recommended period of healing from a recent breakup, or a chosen lifestyle for the long term. Being single is a good way to get to know who you are when you are not trying to fit as the other half of somebody else; learning to live with yourself and enjoy it gives you a lot to share with a partner when you choose to have one. Single sluthood has its own joys and challenges, which is why we're going to deal with it at much greater length later in this book.

Single people can play the field in a variety of ways. One distinguishing dimension is how separate you keep your lovers. So one form of sluttery for the single involves multiple partners who have no interaction, indeed no information, about each other; this avoids complications at the cost of limiting certain kinds of intimacy, such as opportunities for mutual support and the development of community.

Or you may choose to introduce your lovers to each other, perhaps over Sunday brunch. This may sound wild, or impossible, or like a script for disaster, but don't knock it if you haven't tried it. Your lovers have a lot in common—you, for example—and they may very well like each other. Introducing your lovers helps prevent one of the scariest aspects of jealousy, which is the part where you imagine that your lover's other lover is taller, thinner, smarter, sexier, and in all ways preferable to funky old you. When you meet that other person or when your lovers meet each other, they meet real people, warts and all, and so often wind up feeling safer.

Introducing your lovers to each other also makes possible the development of a community, or an extended family of people, who are intimately connected through sexual and personal bonds. As more people connect to each other in a variety of ways, including sexual, networks form, and something reminiscent of a clan or a tribe may evolve. Then the question of introducing your lovers can become obsolete, as they may already know each other.

If you are a single person in any open sexual lifestyle, you must pay attention to how you are getting your sexual, emotional, and social needs met. You can do this in an infinite variety of ways. The important thing is to be *aware* of your needs and wants, so you can go about getting them met with full consciousness. If you pretend that you have no needs, for sex, for affection, for emotional support, you are lying to yourself, and you will wind up trying to get your needs met by indirect methods that won't work very well. People who do this often get called manipulative or passive-aggressive—terms, in our opinion, for people who have not figured out how to get their needs met in a straightforward manner. Do not commit yourself to a lifetime of hinting and hoping.

When you figure out what you want and ask for it, you'll be surprised how often the answer is "yes." Think how relieved you might feel when someone asks you for support, or a hug, or otherwise lets you know how to please him. Think of how competent and just plain good you feel when you can truly help another person, whether it's by offering a shoulder to cry on or that just-right stimulation that leads to the perfect orgasm. Give your friends the opportunity to feel good by fulfilling you too.

Partnerships

There are multiple forms of open relationships for the partnered, including serial monogamy, where one's various partners are separated in time, and the ever-popular nonconsensual nonmonogamy, otherwise known as cheating. We can think of these lifestyles as unconscious free love, but your authors feel both freer and safer when we love right out in the open.

It is axiomatic that open relationships work best when a couple takes care of each other and their relationship first, before they include others in their dynamic. So the slut couple needs to be willing to do the work we will describe later in this book to communicate well and to handle jealousy, insecurity, and territoriality with the highest consciousness. Couples need to know and communicate their boundaries, to make and keep agreements, and to respect their own and each other's needs. Couples also need to make sure to nourish their own connection to keep it happy, healthy, and fulfilling.

Couples can have a secondary relationship outside of the primary, or a number of lovers that don't get ranked in any hierarchy. Relationships vary in how close or distant they are emotionally and physically, and in how much contact is involved. Some may be short-term, while others may last for years or even a lifetime; some may involve getting together twice a week, others twice a year.

Couples new to nonmonogamy tend to spend a lot of energy defining their boundaries. They usually focus more at first on what they *don't* want their partner to do—the activities that make them feel, for some reason, unsafe or downright terrified—than on their actual desires. Setting these limits is, for many couples, a necessary first step out into the disorienting world of sluthood. However, as couples become more sophisticated at operating the boundaries of their relationship, they tend to focus more on what they *would* enjoy, and then strategize about how they can make it safe. How to create and follow this learning curve will be covered in more detail in chapter 16, "Opening an Existing Relationship."

One woman of our acquaintance has a lifetime lifestyle of having two primary partners, one of each gender, with her other partners and her primaries' other partners forming a huge network. Her relationships historically have lasted many years, through raising children and grandchildren, and her exes are still active members of her extended family.

In some open relationships, each partner seeks out other partners pretty much separately, often making agreements about who gets to cruise which club when, or taking care to avoid running into each other on the Internet or in personal ads. They may talk about their adventures with each other and occasionally introduce play partners to their live-in lovers.

Others seek out a close match with another couple so they can play, either as a foursome or by switching partners, with people they have met and chosen together. Many polyamorous couples make a fine lifestyle out of seeking relationships with couples who are most like them, who share their values and boundaries. Such pairings of pairs can become lifelong attachments and generate both hot sex and true family interconnectedness.

More Than Two

People can make commitments to each other in numbers greater than two. The level of commitment may vary, as when an existing couple makes a commitment to a third partner, or even a fourth. Relationships that add, and inevitably also subtract, members over time tend to form very complex structures, with new configurations of family roles that they generally invent by trial and error. Individuals in groups that come together as a threesome or foursome may find their roles within the family developing, growing, and changing over time: the person who feels like the "mother" of the group this year might well transition to "kid" or "dad" over time, or with each different partner.

Triads allow three partners of one or both genders to form a family unit. Some people grow into triadic or quadratic families as they attain deepening involvement with one or more members who started as outside lovers. Others actively seek members for group marriages, to fulfill their ideal of the kind of family they want to live in. We have heard of people who identify as "trisexual" because they are so strongly attuned to the idea of living and loving as part of a threesome.

Balancing triads can be challenging, as in any ménage à trois there are actually three couples, A & B, B & C, and C & A, and each of these relationships will be different. In a triad, as with the siblings of a family, all the relationships will not be at the same level at the same time; we've heard of lengthy arguments over which member of a triad should ride in the back seat of the car. If you get hung up on forcing these relationships to be exactly the same, you may hear yourself starting to sound like a small child screaming about why your sister got the biggest piece of cake (or, in our adult world, the first orgasm). In all forms of ethical sluthood, but perhaps especially in triads, it is vital to find ways to transcend competitiveness: there's enough of everything for everybody.

Hierarchies and Alternatives

Many polyfolk like to use a hierarchical terminology to define their relationships: the people they live with in a marriage-like arrangement are "primaries," the people they love but don't live with are "secondaries," the people they enjoy spending (often sexual) time with, but aren't necessarily in love with, are "tertiaries."

While this terminology is pervasive, and sometimes useful as a shorthand, we have some concerns about a system that inherently ranks the importance of the people in our lives. Janet says, "E is my life partner and Dossie is my coauthor. If I'm buying a house, E's the most important; if I'm writing a book, Dossie is. Each of them has their own place in my life—why do I have to rank them?"

Circles and Tribes

"Circle" is a word we use for a set of connections between a group of people that actually might look more like a constellation, with some people near the hub and connected to several others, and others near the outside and connected to only one or two and, perhaps, part of another constellation as well. (We like the word "constellation" for this, because in a constellation, everybody gets to be a star!) These constellations may be casual or may become extended families, with provisions for raising children, making a living, taking care of the sick or aging, and purchasing property.

Dr. James Ramey, in his wonderful book *Intimate Friendships*, documented his observations that nonmonogamy tended toward the forming of what he described as kinship networks, communities bound together by the intimacies of their sexual connections, perhaps serving the same functions as villages did in a smaller world. Some of us have taken to referring to our groupings as tribes.

Circles of sexual friends are common—gay men call these friends "fuck buddies." Such circles may be open and welcome new members, typically brought in by other members. When you are part of such a circle, new lovers of any member are potential friends and family members of your own, so the focus changes from competition and exclusivity to a sense of inclusion and welcome, often very warm indeed.

Other circles are closed, with new members welcome only by agreement with existing members. Closed circles are sometimes set up as a strategy for safety from HIV infection and other sexually transmitted conditions, and also to deal with alienation in an overpopulated world. In a closed circle, the notion is that you can play with anyone in the circle (all of whom have made agreements about safer sex and are all perhaps of known HIV status), but you don't have sex with anyone outside the group. Thus you get to play around with a variety of relationships and still stay in a limited field. Such lifestyles are sometimes known as "polyfidelity."

Public Sex

Sluts in any kind of relationship may enjoy group sex. Environments for orgies, party houses, sex clubs, swing houses, gay men's baths, the tubs, or the glory holes are available in many major cities in a variety of forms and cater to all sexual preferences. We will tell you all about them in their own chapter. A group sex environment may constitute a safe field of exploration for a nonmonogamous couple. They can attend parties together or separately, cruise singly or as a twosome, meet each other's friends, and play with a variety of people, all the while maintaining whatever connection with each other they feel good about. In this way, sex outside the primary relationship is defined by the specific environment in which it happens.

Group sex environments often develop their own families, people who come regularly and get to know each other and may share other activities, like giant Thanksgiving dinners. The film *Personal Services* shows us a warm and marvelous Christmas get-together of such a family in a British house of domination.

These are just a few of the ways in which sluts have chosen to organize their lives and loves. You get to choose one, or several, or invent one of your own. Relationship structures, we think, should be designed to fit the people in them, rather than people chosen to fit some abstract ideal of the perfect relationship. There's no right or wrong way to do this, as long as everyone's having fun and getting their needs met.

PART TWO

The Practice of Sluthood

CHAPTER SEVEN

Abundance

MANY TRADITIONAL ATTITUDES about sexuality are based on the unspoken belief that there isn't enough of *something*—love, sex, friendship, commitment—to go around. If you believe this, if you think that there's a limited amount of what you want, it can seem very important to stake your claim to your share of it. You may believe that you have to take your share away from somebody else, since if it's such a very good thing, someone else is probably competing with you for it (how could they!). Or you may believe that if someone else gets something, that means there must be less of it for you.

Getting Enough

We want all of our readers to get everything they want. Here are some ideas that might help you over some of the obstacles on the path.

STARVATION ECONOMIES

We call this kind of thinking "starvation economies." People often learn about starvation economies in childhood, when parents who are emotionally depleted or unavailable teach us that we must work hard to get our emotional needs met, so that if we relax our vigilance for even a moment, a mysterious someone or something may take the love we need away from us. Some of us may even have experienced real-world hunger (if you didn't grab first, your brother got all the potatoes), or outright neglect, deprivation, or abuse. Or we may learn starvation economies later in life, from manipulative, withholding, or punitive lovers, spouses, or friends.

The beliefs acquired in childhood are usually deeply buried and hard to see, both in individuals and in our culture. So you may have to look carefully to see the pattern. You can see it in a small way in the kind of complaining contests some people engage in: "Boy, did I have a rotten day today." "You think *your* day was rotten—wait till you hear about *my* day!"—as though there were a limited amount of sympathy in the world and the only way to get the amount due you was to compete for it. Or remember how you have felt looking at the last piece of a very good pie, the secret salivation that made you greedy and territorial and a "selfish" person. When is it okay to want anything? People may think that if you love Bill that means you must love Mary less, or if you're committed to your relationship with your friend you must be less committed to your relationship with your spouse. And then how do you know if you're Number One in a partner's heart?

This kind of thinking is a trap. We know, for example, that having a second child doesn't usually mean that a parent loves the first child less and that the person who owns three pets doesn't necessarily give any less care to any one of them than the person who owns one. But when it comes to sex, love, and romance, it's hard for most people to believe that more for you doesn't mean less for me, and we often behave as if desperate starvation is just around the corner if we don't corner some love right now.

LETTING GO

Getting over past fears of starvation can be one of the biggest challenges of ethical sluthood. It requires an enormous leap of faith: you have to let go of some of what feels like yours, trusting that it will be replaced in abundance by a generous world. You need to get clear that you deserve love and nurturance and warmth and sex. If the world hasn't been all that generous to you in the past, this may be very difficult.

Unfortunately, we can't promise you that the world *will* be generous to you. We think it will, that if you loosen your possessive grip on the love that's already yours, you'll get more, from the person who loves you, and maybe from some other people too. It certainly has worked for us. But, especially in the beginning, letting go of starvation economies can feel a lot like flying on a trapeze: you have to let go of the security you already have, trusting that at the end of the leap there will always be something else to catch you.

Is there a safety net for this kind of daredevilry? Well, yes, but it's going to require another leap of faith . . . because the safety net is *you*, your self-reliance, your self-nurturing, your ability to spend time in your own company. If being alone seems unbearable to you, the courage required to relinquish what's "yours" may be impossible to summon.

On the other hand, what an incredibly free feeling it is to realize that there *is* enough love, sex, commitment, support, and nurturing to go around! Janet used to spend the nights when her partner was out with someone else by securing a date with one of her other lovers, so she wouldn't have to be alone. Now, she says, "I know that option is there for me if I want it, but much more often I choose to spend that time in my own company, enjoying the opportunity for solitary self-indulgence." Knowing that the world offers plenty of companionship, she feels safe enough to not need that reassurance.

REAL-WORLD LIMITS

In contrast to starvation economies, some of the things we want really *are* limited. There are only twenty-four hours in the day, for example—so trying to find enough time to do all the wonderfully slutty things we enjoy, with all the people we care about, can be a real challenge, and sometimes impossible.

Time is the biggest real-world limit we encounter in trying to live and love as we like. This problem is hardly exclusive to sluts; monogamous folks also run into problems finding the time for sex, companionship, and communication.

Careful planning can help—if you don't already keep a fairly detailed datebook or computerized calendar, now is a good time to start. Respecting one another's realities, and staying flexible, is important. Crises happen: a sick child, a work emergency, or even another partner who needs companionship and reassurance during a particularly bad time. You might also want to do some thinking about how much time you need to get your needs met: do you really have to stay over and have breakfast together the next day, or would an hour or two of cuddling and talk be just as nice?

However you work out your schedule, remember that everybody concerned needs to know about it, and that may include more people than you are used to thinking about. A friend of ours, having failed to inform his wife's lover about an engagement that affected her schedule, moaned: "I know I told *someone*."

Don't forget to schedule time to relate to your partner and play with your kids. And don't leave yourself out: many busy sluts find it important to schedule alone time for rest and replenishment. Janet, when she lived in a Grand Central Station–like group household, had an arrangement with her girlfriend that she could occasionally use the girlfriend's house for solitary retreats—a rare and precious gift—when she was out of town.

Space is another real-world limit for many people. Few of us are fortunate enough to live in multiroom mansions with rooms dedicated exclusively to sex. If you're in your bedroom with your friend, and your live-in partner is sleepy and wants to go to bed, you've got a problem. Crashing on a narrow couch in one's own apartment while one's partner disports with someone else in one's bed may be beyond the limits of even the most advanced slut. When you share your bedroom or other play space with a partner or lover(s), we suggest making clear agreements well in advance of any date and sticking strictly to them. This problem may be solved by separate bedrooms or personal spaces if you can afford them. One couple we interviewed said, "Having separate bedrooms is a nonnegotiable need for us; we wouldn't be able to maintain this lifestyle without them."

Dossie once had a very special relationship with a woman who lived across the continent with a partner. They liked to get together for entire weekends every six weeks or so, but where? Part of this book was written in a cabin in the country, where these two went for a writers' retreat and a private place in which to get very noisy. A hotel room can be another good solution.

Possessions can also be an issue. It's only natural to want to share our stuff with the people we care about. But this urge can cause problems when possessions—money, food, art, sex toys—belong, legally or emotionally, to more than one person. If there's any chance that someone feels a sense of possession about an item, we strongly recommend that you talk carefully with that person before you share the item with someone else. This rule is sometimes simple: you don't let your lover polish off the carton of milk that your spouse was planning to drink for breakfast. It sometimes gets tricky, though. While you may have the technical right to give away a gift that was given to you by someone else, the wife who sees her husband's Father's Day tie around his lover's neck may feel understandably miffed. Similarly, it's a good idea to get consent about sharing an item that was made for you by a lover, or something that the two of you bought together during an intimate shopping trip on your anniversary. Many sluts, for the purposes of hygiene and/or emotional attachment, set aside certain sex toys for use with only one person: *my* vibrator, *Harry's* dildo. Lending or giving jointly owned money without discussing it with the co-owner is, we hope it's not necessary to say, unacceptable.

SEXUAL ECONOMIES

The "tyranny of hydraulics" is Dossie's phrase for the biological realities that govern many aspects of sexuality. While it might be nice to think that you're a sexual superman who can generate erections on demand *ad infinitum*, neither of us has yet met such a man. A partner who is looking forward to conventional sexual activities with a male lover may be quite understandably disappointed to find him unavailable by virtue of having ejaculated with another partner earlier that day. And even the most multiply orgasmic of women can't stay turned on forever.

Such problems can often be solved by readjusting your expectations of what constitutes sex—does it really always require an erection? An orgasm? An ejaculation? Practitioners of tantric yoga have developed ways by which many men can experience orgasm without ejaculation. These strategies are only somewhat useful for birth control and safer sex and are certainly no substitute for rubbers. But they come with a wonderful side effect: men who learn to orgasm without ejaculating are able to come many times, like women. Practitioners of many other kinds of sex have developed ways in which enthusiastic sluts can give their partners one or many orgasms and enjoy a surfeit of sensual pleasures themselves, regardless of their physiological state of arousal.

Erections may come and go, but the rest of the nervous system works pretty much all the time. Before you give up on polyamory because of the tyranny of hydraulics, we suggest you investigate at least some of these possibilities (chapter 21, "Sex and Pleasure," and some of the books in the Resource Guide will help).

Remember outercourse. Remember the huge range of sexual delights that don't have any relationship whatsoever to erections. Remember sensuality. Rediscover massage for its own sake. Share a fabulously smutty conversation about what you'd like to do to each other tomorrow.

Are You Really Going to Starve?

When you try to decide what limits you want to the openness of your relationship, it's not always easy to tell which fears are based on reality and which on fear or illusion. First, you have to pinpoint the areas in your life where you feel insecure, where you perceive the possibility of deprivation—which requires a lot of self-searching and honesty. It helps to ask, "What am I afraid might happen?"

Is your partner's fondness for his friend really going to make him fall out of love with you? What if your partner doesn't think you're special any more? What if your partner is so ecstatically happy that she doesn't need you? Why would your partner ever want you, anyway? These are some of the horrible little thoughts that pop up in our minds when we're scared of starving.

You need to decide whether the thing you fear is actually possible or something that probably won't happen. Then you need to choose what you want to do about it. Frequent check-ins, good communication to keep you aware of whether anyone's feeling deprived or overextended, and lots of internal reality checks (is your disappointment that he couldn't get it up really just that, or is it anger or jealousy over his date last night?) can help. We'll talk later about how to get reassurance and support when you're afraid.

Limits Can Stretch

Sometimes, you just have to try it and see. The old chestnut "If you love something, let it go" is sentimental, but more than a kernel of truth lies at its core. In the same way that dieters are sometimes counseled to let themselves get hungry in order to see what that feels like and learn that they can survive the feeling, you may need to let yourself feel deprived, simply to prove to yourself that feeling deprived isn't the end of the world. Sometimes letting go of one pleasure opens your eyes to another that was there from the start; sometimes a new one comes along; sometimes you find out you don't need it all that much right now anyway. We can't tell you what letting go will feel like; all we can do is assure you that you will learn something from it. Scary . . . and satisfying!

Learning new things takes time, so give yourself plenty. It can be useful to get clear with what you are working on learning right now—like how to feel safe and sexy and special when your partner is out on a date—and promise yourself you will learn the next thing, well, next. Every change, small or large, is accomplished one step at a time, so work on this step today, and you'll be ready for the next one tomorrow or maybe next week—working on today's step is how you get ready for tomorrow.

CHAPTER EIGHT

Slut Skills

GREAT SLUTS are made, not born. The skills you need to keep your-self and your partners happy and growing get developed through a combination of conscious effort and frequent practice. There are skills you can learn that will help start your adventure on the right foot and keep it on track.

Self-examination, in our opinion, is always a good idea—when you are journeying without a map, having a clear picture of your *internal* landscape becomes essential. Ask yourself: What do you expect from this way of living your life? What rewards can you foresee that will compensate you for doing the hard work of learning to be secure in a world of shifting relationships? Some people who have already made the journey cite benefits like sexual variety, less dependence on a single relationship, or a sense of belonging to a network of friends, lovers, and partners. The people we interviewed said things like this:

> "I get relief from pressure—I don't have to fulfill every single thing my partner needs or wants, which means I don't have to try to be somebody I'm not."

"People have different ways of knowing and understanding things, so intimacy with various people expands my appreciation of the universe."

"I can have hot erotic experiences without genital sex, and without compromising my emotional monogamy."

"My lifestyle gives me personal freedom, independence, and responsibility in a way that being an exclusive couple does not."

"I don't believe that humans are designed to be monogamous. Monogamy goes against my instincts."

"I never feel that the grass might be greener on the other side of the fence—I've been there."

"Outside partners are an infusion of sexual juice into my primary relationship."

As you read this book, and hear some stories about successful sluts, you may discover special benefits for you. What are your reasons for choosing this path?

Alas, many people begin to explore open relationships because their partner is pushing them into it, or because all their friends are doing it and they don't want to seem prudish. We ask that you get clear within yourself that you're doing this for *you*—because it excites you, because it offers opportunities for learning and growth and fun, because you want to. Make no mistake, this can be a rocky road. If you're navigating it for the wrong reasons, resentment can easily poison the very relationships you set out to improve.

Sexual change can be a path of reprogramming yourself, with the joyous feeling of abundant sex and love as the carrot, and the fear of deprivation, boredom, or self-loathing as the stick. Since we don't believe that the urge toward monogamy is innate, we think you must have learned your negative sexual feelings and your insecurities *somewhere*—from your parents, from your past lovers, from your culture. What you have learned, you can obviously unlearn—or learn something new. Exploring your feelings and changing your reactions to them can be difficult, but what a feeling of power and triumph each time you succeed!

Earning Your Slut Merit Badge

The people we know who succeed at ethical sluthood usually have a set of skills that helps them forge their pathway cleanly, honestly, and with a minimum of unnecessary pain. Here are some of the skills we think are important.

COMMUNICATION

Learning to talk clearly, and listen effectively, is critical. A technique for good listening is to listen to what your partner has to say without interrupting, and let him know you heard by telling him what you think he just said. Use this clarification technique *before* you respond with your own thoughts and feelings. In this way, you make sure you have clear understanding before you go on with your discussion. Similarly, if you're the one talking, it's not fair to expect your partner to read your mind—take the time and effort to be as clear and thorough in your explanation as you can, and be sure to include information about the emotions you're feeling as well as the facts involved.

If your communications often seem to go awry, it might be a good idea to spend some time and effort learning better communication skills: many adult education facilities offer excellent communication classes for couples, and you can check our Resource Guide for further reading.

EMOTIONAL HONESTY

Being able to ask for and receive reassurance and support is crucial. One of Janet's partners used to request, when Janet was off to a joyously anticipated date with one of her other lovers, "Just tell me I don't have anything to worry about." Janet reports that it felt very good to know that he was willing to ask for reassurance when he needed it and that he trusted her to tell the truth about her feelings. If you imagine his feelings if he were insecure and *didn't* ask for reassurance, you can see why it's so important to get your needs met up front.

We have all been afraid to ask, we have all failed to ask, we have all been irked with our lovers when they didn't read our minds and offer us the reassurance we crave, we have all thought, "I shouldn't *have* to ask." Let's remember to honor the courage it takes to ask for support, to share vulnerable feelings. Let's pat ourselves on the back when we do the things that scare us, and then let's do them some more.

AFFECTION

Similarly, it's vital to be able to *give* reassurance and support, both in response to a request and on your own. If you can't tell your partners that you love them, or give them a heartfelt compliment, or tell them what you think is so wonderful about them, it may be optimistic to assume that they'll be able to remain secure enough to accommodate your other relationships. Our friend Carol notes, "If you're already starved for attention, no wonder an open relationship can feel like a problem!"

Put some thought into how you can let your partners know how important they are to you. We recommend lots of hugging, touching, verbal affection, sincere flattery, little "love ya" gifts, and whatever else helps everyone feel secure and connected.

FAITHFULNESS

This may seem like an odd word to read in this context, but even the most outrageous slut can be, in the words of Cole Porter, "always true to you, darlin', in my fashion." Our friend Richard says, "A lot of people describe having sex with only one person as 'being faithful.' It seems to me that faithfulness has very little to do with who you have sex with." Faithfulness is about honoring your commitments and respecting your friends and lovers, about caring for their well-being as well as your own.

If you have a primary relationship, take a look at what you can do to reinforce its primary-ness. Many people in couples have certain activities that they keep only for their life partners—particular sexual behaviors, sleepovers, terms of affection, or whatever. Look at your public behavior—are you comfortable introducing your partner to the cute number you are flirting with at a wild party? We are: we figure any cutie who would be put off by meeting our spouses will likely make trouble in the future, so it's better if we find out now. Make agreements with your partner before the party, and then you need never wonder if you are welcome to join a group or a conversation that your beloved is enjoying.

Pay attention, also, to how you acknowledge your nonprimary relationships. How will a partner you may never live with feel loved and secure? What rights does this partner have to your time and attention? How can you offer affection and reassurance to everyone who is important to you? Make it a point to let everyone you love know it. Make agreements with your life partner about what you will do when an outside partner needs support or has a crisis like an accident or illness. Who makes the chicken soup? How about you? (Both of your authors make great chicken soup.)

LIMIT-SETTING

To be a happy slut, you need to know how—and when—to say no. Having a clear sense of your own limits, and respecting those limits, can keep you feeling good about yourself and help prevent those morning-after blues. Some limits may be about sexual behaviors: Would you have sex with a gender other than the one you usually do? Would you try a kind of sex you think is kinky? Limits about safer sex and birth control are obviously required; there are some things you definitely do not want to bring home with you. Some limits might be about relationship styles, such as frequency of contact or intensity of connection. We also encourage you to think about ethical dilemmas and how you'd react to them. Would you, for example, be a lover to a coupled individual whose partner didn't know about your involvement? Would you lie to a lover? Fake an orgasm?

And then there's the very, very important limit of "I don't want to." "No, thank you, I don't feel like sex right now." Even if it's your anniversary. Even if you're supposed to want to. Even if you haven't for a long time. No excuses needed.

When you respect your own limits, others will learn to respect them too. People tend to live up to your standards when you are not afraid to set them. Only when everyone's limits are out in the open do you become free to ask for your dearest fantasies, secure in the knowledge that if your friend doesn't want to, he won't. From this position we can ask for the earth and wind up getting a goodly chunk of it.

PLANNING

Successful sluts know that relationships don't just happen—they take work, planning, and commitment. Few of us have so much time on our hands that we can simply have conversations, sex, recreation, family time, or even fights whenever we feel like it—mundane reality has a way of getting in the way of such important stuff. And yes, we do think fighting is important and necessary—we'll talk more about the hows and whys in chapter 14, "Embracing Conflict." If scheduling a fight seems a little bit absurd, just imagine the results of letting the tension build for several days because you *haven't* made time to argue.

Get yourself an appointment calendar or PDA and use it (Janet used to schedule sex with her first husband, Finn, with the cryptic note "F.F."—just in case a coworker should glance into her Day Runner). Some families of sluts have discovered complex online calendars that they can keep jointly, and thus everyone can see what everyone else is doing and make plans accordingly. Once you've made a commitment to spend time together for any reason, keep it—we know you're busy, but postponing important relationship work to attend to other business does not speak well of the significance you give your relationships, does it?

KNOWING YOURSELF . . .

And knowing your programming. As we have said before, we are all carrying around a lot of garbage in our minds about sex and gender. No one can grow up in our culture and escape picking up puritanical and inaccurate ideas about sex. Some of these beliefs are buried so deep they can drive our behavior unconsciously, without our knowing it, and cause a great deal of pain and confusion to ourselves and the people we love. All too often, in the name of these beliefs, we oppress other people, and ourselves.

These deeply held beliefs are the roots of sexism and sex-negativism, and to be a radical slut you are going to have to uproot them. To truly know yourself is to live on a constant journey of self-exploration, to learn about yourself from reading, therapy, and, best of all, talking incessantly with others who are traveling on similar paths. This hard work is well worth it because it is the way you become free to choose how you want to live and love, own your life, and become truly the author of your experience.

OWNING YOUR FEELINGS

A basic precept of intimate communication is that each person owns her own feelings. No one "makes" you feel jealous or insecure—the person who makes you feel that way is you. No matter what the other person is doing, what you feel in response is determined inside you. Even when somebody deliberately tries to hurt you, you make a choice about how you feel. You might feel angry, or hurt, or frightened, or guilty (one of your authors was raised Catholic, so she was trained to feel guilty about astonishing stuff). The choice, not usually conscious, happens inside you.

This understanding is not as easy as it sounds. When you feel rotten, it can be hard to accept the responsibility for how you feel: wouldn't this be easier if it were someone else's fault? Then maybe that person could fix it, and if not, well, maybe you can go ballistic and vent a little steam and melt the whole relationship down in the process.

The problem is that when you blame someone else for how you feel, you disempower yourself from finding solutions. If this is someone else's fault, only that person can fix it, right? So poor you can't do anything but sit there and moan.

On the other hand, when you own your feelings, you have lots of choices. You can talk about how you feel, you can choose whether or not you want to act on these feelings (no more "the devil made me do it"), you can learn how to understand yourself better, you can comfort yourself or ask for comfort. Owning your feelings is basic to understanding the boundaries of where you end and the next person begins and the perfect first step toward self-acceptance and self-love.

GOING EASY ON YOURSELF

As prepared as you are, as centered as you are, as stable as you are, you *are* going to trip over problems you never anticipated—we guarantee it.

Perhaps the most important step in dealing with problems is to recognize that they will happen and that it's okay that they do. You'll make mistakes. You'll encounter beliefs, myths, and "buttons" you never knew you had. There will be times when you'll feel pretty awful.

Can we tell you how to avoid feeling bad? Nope. But we think you'd forgive a friend or lover who misunderstood or made a mistake, and we hope you'll grant yourself the same amnesty. (As Morticia Addams says: "Don't beat yourself up, Gomez; that's *my* job.") Knowing, loving, and respecting yourself is an absolute prerequisite to knowing, loving, and respecting someone else. Cut yourself some slack.

A friend of ours, when she trips over some surprisingly intense emotional response, says, philosophically, "Oh well—AFOG," which stands, she says, for Another Fucking Opportunity for Growth. Learning from one's mistakes isn't fun, but it's way better than not learning at all.

TELLING THE TRUTH

Throughout your experience—as you feel pain, ambivalence, joy—you must speak your own truth, first to yourself, and then to those around you. Silent suffering and self-deception have no place in this lifestyle. Pretending that you feel great when you're in agony will not make you a better slut; it will make you bitterly unhappy, and it may make those who care about you even unhappier. Everybody feels bad sometimes, so you are in excellent company. And when you have the courage to be open about a vulnerable feeling, everyone around you gets permission to be open with theirs.

When you tell the truth, you discover how much you have in common with the people you care about. Honesty puts you all in an excellent position to support yourselves and each other in a life based on understanding and loving acceptance. As you dig deeper and share your discoveries, you may learn more about yourself and others than you ever knew before. Welcome that knowledge, and keep on digging for more.

EXERCISE *Some Affirmations to Try*

I deserve love.

My body is sexy just the way it is.

I ask for whatever I want, and say no to whatever I don't.

I turn difficulties into opportunities for growth.

Each new connection expands me.

I contain all I need for a life full of delight.

Sex is a beautiful expression of my loving spirit.

I am on my personal path to ecstasy.

CHAPTER NINE

Boundaries

MANY PEOPLE BELIEVE that to be a slut is to be indiscriminate, to not care about who you make love with, and thus to not care about yourself. They believe that we live in excessively wide open spaces, with no discrimination, no fences, no boundaries. Nothing could be further from the truth. To be an ethical slut you need to have very good boundaries that are clear, strong, flexible, and, above all, conscious.

One very successful slut we interviewed is outraged by accusations of indiscriminacy, pointing out that sluts get a great deal of opportunity to develop exquisitely sophisticated discrimination: "We actually have more boundaries than most folks because we have more points of contact," more experience relating in very different ways to very diverse people.

What Are Boundaries?

It is basic to any relationship, and particularly important in open relationships, that no one can own another person. Some of us who are kinked that way may explore kinds of power exchange that we call "ownership," but regardless of our relationship style it is essential and incontrovertible that we each own ourselves—lock, stock, and barrel. We each have the responsibility of living our own lives, determining our individual needs, and arranging to get those needs met. We cannot live through a partner, nor can we assume that just because we have a lover, all of our needs should automatically be satisfied. Many of us have been taught that if our lover does not meet every need, this must not be true love, our lover must be somehow inadequate, or we must be at fault—too needy or undeserving or some other sin.

If you were brought up to believe that your relationship would provide your other, or (shudder) better, half, or that your destiny is to submerge your identity in a relationship, you will probably have to put some attention into learning about your own boundaries. Boundaries are invariably in the plural because none of them hold still for long and all of them are individual. They are how we understand where I end and you begin, where we meet and how we are separate as individuals. You need to figure out where your limits are, what constitutes comfortable distance or closeness between yourself and others in various situations, and particularly the ways in which you and your lovers are different and individual and unique.

EXERCISE *Your Magic Wand*

Imagine that you could wave a magic wand and make yourself as brave, strong, and independent as you can imagine being. What, then, would you like your boundaries to look like? List your limits, or try drawing a picture. Remind yourself that you have a right to be treated with respect by everyone in your life. Imagine telling the people you love what your limits are, and remember that doing so is an act of self-respect and self-love.

Owning Your Choices

It is axiomatic in communication between intimates that, as we've already discussed, each person owns his or her own emotions, and each person is responsible for dealing with those emotions. Understanding this is the first step to claiming something very precious—your own emotions. And when you grasp your emotions, you have something unbelievably valuable to bring to your relationships.

When you find yourself responding to someone else's behavior, it can be easy to dwell on what that person has done and how terrible it is and what exactly they should should do to fix it. Instead, try looking at your own feelings as a true message about your internal state of being, and decide how you want to deal with whatever's going on. Do you want to find out more? Do you want to discuss a limit? Do you want a little time to yourself to calm down and get centered? Do you want to be heard about something? When you take responsibility, you get these choices, and more.

What you are *not* responsible for is your lover's emotions. You can choose to be supportive—we're great believers in the healing power of listening—but it is not your job to fix anything. Once you understand that your lover's emotions are not your job or your fault, you can listen and really hear, without falling victim to an overwhelming need to figure out whose fault it is or to make the emotion change or go away.

Some people habitually respond to a lover's pain and confusion with an intense desire to fix something. Fix-it messages can feel like invalidation to the person who is trying to express an emotion. "Why don't you just do this . . . try that . . . forget about it . . . relax!" sends the message that the person expressing the emotion has overlooked some obvious and simple solution and is an idiot for feeling bad in the first place. Such messages are disempowering and invalidating.

Being responsible for your emotions doesn't mean that you have to conquer all your difficult feelings bare-knuckled and solo. You can ask for the help you need—reassurance, validation, a shoulder to cry on, an ear to vent in, a brain to brainstorm with—from friends, lovers, and/or a good therapist. And you, in turn, will do your best to make yourself available when your friends and lovers need this kind of help from you . . . right?

Learning to operate our emotional system consciously may require changing some old habits and can feel very shaky, sort of like learning to ride a bicycle. Weird, embarrassing . . . you'll probably fall down a few times, but if you pick yourself up and keep going, eventually you get the feel of it. And once you get your balance, you'll never forget.

Relationship Boundaries

Relationships also have boundaries. The agreements that free-loving singles, couples, and families make with respect for each other's feelings constitute the boundaries of their relationship. In an open sexual community, it is important to deal with each relationship within its own boundaries. For example, you figure out your limits with your partner before you go to the sex party, you don't use your mistress to diss your wife, and decisions are made with input from everybody affected by them and not behind anybody's back.

Communities based on sex and intimacy work best when everybody has respect for everybody's relationships, which includes not only lovers but also children and families of origin and neighbors and exes and so on. Such communities can evolve into highly connected family systems when everyone is conscious of and caring about boundaries.

Be willing to learn from your mistakes. Boundaries can get tricky at times, so we hope you give yourself lots of slack to explore. Expect to learn by trial and error, and expect to make plenty of errors. Forgive yourself for anything that doesn't work out the way you hoped it would. Remember, you can't learn from your errors if you always have to be right!

DUMPING

One place where people often get confused is differentiating between the honest sharing of feelings and dumping. Dumping means using others as your garbage pit, spewing your problematic stuff all over them and leaving it there. Dumping usually carries the expectation that the dumpee will do something about the problem, even if it's simply to take on the burden of worrying so that the dumper can stop. Usually you can avoid dumping by making it totally clear that your need to share your emotional state carries no obligation for your listener: "I don't like your having a date with Paula tonight," followed by a heavy and pregnant silence, carries an entirely different weight than "I'm feeling insecure about your date with Paula tonight, but I want you to go ahead and have it. Are you okay with listening to some of my fears? Can we talk a bit about ways that I might be able to feel a little safer?"

PROJECTION

Another trick to watch out for is projection. No, not the kind you find at the movies on Saturday night! Projection is when you use another person as a screen to run your movie on. You see your fantasy and miss the real person. You imagine you know this person's thoughts, when in fact you are thinking about your fears. Maybe you imagine that they will respond the same way your parents did—"I know you'll reject me if I don't make a lot of money," "You'll never respect me if I show you my sadness." Every one of us learned our expectations of how people will react to us from our parents. Or you might be projecting your expectations, projections that your lovers—who are not mind readers—can never live up to: "You're supposed to take care of me!" "Whaddaya mean, you're not horny? *I'm* horny!"

When you make a commitment to own your own stuff, you can stop projecting and see the people you love clearly, in all their glory. When you find yourself thinking blameful thoughts about your partner, you might ask yourself: "What do I own here?" What you see inside might be something like "Wow, I sound just like my father when he was angry," or "I feel the way I did when I was eight and used to hide in the closet when I was upset." Then you might go to your lover and share how whatever was going on woke up some old tapes of yours, and you can brainstorm what you want to do about that. When you work together to own your stuff, each of you, then your partner can support you in exploring your emotions and, more important, learn to stop projecting on you as well. Then you need never again feel like a puppet in somebody else's show.

ROLE BOUNDARIES

You may find yourself playing out different roles, indeed feeling like a somewhat different person, with different partners. With one partner you might feel young and vulnerable and protected; with another, you are earth mother. With one lover you might feel careful and solid and safe, with another you might be dashing and reckless. These boundaries may seem unfamiliar or confusing when we don't have much experience with living in multiple relationships.

Janet got a wonderful feeling of acceptance for all her parts at a party:

> I enjoy games in which I role-play the part of a little girl, but my last
> partner wasn't comfortable with them. After a bit of searching, though,
> I found within my circle of acquaintances a man who enjoyed being a
> "daddy" as much as I enjoyed having one. My partner was delighted I'd

found a safe place to play that role, and we both felt I'd made a good choice in selecting someone to whom I could entrust such vulnerable parts of me. "Daddy" and I got together once or twice a month for finger-painting, watching Disney movies, eating peanut butter sandwiches, and other slightly more adult pleasures.

At one point I attended a party where both my life partner and my "daddy" were in attendance. From across the room, I saw the two of them chatting, and I headed over to say hi. As I drew closer, my partner held his arm out invitingly and called, "Hey, hon, come over here and hang out with your dad and your boyfriend for a while." The feeling of acceptance, and the warmth of knowing the two men accepted and honored each other's role in my life, was amazing.

One of the things people get out of multiple relationships is the chance to be all of their various selves. When two people meet, they relate where they intersect, where they have complementary roles in similar scripts. So, being different things to different lovers, we might find ourselves having different boundaries, limits, and relationship styles in different circumstances.

Your own internal variety might manifest in many ways. For instance, you might be calm and centered when Lover A is angry, but Lover B's irritability is distressing to you—it "pushes your buttons," perhaps reminding you of a past lover or a punitive parent. Here is an opportunity to take charge of your buttons. When your buttons are your own, it becomes much easier to figure out what your limits need to be with Lover B, and to understand that they may be altogether different from your limits with Lover A.

Forget about fairness. Ethical sluttery does not mean that all things come out equal. Different relationships have different boundaries, different limits, and different potentials. So if your lover has found someone that she can share a certain activity with, and you would like to share that with her too, the question is not "Why don't you do that with me?" but "That sounds interesting, how do you suppose we could make that work for us?"

This is how one woman we interviewed put it:

My open sexual lifestyle gives me personal freedom, independence, and responsibility in a way that being an exclusive couple doesn't. Because I'm responsible, every day, for my needs being met (or not), and for creating and maintaining the relationships in my life, I can take nothing for granted. Every person I meet has the potential for whatever it is that's right between me and that person, regardless of how my relationships are with anybody else. And so this lifestyle gives me a very concrete feeling of individuality that I re-create every day. I feel more like a grown-up, adult, responsible person when I know that my life, all of it—who I fuck, who I relate to, how I relate to them—is all my choice. I promised my partner that I would share my life with him, and that implies to me that I have a life to share—a complete life. And it's clear to me that he's here because he wants to be, wherever "here" is. We are with each other, every day, because we really want to be. Our choices are real.

The Unethical Slut (A Rant)

SOME PEOPLE TREAT SEX as a big-game hunt—trying to conquer the unwilling and unwitting victim, as though the object of their attention would never decide to share sex with them unless tricked into it. Believing that a person would have to be a fool to make love with you is often, we observe, a self-fulfilling prophecy. Someone who tries to use sex to shore up sagging self-esteem by stealing someone else's is a pitiable object: this strategy does not work to build a solid sense of self-worth, and this poor starving individual will have to go on stealing more and more and never getting fulfilled. We hope that such people play the thief of love in some other social circles than our own.

Such people often approach open sexual lifestyles as if keeping score. Set collectors and trophy fuckers treat their partners like prizes in a contest they have set out to win—only what happens after the prize is collected? Is it time to go after the next one?

The concept of set collectors may be new to you, but we assure you that such people exist. Dossie discovered several of them when she lived with two other single mothers in a communal San Francisco household, called Liberated Ladies at Large, and learned that some people's ideal of free love was to make sure they had sex with all three of the liberated sisters. A friend of ours once discovered that a would-be lover of hers had already had sex with her mother and her sister and was hoping to complete the set. Sex that means treating your partners as collectibles does not meet our requirements for mutual respect.

Some people approach "scoring" as if all people can be ranked on a hierarchy from the most to the least desirable and as if the way to make the most points and assure yourself of a high rank is to collect partners as high up the ladder as you can reach. People gain in rank and value in these hierarchies by being thin, young, cute, gym-toned, wealthy, and/or of high social status.

We do not believe that love is a game that you can win by scoring high on a hierarchy of shallow values. We know from extensive experience that appearance and wealth are not predictors of good loving. We try to avoid ranking people as better or worse than each other and are unhappy with those who want to relate to our rank (authors get quite a few points in the status category) more than ourselves. Hierarchies produce victims on the top as well as the bottom, since it is almost as alienating to be approached by too many people for the wrong reasons as it is to be approached by no one at all.

Someone who has a history of nonconsensual nonmonogamy may get attached to the sense of secrecy, of getting away with something. These folks may have a very hard time adapting to the idea of consensual sluthood—they're so used to concealing their activities from their partners that they may even have built that furtive feeling into their erotic life, hooked on the adrenaline rush they get from forbidden fruit. It takes a pretty substantial leap of faith, and maybe some creative fantasizing and role-playing, for such individuals to open up their hidden places and experience the greater joy that can come from knowing that nobody is getting hurt by their fun.

People who refuse to learn to use barriers that get between people and viruses are not ethical sluts. Arguing with lovers about allowing potentially infectious sex, insisting on sex without barriers, or attempting to sneak around a lover's limits about safer sex is, quite simply, playing dirty. Refusing to deal with the realities of viruses and bacteria because of embarrassment is unethical: a good slut speaks the truth even if blushing furiously.

Ethical sluts do not make promises they can't keep. If you are attracted to someone who is looking for a life partnership and what you want is a lighthearted affair (or vice versa), you need to be honest about that, even if that means saying "no, thank you" to sex until your feelings for each other are more on a par. Mistakes can easily be made. Dossie made such a mistake when she was very young and stupid:

> I had just broken up a long-term relationship and was pretty broken up about it myself. I went out to the coffee shops in Greenwich Village and saw my recent ex in earnest conversation with a cute young thing who was not me. I felt horribly betrayed, lost, and worthless. Just then, a young man who had been attracted to me, and for whom I had no serious feelings, came up to speak to me. It somehow seemed appropriate to go home with him and let him soothe my ruffled feathers, but I regretted it the next day when I found myself hurting his feelings and leaving him in the lurch. To further aggravate my guilt, it turned out what my ex was doing with that sweet girl was beating his bosom about how horrible he felt about breaking up with me—we wound up getting back together. I have always felt that I took advantage of the young man who offered me his affection, which I thoughtlessly took and then gave right back to him. It would have been kinder had I just said no.

An older and wiser Dossie has since discovered a couple of limits of her own: she does not share sex with anyone that she's not at least potentially interested in sharing sex with again, and anything worth doing is worth waiting for till the time is right. While we all make mistakes, the hallmark of a skillful slut is to learn from them and keep going.

Which brings us to revenge fucking. It is truly nasty to arrange to have sex with one person to get back at another. To arouse one person's insecurities, jealousy, and other painful feelings on purpose is dishonorable, and to use another person as a puppet in your play is disrespectful and most often downright abusive. In psychopathology, "antisocial" is defined as behaving with flagrant disregard for the rights, and we would add feelings, of others. We prefer to relate to sociable people.

What do you do when someone in your intimate circle is not playing honestly? It helps if the people in your extended family have ways to talk about what is going on, to share experiences and feelings. If everyone is too ashamed to admit to having been misused by someone with an untrustworthy hidden agenda, then no one will have the information they need to protect themselves. There is no shame in having believed someone's lies, and most of us at some time or other have given our trust to someone who turned out not to be worthy of it. It is possible to fool an honest person, but we hope you have enough humility to learn from your mistakes and not get fooled twice.

All these difficult scripts are about somebody not being honest and are also about somebody having sex while avoiding intimacy and emotional connection. When you are not telling the truth you cannot be present, and when you are not present you can't be connected to anyone else, and when you are not connected how can you feel anything at all?

By treating lovers as people, and letting relationships take the shapes they want instead of the forms forced on them by the culture around them, ethical sluts can form friendships that last as sex waxes and wanes.

CHAPTER TEN

Flirting and Cruising

FLIRTING AND CRUISING are fine arts, and skills that you can learn even though few people develop them overnight.

Is there a difference between flirting and cruising? Some people think of "flirting" as what you do in environments that are not erotically oriented, and "cruising" as what you do in clubs, conferences, bars, and other places where people often seek sex partners. Or you might see flirting as a more introductory maneuver and cruising as what you do when you know for sure that you're interested. Both involve an exchange of sexual energy in the form of eye contact, body language, smiles and warmth, and little flashes of erotic energy that can be shared long before any physical contact would be appropriate.

Sex roles can complicate both flirting and cruising. Men in this culture are taught to push, to insist, never to take "no" for an answer; women are taught to be coy, to refuse, never to offer an outright "yes." The more polarized we get in this silly equation, the further we push one another away—with results that range from hurt feelings to date rape.

The good news, though, is that both sets of behaviors can be unlearned and that the more we unlearn them, the less there is to unlearn. When all genders feel free to answer "yes" or "no" with no concern for anything but their own desires, a truer understanding and a more positive sexuality become possible.

Dossie tells the story of a woman friend of hers back in the 1970s who decided to experiment with what was supposed to be every man's fantasy. She sat patiently in a singles bar one night, being approached by many men, until one to whom she felt attracted came along and began to flirt. He asked if he could buy her a drink, and she asked him nicely if he would like to come back to her place and fuck. He swallowed his ice. It took the poor fellow a couple of minutes before he could talk coherently again, and when they actually got to her place he found himself impotent. They did share some perfectly lovely massage. *That's* how deeply ingrained some of these cultural stereotypes can be.

Saying Yes, Saying No

If you're going to put yourself out there and make connection with fellow sluts, it is vital that you get good at saying two simple little one-syllable words: "yes" and "no." For most of us, who have been taught that "yes, please" is overeager and "no, thanks" is rude, these simple words may be unexpectedly difficult.

Sexual sophisticates tend to give each other a lot of credit for knowing what they want. With this assumption, it becomes easier for your potential partners to make very direct proposals that might seem outrageous in any other context; that's because they trust you to say "no" if you're not interested. It is nobody's task but your own to figure out what you want, and nobody can or should second-guess you. So you are going to have to learn to say "no," and to say "no" easily enough that having to turn down a couple of unwelcome come-ons won't ruin your evening.

Men as well as women have trouble with "no"—men are taught that they are always supposed to be eager for sex, so if someone comes on to a man when he is not ready, or not interested, it can feel unmanly and wrong to say "no."

The trick to a comfortable "no" is to structure it in such a way that it's about you, not about them. So instead of "With *you*? Are you out of your mind?" you're saying "No, thanks, you seem nice but I'm not feeling much connection with you," or "No, thanks, I'm not really looking for lovers right now," or "No, thanks, I prefer to get to know people a lot better before I do anything like that with them." Important note: the "thanks" should be sincere. Being asked, even by someone you don't find attractive, is a compliment and deserves a thank-you. If you think someone is ridiculous for finding you attractive, we worry about your self-esteem.

Women have been taught that it is unfeminine to say "no" directly. Ask yourself: when was the last time you said "no" to sex? How did you do it? Was it with a polite and friendly but unmistakable "no thanks"? Or was it with a sort of "Not tonight, I've got a headache" or "maybe another time" or "I'll think about it" waffle? We strongly suggest you work out a "no thanks" that feels comfortable to you; expecting the interested party to read your mind and somehow know that your "maybe . . ." means "no" is neither ethical nor slutty.

Women also need to practice saying "yes." Our cultural myth is that the man in a heterosexual interaction pleads with, or cons, or bullies the woman into saying "yes," or at least refraining from saying "no," and then does whatever he thinks is appropriate. Women need to equalize here, to do more of the choosing, to know what it is that you enjoy and to be able to say clearly what you want to whomever you find attractive. And if you are a man whose programming is more about what you think you are supposed to want than what you actually want, then you need to learn to say "yes" to your real desires when they appear on your doorstep.

Once you've gotten comfortable with "no," "yes" is usually easier (and more fun). Try it, in all its variations: "Yes, please." "Yes, when?" "Yes, but I have some limits I want to tell you about first." "Yes, but I need you to talk to my partner first." "Yes, but not tonight; how does next Tuesday look for you?" "Hell, yes!"

EXERCISE *Practicing Yes and No*

Write down a little speech, maybe a few sentences, that you might use to invite someone to have sex with you. Write down another little speech you might use to decline sex in a polite and nonhurtful way.

The Fine Art of Flirting

Everybody is born knowing how to flirt, and if you doubt it, watch the way a baby or toddler interacts with nearby adults: lots of eye contact, smiles, maybe a chortle of welcome and the offer of a beloved toy (which must, according to the rules, be promptly handed back after due admiration, just like adult toys).

Most of us, though, lose this precious ability by the time we're grownups and need to learn it all again from scratch. Your authors believe that great flirting should be an end in itself rather than a means to an end. Practice flirting for fun, and maybe put aside, for the moment, any specific goals about getting laid. Focus on getting good connection. Watch the way many gay men flirt with straight women—friendly flattery, lighthearted innuendo, nonthreatening intimacy, all made possible by the realization that the interaction is intended simply for mutual pleasure, not in the hopes of a quick dash to the nearest bedroom.

We suggest, then, that you learn to flirt simply by practicing. The sort of behavior you may associate with the word "flirting" ("hey, baby, what's your sign?") is not the sort of thing we're talking about here and is, in fact, its exact opposite. Great flirting is about *seeing*; hunger to be seen is a natural human emotion, and when you show people that you're seeing them, it's natural for them to start seeing you.

A lot of flirting is nonverbal. There's a way of holding eye contact for just a moment longer than usual—more than a passing glance, less than an outright stare—that lets a person know that you find them worth looking at. Turn your body so that you're facing the object of your interest, and stay physically open, arms and legs uncrossed. Smile.

If your flirting proceeds to words, we suggest a sincere, personal, but nonsexual compliment to start. Is the person at the dry cleaning counter wearing a new pair of glasses? Is the person next to you on the park bench leading a poodle that's sporting a fresh haircut? Did you hear through the grapevine that your next-door neighbor just got a nice promotion at work? A sincere compliment on any of these is a way of saying, "I'm paying attention to you; you're not just a face in the crowd to me." This approach may not seem like flirting to you, but trust us, it's a great first step. Commenting on physical appearance, particularly in a sexual way ("hey, those pants make your ass look great!") is *not* what we're talking about here. Your goal is to make your friend feel fully seen, not reduced to an agglomeration of body parts.

Watch for feedback. If we were cruising you and you turned your face away from us, took a step back, or crossed your arms, we'd know you weren't interested in connecting and we'd move on gracefully. We wouldn't like it any better than anyone else does, but we'd do our best not to feel rejected—you don't know us and don't know what you're missing out on. Besides, for all we know, you're on the way to a date with someone you already know and are simply not available at that moment.

One of the most successful flirts we know says he has a never-fail opening line: "Hi, I'm Mike." From there, he and the object of his attention can proceed wherever their interests take them: the weather or scenery, their work, their kids or pets, the sorry state of the world today, their favorite foods, whatever. This stage of flirting is exploration, getting to know this wonderful new person, discovering the ways in which you're similar and the ways in which you're different, seeing how you might connect. The sexy part of this is in the energy—the flash of a smile, a brightness in the eye. You usually can tell when you're talking and when you're flirting—it's the energy.

We recognize that if you are shy, or have been taught that nice girls or boys don't flirt, or are accustomed to a more predatory style of flirting, all this can be difficult to learn. We wish we had a magic flirting wand that we could wave at you, but since we don't, you're just going to have to practice. A willing friend, preferably of the gender (if not the orientation) that you normally flirt with, can be a help here: pretend that you're meeting for the first time and try flirting. The friend can give you feedback about whether you're coming on too weak or too strong and help you refine your skills. When you start enjoying flirting in and of itself, without thinking about where it might lead, you'll know you're on the right track.

Coming Out Slutty

Unless you're doing your cruising in exclusively poly environments, it is reasonable to expect that the object of your attentions may not (yet) have read this book and may not be familiar with slutty lifestyles. At some point, therefore, you are going to have to get it out there that monogamy is not on your personal menu of options.

We can't tell you exactly when or how to do this, except that we vote for sooner rather than later. If both of you are just looking for a quick fling or a party scene, it may not be necessary to discuss such matters at all. However, if the fling leads to a second date, that may be the right time to let your new friend know that you're not interested in going steady, now or ever.

Working this into a normal conversation about software or surfing can be a little tricky, we know. A quick reference to your partners, emphasis on the plural, often does the trick. Or you can start a discussion of relationships in general, in order to get space to express your own opinions and desires.

It may happen that the object of your attention is a devoted monogamist and that you nonetheless find this person extremely attractive. We have some words of advice for polyfolk who fall in love with monogamists in chapter 18, "Couples."

Cruising Challenges

If you're standing in the corner of a roomful of people, feeling like you're the only one there who isn't part of a happy group and like you're never going to be able to connect again for the rest of your life, we suggest finding someone else who's standing in a corner, and starting a conversation. Janet's favorite opening line for these situations is, "Hi, I don't know a soul here, can I stand here and talk to you for a while?"

Beyond that simple opening, which gets easier with practice, cruising strategies depend a lot on your own gender and the gender(s) of the people you're seeking.

FOR MEN
Gay men have their own style of cruising, marked by a straightforward approach based on the understanding that most gay men are able to say "no, thank you" without much discomfort. Without the uncomfortable threat of physical overpowerment that pervades man-on-woman cruising, and free of any requirements beyond following their own desires, gay men often are able to cruise each other with greater reliance on body language and nonverbal cues than their het

brothers, confident, as we all should be, that if body language is not understood, they will use their words.

Het men have different challenges. Few women like to be pushed, overwhelmed, or not listened to in the arenas of sex and intimacy. Most women are particularly offended by men who push too hard for private get-togethers or phone numbers, who insistently move the conversation back to sexual topics when the woman has tried several times to change the subject, or who touch them, particularly in a sexual, paternalistic, or covert way, without permission. Sneaky come-ons are a pain; it works better to simply ask, and if you hear a "no," don't argue.

Many a man has made the mistake of approaching a woman in the way he thinks he would like to be approached if he were a woman. If you're not sure if women find your approach too heavy-handed, imagine being approached by a large, strong man using your exact technique and ask yourself how that feels. Successful male cruisers remain sensitive to verbal and nonverbal cues, conveying friendly interest and appreciation for the fascinating human being in front of them.

FOR WOMEN

Most women are not very good at saying "yes," and not very good at saying "no"—your authors aren't, and we've been practicing both for a long time. We're not sure how things got to this state, where a woman is just supposed to stand there looking adorable until some big strong hunk comes and makes her decision for her, but we don't like it much.

Many women, both gay and straight, can benefit greatly from learning to be more assertive in asking for what they want, both during the meeting process and afterward. If you're used to sipping your drink and waiting for someone to make a move on you, initiating contact yourself may seem terribly awkward, pushy—yes, even slutty—at first. It's also scary as hell to risk rejection like that. It *does* get easier . . . particularly if you do get rejected a time or two and get a chance to find out that it isn't the end of the world. After all, we're not asking you to do anything that men haven't been doing for centuries, and you'll discover, as they have, the many joys of asking for what you want and getting it.

FOR COUPLES

Sometimes couples, or an established group of lovers, may be cruising for somebody or somebodies new to play with, in a three-way or more. Cruising as a couple has its advantages—if you strike out, you still have someone to go home with. However, many cruisees are not used to the idea of openly nonmonogamous relationships and may get a little freaked out when you come on to them with, "Hi, I find you very attractive, and so does my wife." Be reassured that you will also find many lovely people who actually prefer the safety and built-in boundaries of getting it on with one or both members of an established couple . . . and be prepared to find a goodly number of happy shiny needles in your carefully chosen haystack.

Some couples cruise together for someone to play with in a three-way, while others cruise individually for partners who want to play with one or the other of them. When you're coupled but cruising solo, please do remember to mention to your cruisee that you have a partner at home. Some people will be delighted to receive this news and others will not, but full disclosure is the ethical part of ethical sluthood.

If you plan to go home with your spouse when it comes time to leave this party, it is courteous to make sure your other beloveds know this in advance. Reassure new contacts by exchanging contact information and, if appropriate, choosing a place and time to get together in the future, like "May I call you tomorrow morning?" or "Would you like to meet for coffee after work?"

Whether you cruise individually or together, you need to work out your agreements beforehand. Who is interested in doing what to whom? Where? When? If one of you is looking for someone to hit the mattress with right there that night and the other wants something permanent ("She followed me home! Can I keep her? Please?"), you may be headed for a major misunderstanding.

Each member of a couple must have the requisite social skills. Depending on your partner to do all the work of introductions, conversation, flirtation, and negotiation is bad for you and bad for your partner. It may also lead to misunderstandings, since few partners are skilled enough communicators to get across *all* your needs, interests, and personality traits.

A pet peeve of many sluts is the individual who treats one or more of the people involved in a disrespectful or objectifying manner. One example is the couple that sends an innocent-looking woman out as bait, and you may be startled, when you bite, to discover her spouse joining the party. Janet remembers once, in a group sex environment, being invited by a man to help stimulate his female partner. As she happily joined the group, she noticed that the man immediately shifted his focus from his girlfriend to *her*—ignoring the hapless girlfriend as he grabbed Janet's breasts. Needless to say, Janet excused herself immediately from this creepy-feeling scene.

It is disrespectful to treat the third party as some sort of oversized marital aid. Many bisexual women we know are driven to distraction by the "hot bi babe" phenomenon—couples who seek them out, not because they're charming or hot, but because one member of the couple has a fantasy about playing with two women or seeing two women make love as a free peep show.

The fundamental rule for cruising as a couple, or being cruised by a couple, is *respect* for the feelings and relationships of all concerned. You don't want to cruise someone who will try to steal you or your partner for his own, and your cruisee doesn't want to be used, deceived, or mistreated. We may refer to our play partners, affectionately, as "tricks," but actually tricking them into your bed is unethical.

When you treat everybody involved with respect, affection, and intimacy, you can reap very special rewards—anything from a warm happy fling to a long-term multiperson relationship.

FOR EVERYONE

The best, most successful, and least obnoxious cruisers we know, of all orientations, are friendly, curious folks who like most people and are interested in talking to everyone. If some of the people they talk to turn into potential relationships, so much the better.

When you find yourself worrying about how you are seen by others, remember that there is no point in pretending you are anyone except who you are. It does you no good to attract someone who thinks you are somebody else: all you get is someone who is excited about somebody who isn't you. When you are honest, you attract the people who are interested in you, just as you most wonderfully are.

A good conversationalist is usually a successful cruiser and more often than not a skilled partner as well—because the give-and-take of good conversation and sensitivity to nonverbal cues are also important skills for the fulfilling relationships to come.

CHAPTER ELEVEN

Keeping Sex Safe

THE TERM "SAFE SEX," later amended to "safer sex," was coined to talk about how we can design sex to minimize the risk of HIV transmission . . . but sex has *never* been altogether safe. Both your authors grew up in an era when an unwanted pregnancy meant a life-endangering illegal abortion. It's been only a few decades since more reliable birth control became available, and only a few before that since antibiotics began curing illness, insanity, and death caused by sexually transmitted diseases (STDs) like syphilis and gonorrhea. Herpes is still incurable, and we still have only limited answers to cervical cancer from human papilloma virus. No matter what your orientation, your practices, or your risk factors, in today's environment, careless sex can kill—which means that you have to protect yourself and your partners.

Given that sex is never completely safe, ethical sluts put time, effort, and commitment into getting as much sex as they want at the least risk possible. Dedicated sluts have developed a plethora of risk-reduction strategies that can minimize the chances of infection and/ or unwanted pregnancy.

Please research the safer-sex protocols that apply to your life and plan to protect yourself and your lover from HIV, herpes, hepatitis, gonorrhea, syphilis, chlamydia, shigella, human papilloma virus, cervical cancer, unwanted pregnancy, and a host of other nasties. Medical research and recommendations are beyond the scope of this volume, but at the end of the book we have listed some Internet resources that are kept more up-to-date than is possible here.

We don't think you need to cover every portion of your anatomy with latex before you touch another human being. The goal for most of us is risk reduction, sort of like defensive driving on the freeway. Yes, a drunk could kill at any time while you are cruising down the highway, and most of us take our best shot at safety and go on driving. There are ways to have hot satisfying sex without performing the erotic equivalent of skydiving with a faulty parachute. Here are some that we, and sluts we know, have used successfully.

Barriers: The Rubber Fence

Utterly basic technique: put something impenetrable between you and the virus. Today, many people decide to follow their sexual urges to far-out places by being scrupulous about the use of latex or polyurethane barriers. We hope you don't need us to explain this to you at this point in history, but careful use of barriers includes condoms for vaginal sex, anal sex, and fellatio; gloves for masturbation of a male or female partner or for insertion of fingers or hands into vaginas or anuses; and dental dams or plastic wrap for cunnilingus or analingus.

Gloves or condoms make it easy to keep any sex toy that will be used by more than one person nice and clean and bug free. Clean your toys thoroughly after each use, sterilize if you can, and let them rest, clean and dry (most of the bad bugs cannot live long without moisture). If there are toys that you really want to use on each of you within the same little bit of time, we suggest you buy two or more of them.

The use of a good water-based lubricant can do wonders to make latexed sex more pleasurable for both or all partners. Along with smoothing out the friction of rubber on mucous membranes, a single drop of lube *inside* a condom increases the transmission of warmth from one person to another, which feels nice and—well—hot. For tips on how to use barriers in a pleasure-enhancing manner, check out chapter 21, "Sex and Pleasure," and some of the books in the Resource Guide. And if you're not completely comfortable using any of these barriers, practice! Gentlemen can masturbate with a condom (or two, or three) until it comes easy. We have heard of one dedicated fellow who managed to put on eighteen condoms at once—he said the tight squeeze felt really good. And why not get a little playful with your rubber?

If you are inexperienced with condoms and plastic wrap, give yourself some space to learn. Get playful, spill some lube, and roll around in it; invent creative ways to wrap body parts in plastic wrap and then find out what interesting new things you can feel. Plastic wrap doubles nicely as a risk reduction barrier and a bondage toy, and it comes in colors. Explore the taste and feel of your safer-sex equipment, and check lubricants on tender places for allergic reactions—not fun to discover when you are all excited only now it itches inside and you have to go wash that stuff out right now. Pay attention to the sensual qualities: fine latex is wonderfully silky, and the best lubricants feel like liquid velvet.

We want you to have fun and make wise choices: we need all the readers we can get, so we don't want to lose you.

EXERCISE *Practice Makes Perfect*

For a man: Commit to masturbating with a condom on at least once every three or four times you masturbate, until you feel like you have that skill down perfectly.

For anyone who has sex with men: Buy a large box of condoms—the cheap kind are OK for this—and practice putting them on bananas, cucumbers, or dildos, in as sexy a way as you can . . . first with your hand, then with your mouth. Use up the whole box.

For everyone: Make a list of ways you can get off with little or no risk of fluid transmission.

Fluid Bonding

One popular safer-sex strategy used by some couples is called "fluid bonding" or "fluid monogamy." The couple agrees that they are safe to play with each other with no barriers, and to use condoms and rubber gloves very conscientiously with all their other partners. Both of us have made such agreements with life partners. To do this kind of agreement, both (or all) partners get thoroughly tested for HIV and other diseases. You might have to wait six months to be sure, since HIV antibodies don't reliably show up in the bloodstream for some months after the individual is infected. Once you're both sure you're healthy, you're free to practice unprotected sex with one another and to use barriers with your other lovers. Be sure you're in clear agreement about which sexual acts are safe enough to do without a barrier and which ones require a barrier; to reach such an agreement, everyone involved will have to do some homework on the risk levels of various activities and decide together what level of risk is acceptable to you. Don't forget to factor in information from everybody's individual sex histories.

You may wish to restrict certain kinds of sex—often vaginal and/ or anal intercourse, which place the participants at highest risk for disease transmission—to your primary relationship. Any time when you are actively trying to make a baby, you might not want to engage in potentially reproductive activities with all and sundry.

If barriers were infallible, fluid bonding would be a nearly perfect strategy; unfortunately, they are not. Some diseases live on the pubic mound, perineum, outer labia, or scrotum, which latex can't cover. Pinhole leaks can allow virus to creep through, although this happens less often than antisex crusaders would have you believe. Condoms can break or come off during sex. If you are fluid-bonded and experience a condom failure, you and your partner will have to decide together whether to begin again with HIV testing and six months of barrier usage or to risk the possibility that one of you has been infected and could infect the other. If there is any possibility of an unwanted pregnancy, talk together about the morning-after pill.

Avoiding High-Risk Behaviors

Another risk reduction strategy is simply to eliminate some forms of sexual expression from your repertoire. Many people have chosen to forgo forms of sex that involve putting mouths or penises into or near assholes, feeling that the particularly high risks of this form of play are not worth its reward. Others have decided not to engage in any form of penetration with an organic penis. We have never heard of a dildo or a butt plug coming down with an infection.

If all this winds up sounding like no sex at all, please consult a good book about sex—there are hundreds of ways to share really hot sex that don't involve somebody squirting inside somebody else.

Every decision you make requires that you balance your own desires against your assessment of the risks. Remember when you're making your decisions that desire is powerful and important and that there's no point in making rules you can't live with. One friend of ours points out that safer sex can be like dieting—"I can be really good during the week, but then I binge on the weekends." On the positive side, expanding your range of hot sexual expression by learning new and exciting ways to have sex can leave you both safe and satisfied.

Finger-Crossing

Simply hoping for the best, or denying that you're at risk, or pretending that diseases and unwanted pregnancies only happen to other people is *not* an acceptable strategy. If you don't have the honesty and courage to face the genuine risks of your sexual behaviors, you certainly don't have what it takes to be an ethical slut, and we question whether you should be having sex at all.

We are shocked and worried by the levels of denial we see among some sexual communities, who would like to believe that because new treatments have slowed down the progress of HIV that the cure has been found. People are still dying. If your lifestyle seems to make you unlikely to get exposed to HIV, you are still at risk for herpes, hepatitis, HPV, and a host of other diseases. Kinsey's statistics from back in the 1940s indicated that slightly more than half of relationships that are theoretically monogamous in fact involve sexual contact with outside partners. Get educated, friend, and take care of yourself.

Testing and Prevention

We think it's essential for ethical sluts to get tested for HIV and other sexually transmitted diseases on a regular schedule. How frequently depends on the risk factors in your life. Ask your doctor, clinic, or Planned Parenthood office, and follow their advice.

While most STDs are preventable only with barriers and care, recently developed vaccinations can protect you against several potentially deadly forms of hepatitis and, if you aren't already infected, human papilloma virus. If you engage in nonmonogamous anal or vaginal play, these are a *very* good idea; they are expensive, but cheaper than getting sick. You'll still need barriers against all the rest of the microscopic nasties.

Birth Control

Mother Nature is called that for a reason—sometimes it seems like she wants everybody to be a parent. Even when you utterly *know* that you don't want to get pregnant this time, some deeper urge can easily lead you to forget a pill or count the days wrong. Birth control involves tricking the busy little eggs and sperm into not doing their jobs and tricking your own instincts into letting you do the trick right.

Birth control technology is, alas, far from perfect: reliable, reversible, easy, side-effect-free contraception is still a dream. Unwanted pregnancies need no longer be the life-shattering tragedies of yesteryear, but they are still awful, and we hope that none of you ever has to have one.

If you are female, have intercourse with men, and could possibly be fertile, you must take active steps to ensure that you won't get pregnant until and unless you choose to. The possibilities include birth-control pills, longer-term chemical birth control like Norplant and Depo-Provera, diaphragms and cervical caps, condoms, IUDs, sponges and foam, and tubal ligation, among others. Some women with regular menstrual cycles succeed at the rhythm method, particularly if they and their partners learn to enjoy outercourse during their fertile periods. There is a lot of good information available about the risks and reliability of all these methods; your physician, clinic, or Planned Parenthood can help you make a good choice.

For men who have intercourse with women, the choices are (unfortunately) quite limited. If you know you are unlikely to want to father children in the future, a vasectomy is minor surgery that will relieve you of a great deal of worry. If you hope to be a father someday, use those condoms—and lobby for research into better male contraception. The surgery to sterilize women is more involved: the surgeon will cauterize the fallopian tubes—this requires a hospital, and a little recovery, but nothing dreadful. Remember, you'll still need protection from infectious diseases.

When someone gets pregnant unintentionally, this can be, to put it mildly, difficult. If everyone involved agrees that an abortion is the best choice, that can be pretty unpleasant in and of itself; if there is disagreement, it can be shattering. Until such time as science enables men to carry fetuses in their bodies, we believe that the final decision has to be the woman's, but we sympathize deeply with the man who would like to raise a baby and whose female partner isn't willing or able to carry it. We do think that both partners should share in the financial and emotional burden of an abortion or a pregnancy.

If one or both partners is interested in being a parent, and the woman is willing to carry the fetus to term, ethical sluthood opens up a wealth of options for parenting. Please don't feel that the only way to be a parent is to get married and buy a house in the suburbs—perfectly marvelous children come out of shared parenting arrangements, intentional communities, group marriages, and a multitude of other ways to nurture and support a child.

Committing to Healthy Sex

You may notice that we have gone out of our way *not* to tell you what decisions to make about your sexual behavior. Only you can decide what risks feel acceptable to you, and we believe that letting anybody else make that decision for you virtually guarantees that you won't follow through on your choices.

You must, however, *make* choices. You must choose to do your homework and learn what you need to know about risks and rewards. You must choose to do the work of saying "no" to sex that doesn't meet your own safety criteria and of being prepared to say "yes" to sex that does: discovering you're out of condoms at the wrong moment is a recipe for disaster. You must choose to approach your sexual behaviors in a mature, realistic, and *sober* manner—intoxication plays a major role in a shockingly high percentage of HIV infection and unwanted pregnancy.

You must be prepared to share your sexual decision making and history with any potential partners you encounter. If consent is at the core of ethical sluthood—and it is—your partners must be able to give informed consent to whatever risks are involved in having sex with you. You, of course, have the right to expect that same honesty from them.

You won't like talking about this stuff, especially not with a new lover. It's depressing and scary, definitely not erotic, and sometimes horrendously embarrassing. Allow us to reassure you: the first time is the worst. Practice makes perfect, and after you've been over all these ugly and lethal possibilities a few times, you will become less sensitive and learn to deal with what you need to with ease and grace. Many people avoid the discussion on a first date by agreeing upon the safest possible practices for this encounter, then negotiating more specifically later on. If you know you have a risk condition, like active herpes, silence becomes less of an option; you need to invite your lovers to collaborate with you in avoiding infection, and they have a right to enough information to make her own choices.

On a cheerier note, getting good at talking about sex has some very nice rewards, once you get through blushing. Chatting about the fun stuff is a turn-on and the best way to get exactly what you want in the way of pleasure. Then you can learn what your partner gets excited about, which will make you the best of all possible lovers.

We, and most of the people we know, make fairly conservative choices about what health risks we take in our sexuality. We know from experience that it is quite possible to have exciting, satisfying, fabulously slutty sex without lying awake nights worrying afterward. And isn't that the kind of sex we all want to have?

CHAPTER TWELVE

Childrearing

IF YOU'RE RAISING KIDS today, you have it a little bit easier than sluts of yesteryear—images of families in books and television aren't quite as limited to *Leave It to Beaver* and *Ozzie and Harriet* as they were in our childhoods. Still, even though divorce and single parenting are now acceptable topics, our culture is slow to catch up to the other realities of our lives: media images of multipartner relationships, same-sex relationships, and other nontraditional constellations are still rare.

Yet kids take to these relationships quite readily, perhaps more so than to the traditional nuclear family: children have grown up in villages and tribes for most of human history. Janet remembers having some of her first desires for group living during vacations with her then-husband's expansive extended family: she noticed that her kids, surrounded by loving adults with plenty of time on their hands, were happier, more docile, and less fragmented than she'd ever seen them. During her kids' teen years, she lived in a group household and watched her sons adapt quite readily to the comings and goings of a disparate group of adults—one of whom was almost always free to answer a question, troubleshoot a computer program, experiment with a recipe, or play a game.

The single parent ethical slut can check out a number of creative options for maintaining a fulfilling sex life while being a responsible parent. When Dossie was sharing a house with two other single mothers, one of her lovers used to babysit all the kids so all three mothers had a chance to go out dancing together. A friend of ours used to babysit for her younger sister and the kids next door so that her parents could mess around with the next-door neighbors. Dossie never actually lived as a single parent, whether or not she was partnered, during her daughter's childhood; there was always a troupe of friendly people living in sprawling houses, city and country.

We have never had problems creating consistency and security for our children in a sexually interconnected extended family. While you might assume that inclusive relationships might generate massive inconsistency, our experience is just the opposite. Our connections tend to form sprawling extended families that have plenty of energy to welcome all the children, and the children readily learn their way around the tribe.

Some shifts in the population are inevitable, but in our experience children take that kind of mobility for granted and perhaps develop a flexibility that might serve them well later in life. If we prepare them for a life where any change at all is seen as a disaster, how will they manage? Better, perhaps, to learn that loss may be difficult, but we do get through it, pick up the pieces, and go on with our lives. One way parents can offer consistency to children is to role model healthy adaptation to change. Another good form of consistency is to be honest with yourself and with your children—when you live your life in integrity, everyone can count on you to be exactly who you, wonderfully, are.

The binary nature of monogamy-centrist thinking tends, we think, to cause problems: you're either the love of my life, or you're out of here. Both of us have found that opening our lives to other kinds of connections also opens our children's lives. For example, a former lover of Janet's has not been sexually involved with her for quite a while but has become a sort of surrogate uncle and best friend to one of her sons and is still a loved member of her household—as she writes this, he is asleep on a futon on her living room floor.

Still, many parents have a great deal of difficulty bridging the gap between responsible parenting and inclusive relationships. Questions about what and how much to tell your kids, how to prepare them for difficult questions in the outside world, and how to help them relate to the new people who arrive and depart in their lives can be challenging for any mom or dad.

Sex Education for Kids

As you've surmised, we think an abundance of relationships can be highly beneficial to family life and that children gain in role models, attention, and support in the polyamorous extended family. Clearly, children should not be included in adult sexual behavior, and many adults who have been wounded by sexual abuse as children can testify to the damages. Education, however, is not abuse, and children need enough information to make sense out of what the adults are doing, so they can grow up to their own healthy understanding of sexuality.

All parents must make their own decisions about what kind of sexual information their children should have at any given age. For the health and well-being of the child, a balance must be struck between offering too much information, which might seem scary or overwhelming, and too little, which might leave the child with the message that naked bodies and sexual arousal are so dangerous and embarrassing that it's not allowed to even talk about them. We don't want to terrify the kids, and we don't want them to come into their own adult sexual lives with the belief that sex is dirty and shameful.

Remember, sex education is an issue for all parents, whatever their lifestyle. We want our kids to have good information and freedom of choice, and they are often living in neighborhoods and going to schools where many parents believe that kids should be denied all information about sex (or else they might turn out to be sluts like us).

To make matters more complicated, our culture currently is deeply divided about the entire subject of sex information and kids. Some people consider any form of sex education to be somehow dangerous. Some authorities feel that when children have "precocious" information about sex, it must mean that the child is being abused by an adult. We are, however, adamantly opposed to "abstinence-only" so-called sex education. How are we to teach our children to say "no" to an abusive adult if we are not frank about what it is that they should say "no" to? When we try to keep sex secret from our kids, they are aware that something is going on, but they don't know what. And if we leave them to get their sex information in the playground or on the street, from equally ill-informed other kids, we consign them to the jungle. Our kids need and deserve adult support in learning about and negotiating sexuality, as they do in all other aspects of life.

What to Share, and Not

You'll have to decide how much your kids should know about your sexual choices, such as multiple partners, same-sex partners, or alternative family structures. Our experience is that kids figure such things out quicker than you think they do but that they may not figure them out exactly right.

One word of warning: if you are living in a community that does not share your standards about sex education, your desire to educate needs to be balanced against the need for the child to learn what is and is not okay to share with the outside world. When you teach your kids, you will need to talk with them about how other people's standards operate and about what information should and should not be shared.

There are still many places in this country where living a nontraditional sexual lifestyle is considered a justification for legally removing your children from your custody. Even when you are sure you are doing no harm, you still may need to protect your kids from Mrs. Grundy. We can't give you concrete guidelines on this, because only you can know the atmosphere in your particular community and the personalities of your own children.

What Should They See?

We think it's a good idea to model physical and verbal affection for children; that's how they learn to be affectionate adults. But you'll have to make some decisions about the appropriate dividing line between physical affection and sexual demonstrativeness.

Do your kids get to see you hugging your partners? Kissing them? Touching them? These are all decisions we can't make for you. You have to think them through yourself—taking into account such issues as their ages, their levels of sophistication, and their perceptions about your existing relationships—and abide by your own decisions.

Nudity is a gray area. We certainly don't think kids are harmed by growing up in households where casual nudity is the norm. But children who have never been around nude adults may be upset if nudity is suddenly introduced into their living room. Kids can be very sensitive to issues like sexual display, and flashing is clearly a violation of boundaries. Certainly, if a child expresses discomfort with being around your or your friends' nudity, his or her desires should be respected. And we hope it goes without saying that no child should ever be required to be nude in front of others—many children go through phases of extreme modesty as they struggle to cope with their changing bodies, and that, too, deserves scrupulous respect.

What Should They Do?

It is illegal and immoral to allow your kids to engage in any form of sexual behavior with any adult, or to allow your partners to be sexual or seductive with your kids. Many children go through one or more sexually explorative and/or flirtatious periods in their lives—this is natural and common. But it's important that you and your friends maintain especially good boundaries during such periods; learning polite and friendly ways of acknowledging a child's changing needs without engaging sexually is a critical skill for ethical sluts who spend time around their own or their partners' kids. ("Isn't that cute? You're getting to be such a big girl now!") The best way to teach your child good boundaries is to be clear about your own and to respect the child's right to grow up free from violation.

Answering Their Questions

Kids' questions about sex and relationships can often be challenging—from the five-year-old's "But how does the seed get *to* the egg?" to the teenager's "So how come you get to fuck anyone you want, but I have to be home by midnight?"

Here's where the skills you've learned in other parts of this book can come in handy. You owe your kids honest, heartfelt responses to questions like these; this is not the time to come on all high-handed and parental. Particularly with older children and teenagers, it's fine to let them know if you're feeling ambivalent or embarrassed about something: they'll know anyway, believe us. If a situation makes you angry or sad, share that, too. They may need some reassurance that your emotion isn't their fault and some reinforcement that it's not their job to help you feel better.

It's also fine to test their willingness to receive information. Before you start heaping data on their heads, you can try prefacing your communication with a question like, "Do you want to know about [whatever the topic is]?" Janet remembers a conversation with her older son when he was about ten: she'd just done a "birds and bees" rap and had perhaps gotten a little carried away. At the end of her long speech, she asked him, "So, as long as we're on this topic, is there anything else you want to know?" He replied, fervently, "Mom, you've already told me *much* more than I wanted to know."

Good boundaries are important here too. While your kids are certainly entitled to express an opinion about the way you choose to run your life, they don't get to dictate it. The flip side of this is that you owe it to them to help prevent their lives from being unduly impacted by a lifestyle they never chose. Dossie willingly agreed to maintain a discreet closet about her lesbian partner when her daughter's junior high school friends came to visit; her daughter got to come out to her friends about her mom at her own pace. Well, nobody ever said parenthood—especially slutty parenthood—was going to be easy.

Your Lovers' Kids

When your lovers have kids, you are involved with those kids too—one friend of ours refers to the many kids he helped his lovers raise as his "practice kids," helping him learn parenting skills for the child of his own that came along later.

You'll need to make decisions together about what to tell the kids about your relationships, and you need to learn what decisions are conventional in your lovers' families. It may not matter whether younger children know or understand that some of the connections in their families are sexual and others are not. But all adults in families with children have a responsibility to make a connection with the kids we come in contact with, and to foster our own children's connections with our friends and lovers.

Single sluts with no previous connection to children may find themselves in a position of needing to learn how to deal with children in their extended family.

Fact of life: Everyone around children will eventually need to set limits with them. There may be some challenges as you work to reconcile your own limits with the habits and styles of a family that was working just fine before you arrived in it. Expressing your needs can be an opportunity for the kids to learn that different adults have different needs, that Jane can nap through a rousing game of Inside Tag whereas Jean needs an hour of quiet.

It may be that you find yourself disliking one of your lover's kids. Perhaps something about this particular child pushes your buttons: they may remind you of your horrible older brother or maybe even your young self—often the things that annoy us most about someone else are the things we dislike about ourselves or our histories. Or the child may be angry at you, or dislike you, for reasons entirely beyond your control: perhaps you are "replacing" a beloved parent or other adult who has been lost to death or divorce. Whatever the reason for this problem, you are the adult here and it is your responsibility to find a way to solve it. Resolution will undoubtedly take some time, a fair amount of energy, and a great deal of patience, but we believe it will be worth it, for you and your lover and the kids.

Early in Janet's relationship with her spouse E, there was a lot of friction between him and her young adult son, mostly over issues that will sound familiar to any stepparent: housekeeping, noise levels, courtesy. Then, she recalls, "We were visiting my mother for a few days, and the two of them were escaping the domestic whirlwind out in the back yard. E expressed sympathy about a difficult personal situation my son was encountering. They had a beer together and really talked, from the heart, for the first time—and suddenly E could see my son the way I see him, as a socially awkward young man, not always too aware of the physical realities around him, but with a huge heart and a lot to give. From that evening on, they've had no trouble working together on normal household stuff and have in fact become good friends."

When you establish a positive relationship with the children in your environment, they will respond by developing a positive relationship with you. We know of ex-lovers who have maintained close friendships over many decades with children with whom they had no biological relationship. Thus are slut families built and maintained.

PART THREE

Navigating Challenges

CHAPTER THIRTEEN

Roadmaps through Jealousy

Let jealousy be your teacher. Jealousy can lead you to the very places where you most need healing. It can be your guide into your own dark side and show you the way to total self-realization. Jealousy can teach you how to live in peace with yourself and with the whole world if you let it.

—Deborah Anapol, *Love without Limits*

FOR MANY PEOPLE, the biggest obstacle to free love is the emotion we call jealousy.

Jealousy feels really rotten, and most of us will go to great lengths to avoid feeling it. However, your authors believe that most people take the destructive power of jealousy way too much for granted, that they give their jealousy far more power than it deserves. After many years of living free and dealing successfully with jealousy, we tend to forget that we live in a culture that considers it acceptable to divorce or even murder a sexually explorative partner who has committed the unthinkable crime of arousing jealousy in us.

Let us point out here that monogamy is not a cure for jealousy. We have all had experiences of being ferociously jealous of work that keeps our partner away or distracted from us, or our lover's decision to cruise the Internet instead of our bodies, or Monday (and Tuesday and Wednesday) Night Football. Jealousy is not exclusive to sluts; it's an emotion we all have to deal with.

Many people believe that sexual territoriality is a natural part of individual and social evolution. If you believe that, it's easy to use jealousy as justification to go berserk and stop being a sane, responsible, and ethical human being. Threatened with feeling jealous, we allow our brains to turn to static with the excuse that we are acting on instinct. Your authors don't think it matters if jealousy derives from nature or nurture or both. What matters is that we know from experience that we can change it.

Here is a story from Dossie's life about the struggle to cope with jealousy:

My lover is late coming home. I hope she is all right—this morning she left in tears. Last night we both cried until very late. I hope she will not be too angry with me, or then again, her anger might be easier to bear than her pain. Last night I thought my heart would break from feeling her pain.

And it's my fault, my choice, my responsibility. I am asking my lover to go through the fire for reasons most of the rest of the world consider frivolous if not downright reprehensible. I cannot, will not, be monogamous.

More than three decades ago, I left my daughter's violent father, fighting my way out the door, bruised and pregnant, promising anything, promising I would call my parents for money, lying. After I escaped Joe, he sent me suicide threats and threatened murder—one time he set fires around the house he thought we were still in. After I left, I decided he was right—I am a slut, I want to be a slut, I will never promise monogamy again. I will never be a piece of property again, no matter how valuable that property is considered. Joe made a feminist of me—a feminist slut.

My lover is back. She brought me a flower. She still doesn't want a hug. She feels her house has been invaded by alien energy. I was very careful to clean up, all is very tidy, dinner is ready, appeasement and placation, I'll do anything not to feel so awful.

Why did I insist on doing this? My coauthor and I have been patiently waiting to resume this part of our relationship when my newfound and most beloved partner was ready. She has already conquered the terrors of group sex—tomorrow we will have another couple over for dinner and my birthday spanking, which she herself arranged with no egging on from me. Within the last year she has had more new sexual experiences than she'd had in the previous forty-eight years and has taken to it all like a duck to water.

Except her lover having a date with one other person. She hates feeling left out and resents that we are doing it in our home this time, not neutral territory. Maybe this was a mistake. Maybe I make a lot of mistakes.

My friends and lovers have welcomed her into the family with open arms. Loose lovers often form kinship networks from their sexual connections—and customs, even sort of a culture, have begun to emerge. And so it is customary, in my brand-new culture, for one's lovers to welcome a new lover, not as competition but as an addition to the community. But this is not her culture.

My lover is ready to talk now. She is pissed. She is seriously pissed. She resents me for every miserable terrified thought she has had today, she is furious that I would subject her to the unprotected experience of her own feelings, and that's not what she said, that's my interpretation. And that's not what I said either—this was no time to get uppity about clean boundaries and the importance of owning your own feelings. I listened. This time I listened, without interrupting, trying only to let her know that I love her, I feel her pain, I am here for her. She is furious with me, and I am not giving myself permission to defend myself, and I hurt.

This story has no tidy ending—we talked for hours, or maybe I listened, and I heard how difficult it was for her, how she felt invaded, how she felt her home was not safe, how she feared that my other lover would not like her, how she felt attacked by her and me both, how very much she feared I was abandoning her. We came to no pat little answers that make good stories for books—we just poured out anguish, and went to sleep exhausted, and went on loving each other and working on this issue as best we could.

It's been more than ten years since Dossie wrote this story, and she is no longer with this lover. The relationship ended for many reasons, none of them particularly about jealousy. Some readers were upset by this story when we included it in the first edition of this book—it's not exactly cheerful and it doesn't have a happy ending. But we are including it again anyway, because we think it's important that our readers know that even accomplished sluts struggle with pain, miscommunication, mismatched desires, anger, and, yes, jealousy.

EXERCISE *How Do You Experience Jealousy?*

Set aside some time for introspection. Remember some times when you felt jealous, and write about how that felt. You may find your mind preoccupied with thoughts about what those other people were doing. It may take a little patience to go back to your own feelings: rage, grief, despair, desperation, anxiety; feelings of being lost, ugly, lonely, worthless; or whatever other feelings are particular to how you experience jealousy. We are often tempted to accuse ourselves about horrid feelings, as if we needed some sort of proper justification for feeling lousy. Try having some compassion for yourself when you feel so bad.

Or do a freewrite about jealousy—set a timer for five or ten minutes and just write down whatever comes into your mind. When you're through writing, be kind to yourself. You might want to do this more than once, maybe over time, and keep it like a journal . . . to be read by you only, or maybe by a trusted friend or therapist.

Or write a letter to your jealousy. Ask it what it's trying to accomplish. Ask it for advice. Then have your jealousy write a letter to you.

What Is Jealousy?

We cannot ask this question too often. What is jealousy to you? Does jealousy really exist, and is it what we think it is? When we choose to confront the feeling of jealousy rather than run away from it, we can see more clearly what jealousy truly is for each of us. Jealousy is not an emotion. It can show up as grief or rage, hatred or self-loathing— jealousy is an umbrella word that covers the wide range of emotions we might feel when our partners make sexual connection with somebody else.

Jealousy may be an expression of insecurity, fear of rejection, fear of abandonment, feeling left out, feeling not good enough, feeling inadequate, feeling awful. Your jealousy may be based in territoriality, or in competitiveness, or in some other emotion that's clamoring to be heard under the jealous racket in your brain. Sometimes it may show up as blind screaming rage—and being blind can make it very difficult to see.

Dossie, when she first started thinking about and challenging her jealousy, felt an almost intolerable sense of insecurity, along the lines of "nobody will ever love me because something is wrong with me and I'm unlovable." She discovered this about herself in the early years of feminism, so it fit perfectly with her feminist explorations to go to work on her self-esteem and build a foundation of security that didn't need to be granted by another person and that no one else could take away. You can probably figure out how valuable a lesson this was and how many more uses she has found for feeling secure within herself. Thank you, jealousy—without this lesson she wouldn't be confident enough to be writing this book.

If you experience your jealousy as insensate rage, then you might want to read something about anger, how other people are thinking about it, working with it, dealing successfully with it; perhaps you can take a course in anger management. Maybe you can come to terms with your anger. Maybe you can get to a place where you and your lovers need never fear your anger again. Wouldn't that be worth working on?

Many people find forms of jealousy in themselves that are actually pretty easy to deal with—nagging doubts, bits of nervousness about performance or body image. Others find themselves falling into a whirlpool of terror or grief, difficult even to look at, much less to tease apart into separate feelings like fear of abandonment or loss or rejection. Why do we sometimes feel this way? Dossie the therapist has a theory about this, based not only on her own experience but also that of many clients she has worked with on these issues.

Jealousy is often the mask worn by the most difficult inner conflict you have going on right now, a conflict that's crying out to be resolved and you don't even know it. Because it's rooted so deeply, it can be incredibly difficult to stay aware when jealousy peeks over the horizon: we twist and turn and writhe in our attempts to not feel it.

This is when your emotions are most likely to bring you to grief—when you believe that you need to avoid feeling them at any cost.

One way to not-feel a feeling is to project it onto your partner. Projection is a psychological defense that involves trying to move a painful feeling outside yourself by running your emotional movie on someone else, as if that person were a screen for your fears and fantasies and not a human being. It may be that this is the only real definition of jealousy: it's the experience of projecting one's uncomfortable feelings onto one's partner.

But here's some good news. If you recognize yourself in any of this, then some part of you has decided that you are strong enough to acknowledge the underlying emotion, and that means you're in an excellent position to do some healing right now. Use your jealousy as a signpost: "Work on this feeling here!" Take a class, join a group, find a good therapist, start practicing meditation—go to work on yourself. You have a golden opportunity, so make the most of it. You could get a whole lot of bang for your buck if you do the work that's presenting itself now: heal old wounds, open up new possibilities, gain health and freedom from fear . . . and somewhere in there, almost as a bonus, you get to grasp your sexual freedom as well.

Sometimes what we perceive as jealousy is actually something else. Think through the details of how jealousy works in you. What bothers you the most? Is it that you *don't* want your partner to do those things with someone else or that you *do* want your partner to do them with you? Jealousy might actually be envy, and envy is often very easy to fix: why not make a date with your lover to do what you have just discovered you are missing?

Sometimes jealousy is rooted in feelings of grief and loss, which can be harder to interpret. We have been taught by our culture that when our partner has sex with another, we have lost something. Not to sound dumb, but we are confused. What have we lost? When our partners come home from hot dates, often they are excited and turned on and have some new ideas they would like to try out at home. We fail to see what we lose in this situation.

Or the sense of loss you feel might be the loss of an ideal, a picture you have been holding in your head of what a perfect, monogamous relationship might look like. It may be helpful to remember that all relationships change through time: people's needs and desires shift according to age and circumstance, and the most successful long-term relationships are the ones with enough flexibility to redefine themselves over and over again through the years.

Occasionally, our discomfort means that we are becoming aware on an intuitive level that our partner is moving away from us, and it might be true that we are losing the relationship we cherish. That does happen. The fact that supposedly monogamous people everywhere often leave one partner for what they perceive as greener grass with another is not much consolation when it happens to you.

We watched a friend of ours go through feelings of deep grief and loss when she perceived that her partner's lover was trying, nearly successfully, to abscond with her partner. In this case, her pain threw a spotlight on some dishonesty and manipulation on the part of the third party and gave her partner the strength to break off from the outside lover and to find other lovers who had greater respect for his primary bond. On the other hand, this scenario might just as easily have ended in a breakup; we'll talk more about breakups, and dealing with them ethically with care for your own and your partner's feelings, in chapter 20, "The Ebb and Flow of Relationships."

Jealousy might also be associated with feelings of competitiveness and wanting to be number one. There's a reason there is no Olympics of sex: sexual achievement is not measurable. We cannot rank each and every one of us on some hierarchical ladder of who is or is not the most desirable or the better fuck. What a horrid idea! Your authors want to live in a world where each person's sexuality is valued for its own sake, not for how it measures up to any standard beyond our own pleasure. If you find out about something that you would like to add to your own repertoire, you can certainly learn to do it without wasting time trashing yourself for not already having known how.

Fear of being sexually inadequate can add up to a very deep and secret wound. But allow us to reassure you that eventually, when you succeed in establishing the lifestyle you are dreaming about, you will be so familiar with so many different individuals' ways of expressing sexuality that you will no longer have to wonder how your sexuality compares to another's; you'll know from direct experience. Great lovers are made, not born. You can learn from your lovers, and your lovers'

lovers, and your lovers' lovers' lovers, to be the sexual superstar you would like to be.

Unlearning Jealousy

To change the way you experience a feeling takes time, so expect a gradual process, learning as you go, by trial and error. And there will be trials, and you will make errors.

Start by giving yourself permission to learn. Allow yourself to not know what you don't know, to be ignorant; Buddhists call this beginner's mind. You must allow yourself to make mistakes; you have no choice. So reassure yourself: there is no graceful way to unlearn jealousy. It's kind of like learning to skate—you have to fall down and make a fool of yourself a few times before you become as graceful as a swan.

The challenge comes in learning to establish within yourself a strong foundation of internal security that is not dependent on sexual exclusivity or ownership of your partner. This difficult work is part of the larger question of how to grasp your personal power and learn to understand and love yourself without such a desperate need for another person to validate you. You become free to give and receive validation, not from need or obligation, but from love and caring. We suggest most strongly that you put some effort into learning to validate yourself: believe us, you're worth it.

Many people find that as they develop their polyamorous families, they actually get validation from lots and lots of people and thus become less dependent on their partner's approval. Their needs and their sources of nourishment get spread out over a wider territory.

Disempowering Your Jealousy

We can't tell you how to banish jealousy or how to exorcise it as if it were a demon. It may be your inner demon, but it is not a cancer that you can cut out. It is a part of you, a way that you express fear and hurt. What you can do is change the way you experience jealousy and learn to deal with it as you learn to deal with any emotion: work with it until it becomes, not overwhelming and not exactly pleasant, but tolerable; a mild disturbance, a warm summer shower rather than a typhoon.

One woman we talked to had some very good ideas about what you can do about jealousy:

I notice that jealousy comes and goes, depending on how good I feel about myself. When I'm not taking care of getting what I want, it's easy to get jealous and think that someone else is getting what I am not. I need to remember that it's my job to get my needs met. I feel the jealousy, but I'm not willing to act on it, so it mostly goes away.

Once you have made a commitment to refuse to act on your jealousy, you become free to start reducing the amount of power you let your jealousy have over you. One way to do this is simply by allowing yourself to feel it. Just feel it. It will hurt, and you will feel frightened and confused, but if you sit still and listen to yourself with compassion and support for the scared child inside, the first thing you will learn is that the experience of jealousy is survivable. You have the strength to get through it.

A large part of our difficulties with jealousy comes from our attempts to avoid feeling a scary or painful emotion. Perhaps long ago when we were children, truly powerless in the world and with a very limited set of tools for dealing with our emotions, we felt something scary and told ourselves, "I will never feel this again, it's too awful, I'll die, I'll kill myself." So we stick the feeling, and the event that inspired it, into something like a pot, and put the lid on good and tight. As the years go by, whenever something comes along that reminds us of what's in the pot, that rattles the lid a little, we push down on that lid. "Gotta keep the lid on that pot," we tell ourselves—we may not even remember why. And the pressure builds and builds, not so much from what's in the pot as from our frantic struggles to keep the lid on.

When we grow up and we need to take the lid off so that we can deal with our emotional reality as an adult, it can feel really scary. But surprisingly, often when we actually look at what's in our pot and feel it, it's much more manageable than we had feared. You can indeed open your pots, look at what's bubbling away in there, and then put the lid back on. Your old defenses will continue to work just fine when you want them to.

We have heard sluts accuse each other of being jealous as if it were a crime: "See? Look at you! You're jealous, aren't you? Don't try to deny it!" It is particularly important that you own your jealousy, to yourself and to your intimates. If you try to pretend that you are not jealous when you are, others will perceive you as dishonest, or worse yet, they may believe you and see no need to support or protect you—because you're fine, right? If you pretend to yourself that you are not jealous when you are, then your own emotions may try devious routes to bring themselves to your attention, manifesting themselves as intensely irrational anger, unreasonable behavior, crushing anxiety over anything at all, temper tantrums, crying fits, or even physical illness.

When you deny your jealousy to yourself, you take from yourself the opportunity to be compassionate with yourself, to offer yourself support and comfort. When you deny jealousy, or any other difficult emotion, you put yourself in a harsh and difficult landscape, full of pitfalls and land mines. "Acting out" means doing things you don't understand, driven by emotions you have refused to be aware of. Denying your jealousy can lead you to act out harsh feelings in ways you will regret later.

Sometimes acting out takes the form of making ultimatums about what your partner may and may not do or, worse, trying to enforce retroactive "agreements" by getting all righteously indignant about how anybody could have figured out that it wasn't okay to take Bob to the movie you wanted to see, and aren't both of them inconsiderate and rotten? You cannot deal constructively with jealousy by making the other guys wrong. Foisting your feelings off on your partners is a dead end strategy; it just plain won't work. Jealousy is an emotion that arises inside you; no person and no behavior can "make" you jealous. Like it or not, the only person who can make that jealousy hurt less or go away is you.

Listening to someone who is feeling jealous can be difficult, particularly when the jealousy is focused on you. Sometimes when a lover is jealous and in pain, you may find it easier to feel angry and push that person away, rather than staying close, staying in empathy, listening, caring. When you blame this person for being jealous, what you're really saying is that you can't stand to listen to how much your beloved hurts when you're on the way out the door to play with someone else. This seeming indifference is a crummy way to avoid dealing with your own feelings of guilt.

There are easier solutions. Feelings like to be listened to—other people's feelings, and your own. Once you understand that you *are* doing something constructive when you just listen, or ask someone else to just listen to you, you can get those troublesome feelings out in the open and learn to satisfy them. The idea is to be nice to your feelings, to welcome them as guests, till they feel finished and move on through.

If this sounds familiar to you, if you have experienced times like this in your life, we recommend that you practice the skill of staying quietly with both your own and your lover's pain. Remember, you don't have to fix anything: all you have to do is listen, to yourself or another, and understand that this hurts. Period.

Janet and a life partner had a difficult moment when she first told him that she was in love with one of her lovers.

I'd been seeing this woman for a while and realized, much to my surprise, that my feelings toward her had gone beyond simple sexual friendship and into a deep romantic emotion that I identified as being in love. When I told my life partner about this, I think his first impulse was to feel threatened, insecure, and, yes, jealous. I could feel him getting close to exploding. It was hard for me not to try to fix things, to take back what I'd said about being in love, or to simply leave the discussion altogether because I felt scared and guilty.

But he stayed on course, allowing the feelings to present themselves, but not allowing them to drive him into acting angry or defensive. He asked me some questions about what exactly this meant to us, and I was able to explain that I wasn't planning to leave him, that my love for her was in no way a threat to my love for him, that she and I weren't expecting to become primary partners—that, really, nothing had changed except my own emotions and the words I was using to describe them. We went on to revisit this discussion from time to time, especially when our busy schedules permitted me to spend some extra time with my lover.

She and I drifted apart fairly easily later on as we moved on to other things in our lives . . . and, for that matter, so did he and I, less easily. But all three of us who were involved in that particular triangle can look back with pride at the way we gave each other the space and respect we needed to process a change that at first felt terribly threatening to us all.

You can feel jealousy without acting on it. In fact, flying into a rage and breaking all the crockery, or calling your lover's lover and hanging up every fifteen minutes during your first sleepless night, or picking a fight with whoever's handy actually won't help you feel better. All these are things that people do in order to *not* feel jealous, in order to *not* feel scared and small. Anger can help us feel powerful when we use it to push vulnerable feelings away, but it won't actually make us stronger or safer.

When you hold still with your jealousy, you will find that it is possible to feel something difficult without doing anything you don't choose to do. You will have taken your second step at disempowering your jealousy. You've told your jealousy that you will not allow it to drive you to do anything that might destroy your loving relationships.

Khalil Gibran wrote something truly profound about the nature of pain: "Your pain is the breaking of the shell that encloses your understanding."

WHITEWATER RAFTING

So here you are, shell cracked, with waves of pain washing over you. What do you do? Get as comfortable as you can, and see how you can learn to ride those waves instead of drowning under them. Gather up the courage to feel what you're feeling. Explore your feelings, nourish them, treasure them—they are the most essential part of you.

Be good to yourself, and remember that the most important part of love is not loving someone's beauty and strength and virtue. The real test of love is when someone sees our weaknesses, our stupidities, and our smallnesses and still loves us. This unconditional love is what we want from our lovers, and we should expect no less from ourselves.

Experiencing painful feelings is not a moral issue—it is in no way "wrong" to feel what you feel and to want what you want. Only actions can be crimes. Let us repeat that one: emotions are never wrong; only actions can be wrong. Emotions are an expression of our emotional truth, and truth cannot be wrong. Nor do they need to be justified. They just need to be felt.

Remember, as you look at yourself, to look kindly, and also remember that you are not balancing a checkbook: anything you see that you don't like, or that you want to change, is not a debit that you subtract from your virtues. When you learn to reflect on your strengths, it becomes easier to look at your weaknesses with acceptance and compassion. Keep your virtues at their full value, and cherish them.

Start by setting yourself the task of getting through a short period of time with your jealousy, like an evening or an afternoon when your partner may be off with another. Make a pact with yourself that you will stay with your feelings, whatever they may be, for this brief time. If a whole evening or night seems like too long, start with five or ten minutes, then arrange to distract yourself with a video or whatever.

IT MIGHT BE EASIER THAN YOU THOUGHT

One of the possible, and indeed common, outcomes will be that your partner will go off on a date with another and you will feel just fine. Surprise! Your anticipation may have been a lot worse than the actual event. Experienced sluts often find that they feel jealous only now and then. When they do experience jealousy, they examine these specific experiences to see what they can learn about themselves, and then brainstorm strategies to make this particular sort of event safer and easier.

One couple we talked to is working to maintain their primary relationship in a difficult situation: One of them is out of town most of the time on business, and thus much of their activity with other partners takes place under circumstances that prevent them from reconnecting physically afterward. One of their agreements is that they talk on the phone every single night, regardless of where they are or how busy they are. Often, their conversations take place after one of them has spent time connecting with an outside partner. One of them notes that during these conversations,

> He allows my feelings. I don't hesitate to say anything I want; in fact, he encourages me to. I've found that just being allowed to say these things, to talk about my jealousy and sadness, somehow defuses them. They lose a lot of their power because they meet no resistance from him; he just listens to them and lets them be.

FEEL YOUR FEELINGS

Painful feelings, even the most intense of them, have a tendency to run their course if you let them, so an initial strategy is to make yourself as comfortable as possible and wait. Find your jealous feelings—hurt or anger or whatever—and let them flow through you, like a river. Your mind may be racing with nasty thoughts, angry, blaming, focusing on some detail that you're absolutely certain those other people did wrong, obsessing on believing that someone is taking advantage of you or riding roughshod over your naked emotions. You hurt a lot, so surely it must be somebody's fault! But sometimes there is great pain and there is no villain. Allow us to reassure you: we all go through this. Don't die of shame, just let these thoughts run through you, too.

Feelings, once uncovered, can be better understood by reflecting on them. It is useful to have scripts and strategies for self-exploration. Journal writing, preferably with total disregard for grammar and syntax, can be a good way to vent feelings and learn about yourself at the same time. It is okay to cover pages of your journal with FUCK FUCK FUCK FUCK FUCK I HATE THIS! in bright red ink; if this feels good to you, we recommend you get an extra-large journal. Try writing down your stream of consciousness, which means whatever you find in your head whether or not it makes sense, and see what you get. Treasures, jewels of self-knowledge, are often found here.

You can get a big drawing pad and a set of oil pastels, which are crayons for grown-ups. These big crayons encourage expression with bright colors and discourage getting hung up on details (they're too fat to get crabby with). Sometimes you will draw and get squiggles, and that's great; the smallest thing you can accomplish still helps you hold still for a while and rant in color. Other times, you may surprise yourself with a drawing that is profoundly meaningful to you. Both of us use drawing a lot to vent our strong feelings and discover things about ourselves. Dossie quit smoking this way, and Janet used it as an important tool to get out of suburbia and recover her sluthood, and we assure you that neither of us is a great artist.

Some people like to express their feelings with their bodies and might like to run, or work out at the gym, or clean the kitchen, or dig in the garden. Safety note: if your feelings like intense physical expression, you will need to keep a piece of your mind alert to the fact that you're heavily adrenalized and feel stronger than you actually are, so give a little attention to what you can do without injury. Dossie once hiked up a big hill in a stressed-out state and felt powerful and wonderful—she remembers thinking about how she must be in much better shape then she thought she was. The next day was agony of the physical kind, with strained muscles and swollen joints.

Try finding music that fits your mood, angry or sad or frantic, and dancing your feelings out. It can be very satisfying to get a cheap plastic tennis racket and beat up your couch. Kneel in front of the couch, raise the racket above your head, and bring it down with all your strength. Keep your eyes open, imagine anything on the couch that you are angry at except yourself, and yell, loudly, how you feel.

When you express yourself, you get to know yourself better and work out some of the most intense stress constructively. The least you could wind up with would be a clean kitchen, and you might actually feel good after a self-indulgent afternoon on the beach.

POOR BABY

Try focusing on the feelings in your body: where do you feel these emotions, in your throat, chest, gut? Turning your attention to the physical sensations can intensify them and might bring up tears, but they will move on through even more readily if you allow yourself to feel them on the physical level. If rage comes welling up, you can pound on a pillow. If you start to cry, let it flow, remembering the sense of relief that comes after expressing intense emotion in tears. Janet likes to seek out a tearjerker book or movie to help her get tears out when she feels stuck. (*Terms of Endearment* has never failed her yet.)

Some people have trouble doing this because they've been taught that it's wrong to feel sorry for yourself. So who else should you feel sorry for? Stay in sympathy with yourself: you feel bad, so be kind to yourself.

You can talk to a friend, or your other lover, presuming you have made agreements about confidentiality with everybody who might care if you gossip. Janet has a deal with a good friend of hers for telephone support. She can call her friend up and ask for five minutes of "poor baby," and if her friend is available, she pours out her feelings and her friend says, you guessed it, nothing but "poor baby" till she is through. This dialogue may sound silly, but don't knock it till you try it. Comfort is a good thing in hard times.

EXERCISE *Reassurance*

Here's an exercise you can do with your partner to learn how to "poor baby" each other even when times are hard.

Make a list of ten things your partner could do that would reassure you.

Avoid abstractions—focus on behaviors, not emotions. "Love me more" is an emotion and thus pretty hard to act on: how will you know that your partner loves more? "Bring me a rose" is a behavior that anybody with a dollar can perform. Write your list in private, your partner can do the same, and then you can get together and look at each other's lists. You'll be surprised at how easy it is to be reassuring when you have a list.

This assignment may be more complicated than it sounds. Many questions may come up in your mind: How could I ask for that? Shouldn't my partner already know? If I have to ask for it, does it really count? If my partner loved me, wouldn't this be happening already?

If you're having thoughts like these, imagine what it might feel like to be asked for reassurance by your partner. Wouldn't it feel good to know how you could help? We can't read each other's minds, but we do care, and we can help once we know how.

WHO'S TO BLAME?

As you get skilled at finding and expressing your feelings, you can try a more challenging task: see if you can write about or talk to your friend about your feelings without blaming anybody. Not your lover, not your lover's lover, and especially not yourself. This exercise is not easy: you will be surprised how readily we all slip into that blaming mode, but it is very, very worthwhile to learn to have your feelings without foisting them on someone else.

It also helps to pay attention to how we attribute intention. "You're just doing this because you want to make me mad": how often do you suppose that's actually true? We just about never make anybody mad on purpose; the results are usually unpleasant. It's easy to invent other people's intentions for them in order to try to make sense of what you're feeling . . . but it can be very hard for them to speak their truth if someone's accusing them of intentions they never had.

Only when we're all willing to own our emotions, and let our lovers and friends own theirs, does anyone have the power to change and grow.

BABY YOURSELF

When your emotions are overwhelming and chaotic, it can help to ask yourself if there is anything you could do that would help you feel just one tiny bit safer. Let go of the big picture: maybe it's too big to figure the whole thing out right now. A few deep breaths, conscious relaxation of some muscles, soothing music. Try wrapping yourself in a soft blanket. It may not seem like much, but once you manage to do anything that improves your lot even the littlest bit, you are moving in the right direction to build some confidence that you can learn to deal with your jealous feelings.

Give yourself permission to take good care of yourself while you learn to work through jealousy and other hard feelings. Learn to nurture yourself. What are the things you find comforting? Give them to yourself. Hot chocolate? Warm towels after a long soak? A long session with your most beloved movie or computer game? Your favorite teddy bear? Effective self-nurturing often happens on the level of body awareness, so nice physical experiences—massages, hot baths, skin lotion, flannel pajamas—can give a sense of comfort and security even when your mind is anxious and your thoughts are a mess. Give yourself permission to take the best possible care of yourself. You deserve it.

When you anticipate feeling jealous, make plans to occupy your time. It may be too much to ask that you always have a hot date at exactly the same time as your lover: most people's schedules are too complicated, so what do you do when your partner's date comes down with the flu? Do you cancel your date? The people you make these dates with might be counting on you, the time they have with you might be important to them, and their feelings might get hurt. Third parties have a right to some predictability in their lives too.

But even if you can't round up a hot date for yourself, you can probably find a friend to watch a movie with, talk obsessively (with due attention to confidentiality, of course) on the Internet, grind your teeth, eat cookies, chew your fingernails, whatever works. We do not recommend drinking and drugging, as getting high might very well increase the intensity of your disturbance and disinhibit you enough that you might forget your commitment to experience your jealousy without acting on it. A certain amount of escapism is fine, but if you anesthetize yourself so that you feel nothing at all, you will lose the opportunity to develop skills at dealing with all the feelings you're having.

Acquiring these skills takes practice, like meditation or learning to skate. At first you feel stupid and wonder why you're doing it, and it doesn't work very well. But if you practice taking good care of yourself, after a while your view of the world changes a little, and it becomes a much more friendly and welcoming place, because you've created it that way.

EXERCISE *Fifteen Ways to Be Kind to Yourself*

Write a list of fifteen easy things you can do to be kind to yourself: for instance, "Go to the store and buy myself a flower" or "Soak my feet in hot water and give them a rub." Sometimes it helps to ask yourself: "What could I do to feel a little bit safer, or better, or taken care of?" Put the items on your list on index cards. The next time you feel upset and could use a kindness, pull a card and do what it says.

WHEN YOU ARE THE THIRD PARTY

All these ideas about taking good care of yourself apply whether you are single or partnered, but those of us who live alone have to make special preparations to avoid becoming isolated with our feelings. (We've written about this at much more length in chapter 19, "The Single Slut.") You need to reach out to close friends or perhaps get to a support group or a munch in your area. Make agreements with friends to listen to each other's feelings. And don't forget to plan time for serious communication with your nonresidential partner. Being single, or other than the life partner, does not mean you will never feel jealousy or any other difficult feelings. When we are dating, however intensely, we rarely make time for serious discussions of our feelings, our differences, or, for that matter, how we each understand and appreciate the relationship we are having.

To make time, a lot of poly people place a special value on actually sleeping together, and the sharing of coffee, the slow awakening, and even ordinary old breakfast. If each time you connect with your sweetie is intended to be hot and heavy sex, it can be hard to make space for simple conversation, talking about feelings, hearing feelings. If you don't sleep together, try getting together for lunch or brunch at some other time, or make a date to hike in the country or on a beach, or visit a botanical garden or a museum.

Tough It Out

When no better plan is available, there is nothing wrong with gritting your teeth, biting the bullet, and hanging in there till it's over. Dossie remembers her first challenge after she decided to never be monogamous again:

> I had been casually dating a young man and had told him at great length that I was not available for partnering and had no intention of ever being monogamous again. He came over to visit at my home when my best friend was there, we all got a little stoned, and he came on to her. She thought he was neat and didn't know I was involved with him, so they started necking right in the middle of my living room. Eeeek! My thoughts went racing as I watched them, thinking: "Well, it's not like I want to marry him, and I don't think I feel like joining them, and I don't think my friend is bisexual anyway, so what do I do?" Miss Manners has said nothing on the appropriate etiquette for this situation. For a while I sat frozen, to tell the truth, and finally I thought to myself, "Okay, so there's no script, I'll have to make one up. What would I be doing if my friend and my new lover weren't rolling around on the floor with their braces locked?" I guessed I'd be finishing taking the notes from the tarot book I was reading, so I went upstairs

and studied, gritting my teeth. Focusing on my notes gave me at least a little relief by occupying my mind. Eventually they left, and I got through a strange and lonely night, not feeling necessarily great, but at least proud of myself that I had survived. I felt not at all damaged, really okay. What I got a grip on was my own strength, so . . . funky as it was, this was my first successful run through jealousy.

GO FOR THE ICK

Here's a good question to ask yourself as you seek to understand your jealousy: "What are the specific images that disturb me the most?" Chances are you are already imagining along these lines, so you're not likely to make yourself feel worse by thinking about the scary stuff on purpose.

Those disturbing images, the ones that really bother you, are not telling you what your partner is doing—you actually don't know what your partner is doing. The images you see in your mind are the perfect reflection of your own fears. One way to come to terms with your fears is to acknowledge them: "Yes, I'm afraid of that." You can take it even further and work through the fears by envisioning the worst possible scenario that you can imagine. Go ahead, wallow in it. Elaborate it until it becomes ridiculous. Maybe that other guy has a dick three miles long, that girl is a perfect replica of a living Barbie doll. Maybe you can laugh at your fears: that'll take the sting out of them. Silly is the opposite of powerful, so disempower away.

Reality is almost always less terrifying than fiction. You can counter your fears with reality testing. Our minds, like nature, abhor a vacuum. We get nervous. Think of the last time you were waiting for someone to return a call or a family member was significantly late coming home. Did you call the highway patrol? Send out frantic texts? Imagine terrible possibilities? We all do this. Janet and her partner have an agreement to call each other before they leave a lover's house for the trip home, just to help prevent this kind of worry.

When we don't know what's going on, few of us are able to just say "I don't know" and stop thinking about it. We fill in the blanks, and in order to do that we make something up. What you see when you fill in the blanks has nothing to do with reality, it is a picture of your own worst fear. So now you know what you are afraid of, and nothing about what is really happening.

Pay attention also to your imaginings that are less dangerous, less anxiety-ridden. This is where you feel safer. You may be surprised to find that imagining your lover in the midst of sex with someone else is less scary than you thought it would be, or maybe images of kissing bother you more than intercourse, or whatever. Try writing down your imaginings on index cards, then putting them in order from the most to the least scary. Then you will know what parts scare you the most and what the safer-feeling parts are. Now you have something to turn your mind toward that will help you feel a little bit safer, which is your first step on the road to becoming perfectly comfortable.

REMEMBER THE GOOD STUFF THAT YOU CARE ABOUT

Make a list of everything you value about your relationship and put it aside for a rainy day. Be an optimist, turn your mind to the positive end of things. Value what you have and what you get from your partner: the time, attention, and love, the good stuff that fills your cup. Avoid being the pessimist who focuses on what is not there, the energy that goes somewhere else. That energy is not subtracted from what you receive; relationships are not balanced like checkbooks. So when you are feeling deprived, remember all the good stuff you get from your partnership.

EXERCISE *Treasures*

Make a list of ten or more reasons why you are lucky to have this partner. Make a list of ten or more reasons why your partner is lucky to have you. Try carrying your lists around with you for a few days and adding things as they come up. Maybe you and this partner could both make lists and share them.

Sharing

You and your partners need to practice talking about jealousy. When you try to pretend that you're so perfectly enlightened that you never feel jealous, you deprive yourself of the opportunity to work with your feelings and share support with your partner. And when you try to protect yourself and your partner from jealousy, you are engaging in a deception that can only lead to more distance and can never bring you closer.

A couple we know tell us that they have developed a convention in their relationship that each can ask the other for what they call a "jelly moment." In your jelly moment, you get to say what's bothering you. Perhaps you feel scared and jealous, nervous about saying goodbye for the weekend, small and silly, and your knees are feeling like, well, jelly. Your partner's commitment is to listen, sympathize, and validate. That's the response: not "Okay, I'll cancel my date with Blanche," but "Aw, honey, I'm sorry you feel bad. I love you, and I'll be back soon."

When we tell our partners that we feel jealous, we are making ourselves vulnerable in a very profound way. When our partners respond with respect, listen to us, validate our feelings, support and reassure us, we feel better taken care of than we would have if no difficulty had arisen in the first place. So we strongly recommend that you and your partners give each other the profoundly bonding experience of sharing your vulnerabilities. We are all human, we are all vulnerable, and we all need validation.

Your strategies for surviving periods of jealousy will stand you in good stead for the rest of your life, and you will use what you learn about yourself from this practice over and over. All of the techniques listed above are applicable to other difficult events, like job interviews and writing your resume. Now you not only have a repertoire of ways to deal with bouts of jealousy but also to handle other painful emotions that may come your way. So when you get this far, congratulate yourself. Celebrate your successes: Write "I am a genius" two dozen times with lots of bright colors. Buy yourself something nifty. You've done a lot of hard work, and you deserve a reward.

A Spiritual Path?

So when you grow beyond your jealousy by doing the healing that your jealousy is calling on you to do, you're also stepping out of old paradigms and familiar assumptions, into the unknown, which is scary. Working to change your emotions requires that you open up, be willing to feel, flinching when necessary, to become more conscious. Isn't that what spirituality is, an opened and expanded consciousness?

Jealousy can become your path, not only to healing old wounds but also to openheartedness—opening your heart to your lovers and to yourself as you open your relationships to fit in all the love and sex and fulfillment that truly are available to you.

A final note about love: One remedy for the fear of not being loved is to remember how good it feels to love someone. If you're feeling unloved and you want to feel better, go love someone, and see what happens.

Clean Love

CAN YOU IMAGINE love without jealousy, without possessiveness—love cleaned of all its clinginess and desperation? Let's try. We can take some thoughts from Buddhism: What would it be like to love without attachment? Or to open our hearts to someone with no expectation beyond another heart opening in return? Loving just for the joy of it, regardless of what we might get back?

Imagine seeing the beauty and virtues of a beloved and letting go of how their strengths might meet our needs or how their beauty might make us look better.

Imagine seeing another in a clean light of love, without enumerating the ways in which that person does and does not match up to the fantasy we carry around of our perfect mate or dream lover.

Imagine meeting another person in the freedom and innocence of childhood and playing together, without plotting how to make this person give us the kind of love we wish we could have gotten in our actual childhood.

But . . . but . . . but. What if you open your heart to someone and you don't like what happens next? Suppose that person gets drunk? Or treats your open affection with scorn? What if this person doesn't fulfill your dreams? What if this one turns out just like the last one? Suppose all those things do happen. What have you lost? A little time, a brief fantasy. Let it go, learn from it, and go find someone more worthy of your love.

Love doesn't much take to being stuffed into forms, which is what everybody's fantasies and imaginings are: custom-built plans for a constructed individual they've created to solve all their problems. Your authors have dream lovers too. But people are not made of clay or stone, and it won't work well to approach them with a chisel. Look what happened to Pygmalion.

How many times have you rejected the possibility of love because it didn't look the way you expected it to? Perhaps some characteristic was missing you were sure you must have, some other trait was present that you never dreamed of accepting. What happens when you throw away your expectations and open your eyes to the fabulous love that is shining right in front of you, holding out its hand?

Clean love: love without expectations.

Washing your love clean doesn't require advanced spirituality or weekly psychoanalysis. You'll probably never let go of every single attachment—at least we've never managed it. But maybe you can let go just for an instant: your history, worries, frets, and yearnings will still be there to come back to when you need them. Just for now, take a look at the nifty person who is standing right in front of you.

CHAPTER FOURTEEN

Embracing Conflict

NOTHING BUILDS INTIMACY like shared vulnerability. Write this on your bathroom mirror. We'll never discount all the wonderful things that we get from sharing love—laughter and happiness and sex—but nothing deepens intimacy like the experiences that we share when we feel flayed, with our skins off, scared and vulnerable, and our partner is there with us, willing to share in the scary stuff. These are the times that bring us the closest together.

What's in It for You?

Some people find it surprising to learn that a slut can experience overwhelming insecurities, but the truth is that sluts are just as nervous as anyone else, and skills to allay our anxieties were not taught us in our cradles.

Your own freedom might turn out to be a lot easier to accept than your partner's. It certainly does not follow that just because we can date others with equanimity that we will be equally calm when our partner takes off for an exciting evening with somebody else. Going out and staying home are separate functions, like eating and cooking, each with its own rewards, and each requires specific skills to accomplish.

When problems arise, a good question to ask yourself is "What am I hoping to get out of this situation?" Why are you doing all this hard work to become a slut? The answer depends on your own individual situation, but for many of us, the payoff is our own freedom, and we have to learn to give freedom to our partners if we're going to get it for ourselves.

Giving and getting freedom means we also need to have some good ways to deal with the inevitable conflicts that will arise when strong emotions are at stake. There are lots of good ways. Start by checking in with yourself on what you already know about conflict. You already have very strong ideas about this; you learned them, literally, at your parents' knees, if not cringing in the corner.

EXERCISE *Conflict: A Freewrite*

Try writing for ten minutes without pausing—just write down whatever comes into your mind about these questions: How was conflict dealt with in the family you grew up in? What did people do, and what beliefs were they operating on? Did someone use alcohol to deal with tension? Who in your family was likely to initiate conflict, who avoided it to a fault? Whose job was it to placate the angry people, whose job to sweep disagreements under the carpet? Who had the job of opening up conflict? What was your job? How would you describe your style of managing conflict?

Studying the scripts you had to live by in your childhood will explain a lot about how you react to anger and conflict today. Accept yourself: as a child, you had no choices; you had to fit in, somehow, to your family's script. How did you keep yourself safe?

Was this never an issue? People who grew up in healthy families are often both easygoing and unafraid. (We're not sure we've ever met anyone that healthy, but it sounds great in principle.) The downside of growing up in an unusually healthy family is that it can be hard to understand why everybody else gets so scared.

Most people, though, learned to hide for their own safety, or to fight back to protect themselves, or to become small and pathetic so that people would take pity on them. If you have any of these responses to conflict—defensiveness, rage, withdrawal, weepiness, whatever—it is certain that you developed them for a good reason.

Once you understand how you learned your reflexes, more choices open up. Talk with your partners—what are their scripts? What's going on when A really wants to hear how B feels, only B is trying to get safe by hiding? Maybe you each have different skills you learned about dealing with conflict—maybe you could learn new ones from each other.

Fighting Fair

Thinking about how intimate bonds are cemented by sharing vulnerable feelings brings us to perhaps the ultimate act of intimacy: fighting. Many people believe that fighting between partners is to be avoided at all costs, but most relationship therapists would disagree.

Fights between partners appear to be a universal experience; not many people actually enjoy them, but they seem to be necessary, a constructive element in the building of solid relationships, like the fires that make new growth possible in old forests. Only by fighting can partners struggle with their disagreements, express their most heartfelt feelings, and negotiate change and growth in their relationship.

There has to be a way to communicate anger in a long-term relationship, and there has to be a way to struggle with disagreements. How many times have you had a bitter argument with your partner, and when it was over, felt closer than you had before?

So the problem, as we see it, is not to avoid fighting, but to learn to fight in ways that are not destructive, physically, morally, or emotionally. A good fight is very different from abuse: in a good clean fight, there is respect for safety and mutuality so that both people get to express their feelings at full volume and come out the other end stronger and closer than before: bonded by fire, as it were.

The concept of "fair fighting" was first expounded by Dr. George R. Bach in his wonderful book, *The Intimate Enemy: How to Fight Fair in Love and Marriage*. Published in 1968, the book is terribly outdated, but the material on communication, and detailed descriptions of constructive ways to share your anger with a partner, is priceless—this book is a classic. You might also consider reading any of the books listed in our Resource Guide at the end of the book. Whatever book you choose, reading a book together with your partner will put you on the same page, with some of the same information, and get you talking about how you communicate about what's important to you, like how you feel.

So: if feelings like to be heard, and anger is a feeling that can be very hard to hear, how can we vent anger without creating more trouble than we relieve?

EXERCISE *Gibberish Fight*

This will be both silly and very satisfying. Set the timer for two minutes. Stand facing each other, a little distance apart. Express your anger simultaneously with stance and gesture: stamp your feet, wave your arms, and speak to your partner in entirely inarticulate sounds—moans, groans, sighs, growls. (If you're not sure what we mean here, imagine Donald Duck having a tantrum.) It's hard to describe this in words, but when you go for the drama, freed from the need to make sentences, or to figure out who's right and who's wrong, or even to make any sense at all, you'll communicate your feelings very well—and then have a good laugh. This is a great way to vent and break up the tension before a more serious conversation.

Triggering

How is it that we sometimes get triggered into very strong emotions, particularly at times of intimate conflict? We all do it; it's not just you. Dossie recalls at nineteen having panic attacks that seemed to come out of nowhere, until one day she noticed that something had moved fast near her face. Her father was prone to sudden bursts of temper accompanied by a hard slap across the face, and Dossie realized that whenever something moved suddenly near her face—even her lover—some part of her believed that she was about to get hit. Once she understood this, she became able to look around and see that nothing was threatening her in the present, and these panic attacks disappeared.

New research into brain functioning has given us a lot of very useful information about how triggering works on the physiological level. We have an organ called the "amygdala" in the middle of our brains, right under the hypothalamus, that does the job of remembering situations associated with strong emotions, both pleasurable and terrifying, and setting us into action. The most familiar form of this phenomenon is its greatest extreme, the flashbacks experienced by abuse survivors and combat veterans.

The amygdala has a direct line to the pituitary gland and can set off our emergency response systems before our intellects can catch up. Adrenaline pours into our bloodstream, norepinephrine floods our synapses, our cells release all their sugars into our veins to give us energy to fight or run, and everything instantly feels terribly, terribly urgent. Triggering is particularly common, and intense, in intimate arguments, where all of our old triggers we learned as children, when we were truly helpless, may get stimulated.

The first thing to recognize is that nothing can get resolved in this adrenalized state. The flight-fight-freeze responses to adrenaline give us tremendous energy to survive a crisis, but not very much in the way of common sense.

But all is not lost. Two things happen during this physiological stress response that we can learn to use. The first is that if we can occupy ourselves for fifteen or twenty minutes without restimulating the stress reflex, our physiology will return to normal and we will return to sanity. The process of taking a time-out to get calm again is described below.

Better yet, every time we succeed in spending that fifteen minutes taking care of ourselves in the kindest way we can muster, we actually physically heal our amygdalas—by growing more fibers that deliver soothing neurotransmitters—and thus increase our capacity to soothe ourselves in a crisis. So practice, practice, practice being kind to yourself.

Here's how to take a time-out when you and a partner get triggered. Find a way to stop and separate, then find a kindly way to take care of yourself for about fifteen minutes without retriggering your emergency system, until your adrenaline gets back to normal and you feel relatively calm.

There are some agreements you will need to negotiate beforehand with each of your partners. First, everyone should understand that a time-out is absolutely not about whose fault this is. If what you're doing or talking about is what triggered the emergency overload, then both of you need to stop doing that in order to stop the adrenaline. Stopping can be difficult: someone is almost certain to feel abandoned, cut off, interrupted, or unheard. Remember, this is for fifteen minutes, not forever.

Since you will probably need to be at least in separate rooms for a few minutes, a prior discussion as to what room each of you might want to be in is a good idea. Where are your computers, your books, your reading chairs? If someone likes to listen to music or watch television, are headphones needed to provide quiet for the other? If someone needs to go outside, it's useful to agree on a phone call within twenty minutes to check in and make sure everybody's all right.

Some people like to agree on a safeword to call a time-out; maybe "time-out," or perhaps "red," or maybe something silly that might help defuse the anger. If you laugh when you say "pussycat" when an argument has gotten out of control, maybe that's a good thing.

If you have kids, and they are home, who will be responsible for them? Children may get nervous or want reassurance when the adults fight, which is in no way wrong. But they might feel needy or clingy at a time when you'd rather be free to focus on your own needs.

Make an agreement to honor a time-out with silence. Trying to get in one more thought is likely to trigger another adrenaline release and prolong the problem.

You'll want to talk these things over with your partner to plan your initial practice at time-out. Then, look for an occasion to practice. You might decide to call a time-out over an issue that is only a little bit disturbing, just for practice.

When you feel your most familiar uncomfortable emotions flaring up and you recognize you're being triggered—perhaps at the level of irritation or frustration, perhaps rage or grief—call a time-out. Strong emotions often appear very fast and can be very hard to predict, so as soon as you remember the option when you start flooding with feelings, call a time-out.

Wrench yourselves out of the conversation and go to your agreed-upon places. Do whatever you've thought might be calming, and not retriggering. Take a few deep breaths and remember to exhale thoroughly; reducing the carbon dioxide in your lungs will help the adrenaline subside. We like activities that occupy the mind—neither of your authors has much luck with meditating when we're feeling triggered; if you can do it, go for it, but don't put yourself down if you can't empty your mind right now. We tend to turn to a novel or magazine, surfing the Internet, solitaire, music, or maybe an old movie. Try to steer clear of things that create more adrenaline: be careful of "shoot-'em-up" games or music with violent lyrics. Some people do very well with dancing out anger to raging hip-hop, while others find it too stimulating. You will learn from experience what works for you.

You might want to write out your feelings, or draw them. The quality of the art is irrelevant; this is for you. One of your authors has journal sessions that start with frankly insane projections complete with terrible accusations and gradually grow into a remarkably nonjudgmental investigation of what she and her partner were fighting about, sometimes ending with new insights about what upset her so much.

After fifteen minutes, check in with yourself—are you feeling better? Your time-outs could take longer the first few times until you learn what works for you and gain some confidence in your process.

When you are ready to come back together, do something easy and comforting. Go for a walk in a park, or get your favorite takeout, or cook something together, or watch a video in a companionable way. Make an appointment to resume the discussion that triggered the time-out.

The process of a time-out is seldom elegant, pretty, or even remotely resembling okay. We need to take time-outs when we are in emotional overwhelm and definitely not at our best. Be ready to forgive each other for being human. Be ready to forgive yourself. The results are well worth it when you come back together ready for harmony and understanding.

Win-Win Solutions

A good fight starts with the understanding that in order for a fight to be successful, both people have to win. If one person wins a fight and the other loses, the problem that caused the fight has not been resolved. It is naive to imagine that just because you've "lost," you've given up your interest in whatever issue is at stake. When you feel overpowered, outgunned, or shouted down, you will be resentful, and the problem will go on being a problem. The only real way to win is to come to a solution where all parties concerned feel that they have won. So in a good clean fight, each person's feelings get heard and considered, and solutions are decided on by agreement, not rhetorical "might makes right."

We make a fight fair by agreeing on rules and limits, and by respecting everyone's right to express their feelings and opinions, including our own. It is usually helpful to schedule a time to fight and make an agreement to do so; it does not promote constructive hostilities if we waylay our partner in the bathroom or on the way out the door to work. We need to schedule discussions at a time when we can give them our full attention.

Scheduling fights has the added advantage that you can prepare for them, organize your thoughts, and know you have a time when this particular issue will be dealt with. If you feel bad about the grocery bills on Tuesday, and you know you have a date to fight about it on Thursday, it's pretty easy to put your stuff aside until then. Most people don't put their stuff aside very well when it seems that their issues will never get dealt with.

"Whaddaya mean, schedule a fight? Don't they just erupt, like volcanoes? And when we have a fight, we are not likely to obey any rules or respect any limits, right? Aren't we talking about intense emotional outbursts?" Well, yes, we are, but we don't believe that you can settle any issues when you are in an intense emotional state. When your feelings erupt, it is important to acknowledge them and pay attention. However awkwardly you may be expressing yourself, this is your truth; you obviously feel strongly about it, so it's an important truth.

I-Messages

Good communication begins with everybody talking about their feelings, long before they get to discussing the pros and cons of any solutions. Good communication is based on identifying our feelings, expressing them, and getting validation that our partner hears and understands what we are saying, whether or not they agree. Emotions are not opinions, they are facts—truths about what people are experiencing.

Try speaking in sentences that begin with "I feel." There is an enormous difference between saying "you are making me feel so bad" and "I feel so bad." The I-message is a pure statement of feeling, and there is no accusation in it. When your lover doesn't feel attacked and doesn't need to feel defensive, he or she is free to listen to what you're actually saying. Conversely, if your sentence starts with "you," and especially with "you always," your partner may well perceive an attack and respond defensively.

The words "I feel" then need to be followed with an emotion—sad, mad, glad, angry—or a physical feeling like queasy, tense, wound-up, shaky. Messages that begin with "I feel that" more often express a belief than a feeling, as in "I feel that we should not be enjoying so much sex," or a covert you-message, like "I feel that you are crazy." We are often tempted to describe our emotions in words that end in "-ed," as in "I feel judged/attacked/betrayed." This is a covert you-message: "You are judging/attacking/betraying me."

Most of us resent it when another person tells us how we feel—whether or not they are correct is immaterial. It is a violation of our boundaries when another person presumes to tell us what our inner truth is. Dossie trained with a supervising therapist who used to point his finger at clients and say, "I know what your problem is!" You probably already know how you feel when someone does that to you. Try, instead, asking a respectful question. "How are you feeling right now? I'm wondering if you're sad."

We can't ask our lovers to hold still while we sling accusations at them, using them as a target for our frustrations; that would be asking them to consent to being abused, and they would be right to resist. But we can ask them to listen to how we feel, because putting aside their own agendas for a few minutes and listening to our feelings is a doable task for the listener. To learn how to use I-messages, try talking about an issue that is current for you without ever using the word "you," and without talking about what anyone else is doing, but only about your own feelings. This technique takes a little practice but is less difficult than it may seem at first.

When it's your turn to listen to how your lover feels, put yourself in listening mode. Remember, feelings like to be heard and validated, so don't analyze or try to explain things. Just listen, and you may be surprised to hear something you didn't know. You can learn how the world looks from someone else's shoes, you can appreciate that person's feelings, you can validate that person's position and express understanding.

Then the solutions can flow more freely and more naturally. There are no wrong solutions, and no right ones: only the agreements that fit well with how we all feel.

EXERCISE *Feelings Dyad*

The purpose of this exercise is to speak about your own feelings in such a way that your partner can hear you, and to listen carefully to your partner's feelings. Each person gets three minutes to speak while the other listens.

Choose a time when you and your partner(s) can spend half an hour or forty-five minutes with no interruptions. Choose who will speak and who will listen. Set a timer for three minutes—five if you're feeling adventurous, but no more.

Remember, feelings like to be heard. So while you are listening, all you are going to say are things that indicate listening, like "Okay," "Yes," "I hear you," and "I understand."

Read about I-messages, earlier in this chapter. Remember that we can ask our beloveds to listen to us talk about our feelings and how we are doing. It's not fair to ask anyone to stand still and be a target for accusations and blame, so for this exercise, sentences beginning with "You" are out of bounds. Both of you should try to maintain eye contact during this exercise.

Try this as a script to talk about jealousy, and you can later use it to discuss any emotional situations. Here is a script you can follow:

Listener: "About jealousy, what would you like to tell me?"

Speaker: "When I look inside, I find . . ." (speaking as long as is comfortable)

Listener (throughout): "Yes." "I hear you." "Okay." "Uh-huh." (and so on)

Listener (when Speaker stops): "Is there anything else you'd like to tell me about that?"

Speaker (may continue, or say): "No. I'm through for now."

Listener: "Thank you."

Listeners will often find themselves full of ideas, suggestions, and so on, which they need to keep to themselves. Put your own ideas aside for these few minutes, and pay attention to what it's like to just focus on listening. Because you may be full of responses to what you have heard, we suggest waiting a bit or doing something else before switching roles.

These are intimate conversations. Show your appreciation to your partner for being brave enough to talk about these struggles. Hugs work great.

Help Is Available

You don't have to do all this on your own—many wonderful books, classes, workshops, and other resources are available. It's a good idea to put aside some time and energy to learn about communication and to do it with the person you're trying to communicate with.

There are many excellent weekend workshops focusing on communication for couples; many churches offer weekend marriage retreats, and some medical centers offer classes in couples' communication and anger management. Workshops and classes are worth attending even if they don't specifically address sluttery. We've never known a couple who went to a communication or intimacy workshop and didn't gain some good new skills and insights from it. Some workshops exist specifically to work on issues arising from nonmonogamy. Don't hesitate to take these workshops, and remember that the facilitator has expertise in creating safe environments to explore highly charged issues. Many couples repeat these workshops when a new issue has arisen in their lives. We encourage you to take a class or a workshop, or to join a support group suitable to your needs. Just knowing that others struggle with some of the same issues that you do can help.

Support, ideas, and information can also be found through online groups and tribes. See chapter 17, "Making Connection," for ideas on how to find these.

A more expensive, but still excellent, option is to do some sessions with a couples' counselor. In general, we recommend this as a second-level alternative, after you've already done some classes and workshops, unless you have privacy concerns that make classes and workshops difficult for you.

Screen any of these resources about whether they'll be accepting of your open relationship. Some old-fashioned psychologists, and the leaders of some workshops and retreats, may believe that your lust for many people is a symptom of psychological disturbance; you may not feel adequately safe and supported in such a hostile environment. If you need help finding a sympathetic therapist or group, try asking your friends or checking the Resource Guide at the end of this book. Most therapists now have websites where they list their skills and experience and something about their philosophy: you can email them to ask what their experience is in working with polyamorous relationships.

We strongly recommend that you investigate these types of help sooner rather than later. Just about everyone can use an occasional communications skills tune-up, and if you wait until your relationship is in crisis, you'll face much harder work than if you'd been practicing your skills all along.

Time Is Your Friend

In some Native American cultures it is customary to wait several minutes after a person speaks before responding: it is rude and disrespectful to fail to think about what the person has said, and to speak immediately would indicate that you have simply been waiting for the speaker to be quiet so that you can then attempt to change his or her mind. We recommend taking some time before responding to any serious communication, especially when it's important to the speaker. Maybe if you pay attention you'll hear something new.

People often approach a disagreement as if it were urgent that it be resolved right away. They strive for a resolution within minutes of discovering that they don't agree about something—something that they have in fact never agreed on.

But you've probably been living with that disagreement for a long time, and a little while more is not going to make a lot of difference. Thus, consider this strategy: acknowledge the disagreement, give each of you a chance to state your feelings using the principles you've learned in this chapter, and then take two days to digest what you've learned.

When you return to discuss the disagreement, you will probably be in a much calmer mode. You may have a clearer understanding of what is important to you and an appreciation of what is important to your beloved and why. Thus you may find yourself in a much better state to negotiate a solution that might make everyone happy.

Dossie sees this phenomenon all the time in her therapy practice, when she sends clients home from a session in a state of disagreement that seems intolerable. She instructs them to hold this new knowledge for a couple of days and then see how they feel. Often they come back the next week reporting that it became easy to find a solution. So sometimes it will be most fruitful to wait two days before going on to consider solutions you might want to try, as in the "Eight Steps to Win-Win Conflict Resolution" exercise on page 153.

Or after two days, maybe it will have become so easy that you won't need a special script to come to an agreement. Remember, where emotions are concerned, time is your friend.

Writing It Out

Sometimes our feelings are so complicated that it seems impossible to deal with them in face-to-face conversation with our beloved. Under such circumstances, you may want to write a thoughtful letter, either snail mail or email, to let your honey know the entirety of your concerns in a measured way that can be absorbed and processed at the recipient's own pace. This correspondence isn't a substitute for actual conversation, but it can be a good precursor to it, a way to open up the discussion that may feel a bit safer to start.

It is vital, however, that you send this letter only after you've had time to think about it. The downside to correspondence is that it can't convey all the fine points of communication—facial expression, body language, touch. The upside is, or should be, that a letter can be composed carefully, without undue emotional overload. If you click "Send" or drop the envelope into the mailbox before you've had a chance to think about its contents, you're taking on all the downside without any of the upside.

Try writing a letter you're not going to send, expressing all your feelings and concerns. Janet keeps letters like this in the "Drafts" folder of her email program; Dossie writes them in her word processor (which doesn't have a Send button) and pastes them into an email later. Write out all your feelings, and then close the file and go do something else. Come back and add stuff, or edit things out, for a couple of days, and then check what you've written, making sure you're owning your own stuff and using I-messages. We usually delete sentences that begin with the words "You shithead." Later, when you can read the message and imagine your friend truly understanding whatever you are disturbed about, it's time to send it.

We hope we do not have to remind you that your blog, or your MySpace page, or your private email list of a few dozen very intimate friends is not the place to rehearse this private correspondence. Struggle with it yourself—or, if that seems impossible, perhaps you can run it past one trusted friend, someone who would be acceptable to your lover too, to make sure you're saying what you're trying to say.

Dossie wrote such a letter recently to a lover of hers. She wrote the first draft at a time when she was terribly upset, on a Friday. She was busy over the weekend but managed to revisit her letter from time to time. By Monday, the issues were still there but, after some processing, seemed more manageable, so she called her friend on the phone and they talked . . . and resolved the issues quite easily and peacefully. The letter never got sent.

Owning What's Yours

When you are willing to own your distress, it becomes possible for your lover to comfort you, to offer you reassurance and love, when things are hard. Even when you don't agree about how you are going to handle an issue, you can still exchange love and comfort. We recommend that everyone be open about asking for reassurance, love, hugs, comfort, and stuff like that. Many of us grew up in families where we were taught not to ask for what we needed and were scorned, perhaps, as only wanting attention.

So what's wrong with wanting attention? Isn't there plenty? Remember about starvation economies: Don't shortchange yourself. You do not have to be content with little dribs and drabs of comfort, attention, support, reassurance, and love. You get to have all the comfort and reassurance you want. You and your intimates can set yourselves up to share lots and lots and lots and in the process learn how much more you have to share than you ever thought. So focus on abundance, and create a relationship ecology rich in the good things of life: warmth and affection and sex and love.

CHAPTER FIFTEEN

Making Agreements

MOST SUCCESSFUL RELATIONSHIPS, from casual acquaintanceship through lifetime monogamy, are based on assumptions that are really unstated agreements about behavior: you don't kiss your mailman, you don't tip your mother. These are the unspoken rules we learn very early in our lives, from our parents, our playmates, and our cultures. People who break these unspoken rules are often considered odd, sometimes even crazy, because the values and judgments behind the social agreements about how we relate to one another are so deeply ingrained that we are usually not even aware that we have made any agreement at all.

In many day-to-day relationships, like your relationships with neighbors and coworkers, it's probably fine to rely on those implicit, built-in agreements. But when you're trying something as complicated and unprecedented as ethical sluthood, we think it's very important to take nothing for granted. Talk with the people in your life about your agreements, and negotiate the conditions, environments, and behaviors that will get your own needs met and respect everybody's boundaries.

You'll often hear people talking about the rules of their relationships. But "rules" implies a certain rigidity, that there is a right way and a wrong way to run your relationship and that there will be penalties if you do it wrong. We understand that there are many different ways that people may choose to relate to each other, so we prefer to use the word "agreements" to describe mutually agreed-upon, conscious decisions, designed to be flexible enough to accommodate individuality, growth, and change. These agreements are sometimes a little fuzzy, particularly if you're used to the hard edges of rules. A little fuzziness is okay; your agreement will either get clarified later if it needs to be—or it won't, in which case it's probably clear enough.

How do you know when you need an agreement? You can tell by listening to your emotions. If something comes up that leaves you feeling upset or angry or unheard or whatever, that's an area in which you and your sweetie may need to discuss making an agreement. We suggest that you let go right now of the idea that you can predict every single situation that might come up in your relationship and make a rule to cover it—just forget it. Many perfectly good agreements get made by twenty-twenty hindsight: a problem comes up, and instead of arguing over whose fault it was, the people simply make an agreement to try to prevent that problem from coming up again or to deal with it when it does.

Our friends Laurie and Chris have become extraordinarily flexible agreement makers through practicing a lot:

We met at the Renaissance Faire and made a pretty deep connection right away. Although we didn't feel ready to jump into marriage right off, we did get handfasted [an ancient Celtic rite of romantic commitment] about five months after we met. Our handfasting included an agreement that if we still wanted to be together a year and a day later, we'd get married. And we did.

When we first decided to get handfasted, Chris proposed an agreement in which we'd be free to be sexual with other people during Faire, but at no other time. Laurie felt shocked by his desire to do this, and insecure about what might happen. So we decided to postpone a decision until the next summer's Faire, after we'd gotten married.

During the first year of our marriage, the agreement was for Faire only, and then after that we extended it to the weekend preparatory workshops as well as to Faire itself. At one of these, Laurie met a guy with whom she got fairly seriously involved—it was our first ongoing relationship outside the marriage. At that point, things opened up all the way to where Laurie was spending a lot of her time with her other lover, and Chris didn't like it much; he felt that he wasn't getting enough time with Laurie.

So we renegotiated. We decided that either of us could sleep over with another partner twice a month. We felt that twice a month was often enough for fun, but not so often as to encourage a threateningly strong bond with someone else. That's been working pretty well for a while, although we've compromised on a case-by-case basis a time or two.

We're still working out the bugs—among other things, we're hoping to become parents pretty soon, and we're not sure how a baby will affect our relationship. But our agreements have always been at least tolerable, and at times they've offered a relief valve that's kept us from fleeing the relationship in terror!

Chris and Laurie have had two children in the eleven years since this interview and are still together and still happily slutty.

Consent

So what constitutes a good agreement? In our opinion, the single most important hallmark of agreement is *consent*, which we define as "an active collaboration for the pleasure and well-being of all concerned." In the case of polyamory, this consent often includes that of people not directly involved—other partners, children, and other people whose lives are affected by our agreements.

Defining consent can sometimes be tricky. If someone consents under pressure, we don't think that meets the "active collaboration" criterion. And you can't consent to something you don't know about: "Well, you didn't say I *couldn't* fly to Boise for two weeks with this flight attendant I just met" does not constitute consent.

In order to achieve this kind of active consent, it is critical that everyone involved accept responsibility for knowing their own feelings and communicating them—but this isn't always easy. Sometimes feelings don't want to be pulled to the surface and examined—you may simply know that you feel bad. Give yourself the time and support you need to get to know that feeling, perhaps using some of the strategies we discuss in chapter 13, "Roadmaps through Jealousy." If you feel that you need help in defining what's going on for you, it's okay to ask for that help, possibly by asking a partner or a more neutral friend who understands multiple relationships to devote some time to hearing you out. Physical or verbal reassurance often makes a huge difference, and sometimes a wise friend or therapist can ask the right questions to help you untangle a complicated feeling. Once you start listening to your own feelings, you'll have a much easier time getting your needs and desires out there where everybody can hear them and make agreements to help meet them.

Most of us need some support in asking for what we want. When we are involved in making agreements, we need to feel sure that the needs we reveal will not be held against us. Most of us feel pretty vulnerable in and around our emotional limits, so it's important to recognize that these limits are valid: "I need to feel loved," "I need to feel that I'm important to you," "I need to know that you find me attractive," "I need you to listen and care about me when I feel hurt."

Blaming, manipulation, bullying, and moral condemnation do not belong in the agreement-making process. The process of making a good agreement must include a commitment from all concerned to listen to one another's concerns and feelings in an open-minded and unprejudiced way. If you are waiting for your partner to reveal a weakness so that you can exploit it into ammunition to "win" your argument, you are not ready to make a satisfactory agreement.

Legalistic hairsplitting is another enemy of good agreements. We know one couple whose agreement was that either of them would let the other one know within twenty-four hours if they were going to have sex with someone else. One of them called the other one from another city to let her know that he'd had sex with someone else the night before. "But you said you'd give me twenty-four hours' notice!" she cried angrily. "I never said twenty-four hours *before*," he pointed out. This loophole-finding legalistic behavior left neither individual feeling that their agreement had worked for them. The moral: be clear, be specific, and above all negotiate in good faith; this is not about cheating any more.

Agreements need to be realistic and clearly defined—if you're not sure whether you're keeping an agreement, it may be time to redefine that agreement. It is unrealistic, for example, to ask your partners never to enter into sexual interactions with people that they care about "too much." There is no way to define "too much," and few of us conceive of our polyamorous utopia as a world in which you are only allowed to share sex with people you don't care about at all. None of us can truthfully agree to feel only this way or that way: our agreements need to have room in them for real emotions, whatever they may be. A more concrete agreement would be to limit outside dates to once a month, which might serve the same purpose.

Agreements do not have to be equal. People are different and unique, and what pushes my buttons might be perfectly okay with you. So one person might find it very important that his partner not stay out overnight, whereas said partner might actually enjoy an occasional opportunity to watch the late movie all alone and eat crackers in bed. One friend of ours says,

> Bill and I have very different needs when it comes to relationships. I feel no need to be monogamous; I'm quite comfortable having sex with people I like, but they're not affairs of the heart—whereas his sexual connections are either very casual, like at parties, or very deep and long-term. We've formed agreements that meet both of our needs—mine for friendly partners and fuck buddies, his for long-term secondary relationships.

Fairness does not mean perfectly equal. Fairness means we care about how each person feels and make agreements to help all of us feel as good as possible.

When thinking about agreements for an open relationship, most people start out by listing what their partner should not do: don't kiss her on the mouth, don't treat him better than you do me. Some "thou shalt nots" *are* necessary: agreements need to be made, for example, about sexual connections with relatives, neighbors, and coworkers. But many negative agreements are really about protecting your partner from feeling hurt or jealous, and we're not big fans of these, although we recognize that they sometimes have their place as an intermediate step. We think that the best agreements to protect your partner from emotional pain are positive: let's have a special date next weekend, I will find time to listen to you when you hurt, I'll tell you how much I love you again and again.

Everyone needs a sense of emotional safety to succeed at feeling secure in open relationships, but thinking up agreements that will help both partners feel emotionally safe can be confusing. In the process of unlearning jealousy we will all at some time be asking our partners to take some risk, to agree to feel some painful feelings, to fall down a few times in order to learn how to ride the emotional bicycle of truly free love.

EXERCISE *Eight Steps to Win-Win Conflict Resolution*

1. Take time out to ventilate anger.

2. Select one issue to work on.

3. Make an appointment to talk.

4. Each person takes three minutes to state how they feel while their partner listens. Hint: Use I-statements, avoid you-messages, and consider allowing time between each person's statement. Try as hard as you can to describe your emotions about the issue.

5. Brainstorm. Write a list of all possible solutions, even silly ones.

6. Edit the list. Cross out any suggestions that either person feels they could not live with.

7. Choose a solution to try for a specific period of time—perhaps two to four weeks.

8. Re-evaluate when that time is up.

One way you can make agreements to respect emotional limits is to ask for whatever might make you feel a *little bit* safer—reassurance, compliments, affection, a special ritual for homecoming after a date—and then when that works and you feel a little safer, take another step toward even more safety, and soon you will feel safe enough to expand your explorations further and further. Each tiny step in the direction of freedom will eventually get you there. One of the things that works about reassurance is that once we understand that our partner, or partners, or maybe even also their partners, are willing to help us with our feelings, we feel more secure and need less and less protection as we go along.

The single most important thing to remember about agreement making is that the purpose of an agreement is to find a way in which everybody can win.

Some Agreements

We've done some asking around among our friends and colleagues to find out what kinds of relationship agreements have worked for others. Here is a partial list of agreements we've heard from some very successful sluts.

Notice as you read it how many different kinds of agreements it contains—some are sexual, some are relationship-oriented; some thou shalts and some thou shalt nots; some logistical and some sentimental. Just so you know that we're not recommending any of these, you should also note that some are mutually exclusive. We're presenting this list as a discussion opener, not as how it ought to be. Everybody *has* to make some agreements about sexual health and safer sex.

- We always use condoms and barriers for all possible fluid exchanges.

- We always spend the night together except when one of us is traveling.

- I'll watch everyone's kids this weekend, you do it next weekend.

- Neither of us will [specific sexual act] with other partners.

- Either of us can veto the other's potential other partners.

- We always provide advance notice of potential other partners.

- Don't tell me about other partners.

- Tell me everything you did with other partners.

- Other partners must be same-sex/opposite-sex.

- We always meet each other's partners—no strangers.

- Outside sex will only be: group sex / party sex / anonymous sex / committed sex . . .

- We must check in with each other to confirm safety after a get-together with a new partner.

- Everybody chips in for the babysitter.

- We see others on Friday nights only.

- Saturday nights are for us.

- Be sure to save some hot sexual energy for me.

- Sex with other partners is off limits in our bed/house.

- We set limits on phone calls, Internet time, etc., with other partners.

- We establish quality time with each other.

- We establish agreements about who can talk about what to whom.

- Don't take off the ring I gave you.

- Little gifts and cards help me feel less abandoned.

- Who is too close to have sex with? Neighbors? Schoolmates? Coworkers? Close friends? Former lovers? Your doctor? Your lawyer? Your partner's therapist? Your sibling? . . .

- We'll spend an hour cuddling and reconnecting afterward.

Predictability

Our experience is that we need some kind of predictability to deal with the stresses of open relationships. Most people can handle a nervous-making situation much better if they know when it is going to happen and when it is going to be over. You can plan to do something supportive with a friend, go to a movie, visit Mom, whatever—and tell yourself that you only have to handle things for this chunk of time, and then your sweetie will come back and maybe you can plan a celebratory reunion.

Most people have a hard time dealing with surprises, which can feel like land mines exploding. Very few of us would be comfortable living with the possibility that our partner might go home with someone else at any time, from any party we go to, from the restaurant where we thought we were just going for a cup of coffee—no place, no time would be secure. One partner of our acquaintance was working across the country from his spouse during a time when he was first struggling to deal with his jealousy. He made an agreement to know when his partner was playing with someone else because, as he put it, "If I know when she is out with someone else, I also know when she isn't, and then I can relax most of the time."

If you feel that planning takes too much of the spontaneity out of your life, then think about declaring one night or one weekend a month to be open season—then you can make a decision whether to join your partner in cruising or sit this one out in a quieter milieu. An agreement to be unpredictable at some specified time is, after all, predictable.

When There Is No Agreement

There are probably a lot of things in your life on which you feel no need to reach agreement. Everyone deals with differences in relationships all the time, as any night person married to a morning person can tell you. However, lack of agreement can feel less comfortable in the close-to-the-bone field of sexual relationships. When feelings run high, particularly about sexual issues, it's easy to want to believe that your way is right and that all other ways are wrong.

One way to avoid the trap of turning a difference into a moral argument is to look carefully at ownership: who owns what in this disagreement anyway? What is A's investment in this particular choice, how is B feeling different about it, and what are we afraid might happen if we can't agree? Try to get really clear on how each person feels before you even think about what you want to do about this issue at hand. Understanding your own and your partner's emotions will lead to new and better ideas for agreements or resolution.

It can help to remember that you have been living with differences and disagreements with everyone in your life ever since you met them.

When you discover a sexual difference with one person, it has probably been there all along, and yet you still like each other and share a lot of good stuff. Remember that you've been getting along fine without this particular agreement. If you've made it this far, you can live with the lack of agreement a little longer. Let time be your friend, and when difference is difficult, allow yourselves the time to thoroughly explore the feelings that are driving the disagreement and arrange to lead a rewarding life while you do it. You really can agree to disagree. Between the "yes" of full agreement and the "no" of full disagreement is a whole big gray area of no-agreement-yet, or tolerable-disagreement, or even who-cares?

Sometimes you will eventually find it possible to make an agreement, and other times you won't. Occasionally, however, you will hit an area in which agreement is both necessary and impossible. For many people, the whole issue of nonmonogamy may be one of these; childbearing is another frequent point of contention. We suggest flexibility, and compromise seeking, possibly with the help of a qualified therapist.

But if agreement simply cannot be reached, we think the skills you learned in trying to reach agreement can come in very handy as you practice not-blaming, not-judging, and not-manipulating, as you work to change or even end a relationship that cannot reconcile its differences.

Some people agree to end a relationship and then discover that later on, when the stress of parting has eased, they can agree on a new kind of relationship with the same person. Others cannot. But either way, forthright and open-hearted discussion of disagreements and agreements will lead to a cleaner and less stressful outcome.

MAKING SPACE FOR DIFFERENCE

You and your sweetie might have different visions about what polyamory will be for you. For one person, it could be a lot of recreational sex, one-night stands, or party play; another might yearn for one primary and one special secondary relationship. Some people enjoy many relationships that make extended families out of their lovers and their lovers' lovers; others look for a three- or four-person group marriage.

Negotiating difference, however, can be done and is being done successfully every day. So what if one person wants S/M, or tantra, or wild orgies, and the other wants walks on the beach at sunset? Once you've opened your relationship to other people who may be more accepting of those desires, anything is possible—Dossie has worked with a number of couples with these kinds of differences. Agreements may be asymmetrical, to account for different desires and different feelings, and each individual may need a different kind of reassurance. The relationship-lover may feel shy and unhip, the party animal may feel judged or threatened by long-term partners, and each needs to have their own feelings validated and cared for.

Reaching Agreement

So how do you find an agreement that will work for everyone? A good place to start is by defining your goals. A goal is not the same as an agreement; your goal is what you're trying to accomplish, and your agreement is the means you're using to try to get there. For example, if your goal is to prevent anyone from feeling taken advantage of, your agreement might be to ensure that nobody's personal time, space, or belongings are being infringed on. So start with getting clear on what feels like infringement to each person involved, and use that for your guidelines.

Often you will discover a goal by tripping over a problem: "Last night, when you and Sam were in our bedroom together, my feet were freezing and I couldn't get in there to get my bedroom slippers." The goal is to prevent this problem from coming up again—what kinds of agreements might help achieve that goal? Answering these questions will require an honest (and often difficult) look at what the *real* problem is: is it that your feet are cold, or that you resent being kicked out of your own bedroom, or that you're feeling threatened and left out?

Once you've defined your problem and your goal, it's time to start figuring out a good agreement. It might be appropriate to do a trial agreement, to put a time limitation (a weekend, a week, a month, a year) on your newborn agreement to see how it feels to everybody concerned. After the time is up, you can sit down again to discuss what worked, what didn't, and whether to continue your agreement or revise it or scrap it.

In our experience, it's rare for an agreement to last a lifetime without change: human beings change, and so do agreements. The way you can tell that your agreement needs to change is when someone doesn't agree to it anymore. Janet and one of her partners, for example, began their relationship with an agreement that they could be sexual with other people, but that they couldn't fall in love with anyone else. Then one of them did. (In hindsight, this seems like a fairly silly agreement—as though you could simply decide not to fall in love!) She remembers,

> There was a period in which we were having "check-ins" one or two times a day. This was a situation neither of us had ever planned on. We found it was very important to stay in the moment and to stay with tangible things—yes, it feels okay if she sleeps over while I'm out of town; no, it doesn't feel right for you to bring the two of us to the same party. We found, during that experience as well as similar ones that came later, that the words "in love with" made us both feel kind of panicky—that agreements that dwelt on measurable factors such as time, behavior, and space worked better for us.

Expect to try out some agreements and find out that they don't work, and expect to need to change them. You will get better at this process with practice, and in time you may know your own and your partner's needs so well that negotiating agreements will be easy. But in the beginning, while you are learning, tidiness won't count anywhere near as much as tolerance.

When you first set out, some of these discussions may get quite heated: remember, anger is an emotion that tells you what is important to you. What is constructive about these difficult times is what you learn about your partners and about yourself.

Remember that there are many good ways to structure your sluttery. Structure is not what makes you safe from hard feelings—your ability to take care of yourself is what counts. So whatever structure you choose, hold it fairly loosely. Your agreements are not taking care of you; you are.

Don't get discouraged—all the successful sluts you see who seem so carefree have fought over their agreements. You too can work your way through this tangled web of assumptions and emotions and learn to love with openness and freedom.

CHAPTER SIXTEEN

Opening an Existing Relationship

MANY PEOPLE come to a time when they want to open their relationship to more sexual partners. But when your relationship was established under conventional monogamous agreements, you can't expect to proclaim "Open Sesame!" and have everything fall magically into place. Like everything else about ethical sluthood—and perhaps even more than other ways of relating—opening an existing relationship requires care, thought, practice, and work.

The relationship that you want to open may or may not be a life partnership; you may or may not be living together. You might have been practicing serial monogamy, with the usual occasional overlap. Or you may be dating and keeping all your lovers compartmentalized and want to move toward something more like a family or tribe. You may be looking for adventures outside of a triad or a group marriage. The work of opening is still work, no matter the nature of your relationship.

For the sake of simplicity, we are going to talk about opening a relationship between an existing two-person couple—but the principles and skills we discuss here can apply to lovers in any configuration.

Turning Two into Three

If you and your lover are beginning this work with equal agreement that you both want to create this expansiveness in your lives, then congratulations, and welcome to the path. You will probably encounter some unexpected disagreements about the way this new life will look—so you still don't get to skip this chapter.

In our experience, though, it's much more common that one person wants to open the door to outside connections and the other hasn't ever even considered it and is appalled by the idea. This situation is definitely more difficult, especially when the third member of the triangle, the outside partner—potential or actual, open or secret—is waiting in the wings and probably cares a lot about the outcome of this process. A lot of people don't really think about monogamy until they make a connection with someone who feels important to them and they don't want to give up their beloved life partner, or get a divorce, or split up the kids. You could be in any of these roles in the triangle: the one with the lust for adventure, the new love who is not a partner, and the sometimes stunned partner to the would-be adventurer.

In physics, the triangle is considered one of the most structurally sound and well-balanced structures—but in relationships, the very phrase "love triangle" carries a whiff of tabloid drama. This particular situation is not made any easier by the fact that it's been happening for as long as there have been relationships. It can help to remember that it is utterly normal to have differences in desire in any relationship—you don't need to both get excited about the same flavor of ice cream. Making room for everyone's desires *can* work for all concerned—we know many people who have done so, reaching accommodations that work for all three people involved. Let's look at the dilemma from all three points of view.

THE ADVENTUROUS PARTNER

The advantage of being in this position is that you know, more or less, what you want. Perhaps you bought this book for your spouse, hoping for some freedom down the road and probably hoping that there is some way that you and your spouse can reach agreement without going through a whole lot of agony. However, you and your spouse are both, like all of us, products of our culture, and it takes hard work to step out of the paradigm upon which your entire previous existence was based. Good work, rewarding work, life-changing work, but still hard work.

Guilt is a dreadful emotion, one of the most uncomfortable ones we can feel. Most people feel guilty when something they do causes pain to the people they care about. When you place your desire for an open relationship on the table and your partner has a hard time with it, you will probably feel very guilty. There are no easy ways to allay your guilt by fixing how your partner feels.

You can't wave a magic wand and change your partner's mind—that's the hard work we must each do for ourselves. It will hurt. There may be tears and rage and bitterness, and you will feel guilty. If you already have two partners, then both of them might feel bad, and you will feel doubly guilty.

Don Juan and Doña Juana are portrayed in fiction as carefree explorers—and also heartless and free of care for any pain they may leave in their wake. We don't believe that you want your freedom at the cost of becoming a callous jerk. If you have invited your partner into this exploration, that means you don't want to cheat, you want to live your life honestly and honorably. We respect you for that. A lot of other people won't.

THE OUTSIDE LOVER

We don't even know what to call you, which makes it hard to talk to you and may make it hard for you to think about your situation. Your role—a potentially loving, giving individual who's sexually involved with one member of a committed couple—is so distant from most people's conceptual framework that a nonloaded word for you does not exist. Homewrecker? Mistress? The other woman? (There isn't even a phrase for "the other man," in spite of the fact that many, many such men exist.) More civilized, but often equally problematic, are concepts like "secondary" or "tertiary": this language does define the situation, but we think the implied hierarchy can be demeaning. Do you only count when you are number one? Or does everybody have rights in this constellation?

Whether you are the sweetie, the squeeze, the lover, or whatever, your position in the triangle comes with advantages and disadvantages. On the positive side, nobody expects you to wash their socks, and most of your time with your lover can be spent having fun. You are not expected to support your lover, nor to give up your career to stay home with the kids. On the downside, who do you call when you need a drive to the emergency room? Who do you call when you are sad? When you need support? Do you have any rights at all to your partner's time, or is there somebody who sees you as the competition, with whom you may never speak or negotiate? While your position conveys few responsibilities, it often also carries very few rights.

THE ONE WHO CHOSE NONE OF THIS

We really hope you didn't get this book as a Valentine's Day surprise, but we know that could be the case. It is utterly no fun to be called upon to expand your relationship in ways you never asked for, nor to deal with your beloved's desires for other lovers after you'd promised to forsake all others. You may be feeling like you've had an abyss open up under your feet, with no solid ground anywhere to stand on.

Of course you are distressed, and angry as well—you did not choose this path. Here you are, in a maelstrom of scary feelings you never agreed to undertake. It may take a while for you to get that this is really happening. Eventually, though, this situation must be dealt with: once the subject of opening a relationship is on the table, it cannot be shut away in a drawer again. One way or another, you must find a way to cope with what's been handed to you and begin considering what may happen next.

It is unfair, of course, that you're being asked to do hard emotional work that you never chose to do. Is there any reason why you should have to work so hard? Is there anything in it for you?

Well, quite possibly. Perhaps this work will make you stronger. Perhaps you will make an unexpected journey into your own capacities: Maybe you too have the ability to love more than one person. Perhaps it will deepen your relationship with your partner. Perhaps it will improve your sex life. Perhaps you will find a path that allows your relationship to continue, that allows you to grow and change together. Perhaps you can see a faint gleam of a possible freedom somewhere on the horizon.

We can't promise that any of these will happen for you. But there's one thing we *can* promise. If you tackle this difficult situation, and learn whatever you can about yourself and your relationship from it, at the end of it you will have a choice. You may choose to separate, or you and your partner may choose to go back to monogamy, or you may try a more open relationship . . . but whatever you do, it will be because you're looking at all your possibilities and *choosing*. Not reacting blindly, not doing what you've been told, not choosing the easy way just because it's easy, but making your own, informed, heartfelt choice. We truly believe that consensual monogamy is a fine choice.

Later in this chapter, we'll give you some ideas about ways to keep this difficult negotiation as productive as possible. But first we want to talk about a situation that we know some of our readers are confronting.

Cheating

Sometimes the relationship is already open, only one partner doesn't know it yet. This situation can be very hard to deal with, but it does happen, and often. Discovering that you have been and are currently being cheated on can be utterly awful. Feelings of betrayal, of lost trust, and often of shame are frequent consequences. Many people in this painful position are plagued with questions: "Am I not desirable?" "What did I do wrong?" All these feelings are legitimate, and we don't believe you did anything wrong beyond accepting the stories you grew up on about what "happily ever after" is commonly supposed to mean.

It can help to remember that a cheating spouse who wants to open up a primary relationship is taking steps toward *more* honesty, showing respect for the partner and the relationship. They wouldn't go to all this trouble if they wanted to get rid of you.

Our stereotypes paint the cheating partner as the villain, the greedy prick or bitch who wants to have their cake and eat it too, at your expense. But we know way too many people who have gotten into this position and are trying, often desperately, to find a way to make things right for everyone. The truly callous cad would just keep it all secret.

It can be hard to remember your partner's goodwill while you are struggling to digest this unwelcome news. Discovering that your partner already has an outside love can be very close to catastrophic, simply because it feels so terribly bad. And although it may be comforting to focus your pain into righteous outrage—and you are justified in doing so—something more needs to happen if you and your relationship are going to survive and thrive.

What do we see when we look at cheating with an open mind and with compassion toward everyone involved? Our culture would like to have it that cheating happens rarely, that it's an anomaly. Kinsey discovered otherwise more than half a century ago: slightly more than half of theoretically monogamous marriages back then actually were not. So cheating is not unusual and is not perpetrated only by heartless sex addicts.

Conventional therapeutic wisdom is that cheating is a symptom of something wrong in the marriage and that working on the marriage will make the cheating go away. Sometimes this is indeed true. But cheating is not necessarily about some failure in your connection, and it is cruel to tell people that something is wrong with a perfectly good relationship just because sexual desire has a way of squirming out of bounds.

You may feel betrayed, or grief-stricken, or furious. You've been launched into these feelings without any warning, and without your choice. It can be particularly hard to learn that your partner has been engaging in far-out sexual activities like kink or cross-dressing—if you're struggling with this, please look at some of our other books, particularly *When Someone You Love Is Kinky*.

Working to open a relationship under these conditions is far, far less than optimal—how is the nonconsenting partner supposed to find a way to feel secure and loved when the rug has been pulled out from under? But many couples do eventually find their way through this particularly thorny thicket. If you find yourself so angry that you can't begin to think about anything else, here's a way to make it easier to listen to your anger.

We are talking about a life situation in which many people experience particularly fiery anger. This exercise can be a first step in getting

EXERCISE *What Is Anger Good For?*

For this exercise, you start out thinking like an ecologist. Remember in school how they taught you that everything in Nature has its job, its contribution: the maggots eat the dead mouse and turn it into rich soil and then the rose can bloom, right?

So why do we all experience anger? What is its contribution to our individual ecologies and to our relationships? How does your anger help you? How does it protect you? Write a list. Examples might include: helping you discover your limits; energizing you to action; letting you release tension.

You might put this list on the refrigerator and add items over a week or two as you experience them.

Then, the next time you feel angry, you can ask yourself: "How is my anger trying to take care of me?"

to know that anger and understand it, rather than just avoiding it like the plague and then erupting when you can't stand it any more.

Intellectually understanding cheating doesn't make it that much easier to handle when you discover that it's *your* lover who is doing it . . . but it might help you figure out where you want to go from here. The challenge of rebuilding trust can be hard to contemplate, and you need to figure out how you can meet your partner halfway. Your spouse can't make you trust, can't really even earn your trust as though it were a salary—you have to decide that it's worth your while to grant it.

Furthermore, there is the problem of your partner's outside lover waiting, patiently or not, in the wings while you are starting from scratch trying to orient yourself to the situation. This person that you just found out about has feelings too and has perfectly good reasons for not wanting to remain a dirty little secret.

If the situation you're negotiating is one in which you or your partner has been cheating, you will probably have to spend some time together working through feelings of anger, betrayal, and guilt. But when you have those feelings under some degree of control, you will next have to look at the future and begin working—preferably together—on some solutions.

It may be that you will wind up separating, or perhaps the two of you will return to monogamy. Your local bookstore offers many excellent books to support you through either of those alternatives. But this book is called *The Ethical Slut*, so let's assume for now that you are at least considering the possibility of more openness in your relationship.

First Openings

In order for everyone involved in this situation to get from where you are right now—perhaps angry, perhaps scared, almost certainly confused—to somewhere new, you need to make a commitment to push yourself a little beyond your comfort level. Just a little, but still you need to push yourself. It doesn't work if your partner has to push for you, and it doesn't work if you are pushing your partner. You each have to push yourselves so you can discover how much stronger you are than you thought you were. It's sort of like working out—you have to push and pull those weights in order to strengthen your emotional muscles.

A good way to start would be to sit down with your partner in a peaceful place and compare your visions of a more open future. Perhaps you could each write down a little about what your relationship would look like if it were perfect, and perfectly easy. When you compare notes you may find out that you have very different visions: one partner may want to be the Queen of Sluts at sex parties, the other may be looking for a lover who wants to go backpacking and make out on a mountainside. One of you may be yearning for zipless fucks with no obligations, the other may desire an ongoing relationship with one or two people who stay connected and join the family.

Don't panic. You don't have to want the exact same thing, and you can figure out agreements that make it possible for you both to make your dreams come true. Look back at chapter 15, "Making Agreements," to get some ideas of possible ways the two of you might want to structure your poly constellation.

It can be pretty overwhelming to look at the dream with no idea how it can possibly be brought into reality—but, again, don't panic.

The next part is to figure out how you are going to get from here to there. As with any journey, you don't have to teleport to your destination in an instant—you will get to where you are going one step at a time. You don't learn to swim by jumping into the ocean, and you won't get comfortable with any of this by castigating yourself for not being comfortable already.

EXERCISE *Hierarchy of Hard, or, How to Get from Here to There in However Many Absolutely Easy Steps*

Here's an exercise about choosing the first step you want to take.

Choose a very concrete goal to focus on, one about which you have some anxiety. Poly issues might include: looking at personal ads together, introducing your lovers, making a date, having a sleepover, talking about safer sex. Choose an issue to practice with that is relatively easy for you today.

Think about the steps you would have to take to get from here to there—agreements, negotiations, honesties, asking for what you want, scheduling time, finding a babysitter, and so on. Write each of these steps on an index card. If any step looks too enormous, break it down into a few steps. Sort of like teaching three-year-olds to bake cookies, make each step utterly simple before you go on to the next one.

Then lay out the cards and put them in order from the easiest to the hardest, or the safest to the scariest, according to how intense it feels when you think about that step. You may get new information about yourself when you do this.

Then pick up the safest, easiest card, figure out how you could take that step, and march onward! When you've accomplished that, and learned whatever you learned from doing it, put the card away and go to work on the next step, which is now the easiest step.

Never take anything but the easiest step.

Kinds of Agreements

We look at the kinds of agreements that sluts make to deal with emotional comfort zones as falling, loosely speaking, into two categories:

agreements that avoid scary feelings, and agreements to take a risk of feeling something that might be uncomfortable or scary, but not terrifying. Make a list of all the agreements you might consider entering into, and divide them into avoidant and risky. Avoidant strategies might include don't ask, don't tell; don't rock the boat; don't let me find out; I will never meet your lover; only on Thursday nights when I'm out with my lover, so I'll never be home alone. These might be good agreements for the couple who are starting out on this path, in that they are taking the very smallest risks with the tightest possible containers. This is how we form a learning curve.

If you choose only avoidant strategies, however, you can wind up keeping yourself frozen in your present state. If you don't talk about what you are doing, then how can you think? If you can't think, how can you negotiate? How can you reassure yourselves without knowing what is happening? People don't do well in a vacuum, and many people find that the stories they make up in their heads in the absence of information are scarier than the reality.

In a worst-case scenario, you could wind up not knowing something that everyone else in your community knows, and then you might find out about it from a friend who thinks you already know. Most people don't much like getting blindsided, so basing your safety on keeping yourself blind is not going to work forever. And if you and your partner have to keep your activities secret from each other, then you have, well, a big secret. Secrets will not bring you closer together— they often create more distance. Suppose you have a fight with your outside lover, and your life partner can tell that you're upset. How do you deal with these realities and not disclose anything about your outside connections?

Many people find it easier not to hear about the specifics of their partner's lovemaking with others, and we don't see a lot of problems with that. Eventually, you might find it a turn-on, but there is no need to start there, or even get there, unless such sharing is important to one of you.

Think very hard about any agreements that add up to "don't have too much fun." Agreements about safer sex, of course, are absolutely required. But in the long run it's not going to make you feel very safe if your lover agrees not to, for instance, kiss someone, or not do any of a long list of activities. All you will get for that is a lot of wondering if this agreement will be kept and a lot of uproar if you suspect it is not.

You have the right to expect your spouse to be open with prospective partners about having a life partner already. You may be surprised to learn that this will make both of you more attractive to some people than a single person would be—an outside partner can play with either one of you and not have to worry about whether you are going to show up with a U-Haul. By being honest about the relationship you are looking for, you will attract people who are ready and willing to deal with the realities of your life.

There are distinct advantages to connecting with experienced sluts— their knowledge can be very helpful. When a prospective outside sweetie is new to polyamory, you will negotiate another set of agreements and establish a learning curve for this relationship.

Risk-taking strategies might include things like full disclosure or checking out personal ads on the Internet together: your first steps on your learning curve can be virtual steps if those feel like the easiest to take. What photos in the ads does your partner respond to? How do you feel about that? What does your partner think about the people you find attractive? What happens if you field a couple of characters on Second Life or flirt online in one of your fantasy identities? Or you might go out to a club together and talk about what it would be like to flirt with any of the hotties you might find there.

You can take the risk of arousing one of those scary emotions almost as an experiment, to see how it feels, learn about yourself, and explore how you can take care of yourself and reassure each other when jealous feelings are being felt in the present.

One risk that we advise you to take involves making the time in your busy lives to talk about how you are feeling about all this. There are a lot of exercises in this book about communication: try them. On the next page you'll find another script for talking about difficult feelings.

We have said before that nothing creates intimacy like shared vulnerabilities—so we advise you to savor all the closeness that you open up with each other when you start taking risks.

You can also use the "Yes, No, Maybe" exercise in chapter 21, "Sex and Pleasure," only this time list all the poly things: coffee dates, answering an ad, exchanging phone numbers at a party, flirting, all the way up to actual dates, sleepovers, and sex. The items that wind up on your Yes lists are the ones to start with, and then you can negotiate what it would take to make it safe enough to try something on your Maybe list. The No list states your absolute limits at this time and maybe forever. Compare this to your "Hierarchy of Hard" cards we talked about in the exercise earlier in this chapter. These two exercises you will use over and over again, because each time you get good at any part of what you are attempting, the scary level of all the items will change. Every time you learn something new, you become stronger and more confident.

EXERCISE *The Twenty-Minute Fight*

Make an appointment with your partner to discuss something you don't agree on for twenty minutes. Find a good time when you can focus, and when you won't have to do anything stressful right after— perhaps plan to watch a movie.

Try this first with a small disagreement, something not terribly heated, just for practice. How do you manage to stop after twenty minutes when the discussion isn't finished? Our most difficult disagreements are not going to be resolved in hours of talking, arguing, or yelling—maybe not even in weeks or months. Difficult issues take time to work on. So one important skill is to open up the controversy, and then figure out a way to stop and close it back down till the next time.

Use good communication tools, and set the timer. When the twenty minutes are up, take a few deep breaths and let go, let go, let go of wherever you are in the argument. It is a terrifically useful skill to know how to stop. It is much safer to start talking about a controversy when you have agreed not to yell at each other till you are exhausted and go to bed in a huff. You may find that after you stop talking you will be thinking about what you said, and what your partner said, and in a day or two you may very well get some new ideas about how you feel and what might work. By the time you come together next week for Twenty-Minute Fight round two, you may surprise yourselves by how much closer to understanding or accepting each other's positions you have come.

We have deliberately suggested some extremely easy places to start with—like looking at ads, or talking about all the cuties dancing at the club. These are very safe places to take a tiny risk, and pay attention to what feelings come up, and talk about them. Remember that feelings like to flow—don't look for answers, just watch them move on through. Please don't assume that how you feel today is how you will always feel: the whole purpose of this endeavor is to open up your options about your feelings.

You may be surprised by what's difficult, or by what's easy. Give yourself a gold star for what's easy—that's a strength you already have. Give yourself another gold star for even thinking about something that's hard—this is the work you are setting out to do.

Keeping It Hot

Regardless of what decisions you make about other people in your life, it's a good idea to start from a relationship that feels fulfilling and exciting. If you are delighted with your sex life with your partner, perhaps you don't need this section. But if your sexuality as a couple has become infrequent, perfunctory, unsatisfying, or nonexistent, please know that this is utterly normal (although not inevitable) in mature relationships. Most of us, when we get settled into a comfortable relationship, find wonderful ease and safety, but as our days get filled with careers and kids and softball and mortgages and building the studio in the garage, there is less energy for sex, and passion may lose both its ease and its urgency.

Before you read on, think for a minute: is the sex in my partnership okay the way it is? Maybe having somewhat less sex these days than you did on your honeymoon is fine for you. It's a myth that your relationship is a disaster if you're not getting it on three times a week or for three hours at a time. There are perfectly marvelous partnerships that last for decades and are very satisfying to all concerned, with little or no sex, or with comfortable, routine sex. Don't feel like you have to change something that feels okay the way it is: when it's not broken you don't need to fix it.

If, however, there are changes you would like to make, the first thing you need to do is find some time to talk with your partner, maybe read this section together, and negotiate your learning curve. If this opens up some hard feelings—and it may—go back to chapter 14, "Embracing Conflict," and consider how you can listen to each other's feelings without making anyone into a villain. Both of you got you here, and it's going to take both of you to get somewhere better. So start with what you need to do to get on the same side. We'll start with discussing a few common problems and some solutions to try.

Where you start depends somewhat on the nature of the problem. Some couples fall out of sexual synch because of a physical difficulty with sex that has eaten away at their sense of intimacy. For others, it can have more to do with the distance caused by the pressures of day-to-day life, or about small resentments that have built up over time and that can make it difficult to find the passion and romance that once inspired you. For many, it is some of each.

Let's start by talking about sex. It may be that one or both of you has kept silent about some aspect of your sex that isn't working right, out of some sense of trying to protect your partner's feelings. Silence will not help: the loving way to treat a sexual problem is to work together on fixing it, and your partner can't join you if you won't say what's wrong. If your partner tends to stop that perfect stroke right when it's getting good for you or initiates orgasm-seeking activity long before you're ready, you have to ask for what you want or else you are going to get frustrated and eventually resentful. And if you've never told your partner what you need to make you happy, you are depriving both of you of a blissful sex life. Similarly, when your partner has a concern, please don't take it as a deliberate blow to your sexual self-esteem. Most of us have to learn what our partners like from our partners—there are no clever tricks that work for everyone.

Pay attention to practical matters. Has sex become uncomfortable or painful? The first step here, too, is communication. If your back hurts in some positions, talk to your partner and choose some positions that are comfortable for both of you. Bad disks are not very sexy, but a pillow under the hips or the belly can change what gets strained or stretched. If friction feels unpleasant, pick up samples of some nice lubricants (many erotic boutiques sell sample packs), test them out to find your favorite, and enjoy yourselves. Lubricant is an asset to vaginal play for many women, and an absolute necessity for women in midlife and beyond, or for any form of anal play. If you haven't tried it before, you'll be stunned at how good it can feel for both parties. If penetration still hurts, get a medical checkup to deal with anything that needs medical attention. And if you both want penetration, but his penis isn't cooperating, consider trying one of the prescription medications now available to help maintain the hard-on once you've taken care of the turn-on. Once you start talking about physical issues that can affect sex, you'll be pleasantly surprised at how many of them are easy to fix.

Alcohol and other intoxicants are not really your friend. Although a small amount of wine or whatever may help you feel less inhibited, nervous people tend to overindulge, and getting hammered will leave you unable to feel anything at all and no fun to play with. We are going for sexual consciousness, not sedation.

For more problem-solving information, we have listed some good books about sex in the Resource Guide at the end of this book, and you can call or email San Francisco Sex Information (also in the Resource Guide) to discuss your question with a trained peer counselor.

DESIRE

Both men and women can develop some resistance to sex, either from fear of not doing it well themselves or from disappointment in not getting their needs or their dreams fulfilled. Once any part of sex has become difficult, if it isn't discussed and dealt with, resentments can build up. Responding to resistance by getting so pushy that you're ignoring your partner's signals to knock it off is definitely not an answer. Sweeping someone off their feet when they don't want you to only works in movies. Avoid treating your partner as a resource for getting your rocks off: just because you got married does not mean you have a right to demand sex whenever you want it. What you can do is invite your partner to collaborate with you on a meander through the garden of earthly delights and discover what pleases both of you.

It is very rare that both partners have exactly the same desire for sex—that would be like insisting that you and your partner should have identical patterns of tidiness. To get through times when one partner is hungry for sex and the other is starving for sleep, a positive attitude toward masturbation is an utter plus. Sex with yourself doesn't mean you're a failure, it means that you enjoy yourself; it can make your relationship a lot easier, especially when you don't have to hide it. One of your authors regularly goes to sleep with her partner curled up around her beating off while she reads herself to sleep with a good novel, both of them getting drowsy in their favorite way and all warm and cuddly.

So your first slut skill in keeping it hot is to talk to each other about the practical aspects of what works for each of you and scheme together to overcome any problems. Knowledge is the most powerful aphrodisiac.

EXERCISE *The Great Sex Story*

Write a story about the best sex you ever had with your life partner. Get into the details, describes the sensations: the sounds, the smells, the pounding pulse, and such. Both of you write your stories—it might be a different episode, and that's fine—and then share them. Talk about what made it so good for you.

WHAT DO YOU WANT?

Some couples develop a groove, a satisfying script for sex that reliably works for both of them. Experimenting with new sensations in your sex life doesn't mean giving up your groove, but rather adding some new tricks to your excellent repertoire. What's already a good thing will remain good, and you will return to it again and again like a well that has very sweet water.

If the groove has become a rut, if it feels like a chore, if it is a source of repeated disappointment, it's time to talk about expanding your options. Now might be a good time to do the "Yes, No, Maybe" exercise in chapter 21, "Sex and Pleasure," being sure to include things that you've never tried but might like to. Looking at your partner's list may be a mite shocking for starters—"I never knew you hated that!"—but after you recover from any surprises, you get to start into the future with a lot of really useful information about what works for both of you.

Compare your patterns of desire, and particularly look at the spectrum from brief encounters to production numbers. Do you like to have friendly, warm, cuddly sex on weeknights? Swift rocket trips surging to release? Do you dream of ecstatic journeys that could take up most of Saturday and maybe some of Sunday morning? Good sex travels the range from what Dossie calls "bread and butter" sex, the nourishing part of every meal, to fancy desserts that take enchanting hours to concoct. Production numbers obviously can't happen every day, but luckily you don't have to choose—you can have some of each.

Start by setting aside some time for pleasure—this may be harder than you think, but it's very important. Waiting until the kids are in bed, the emails are answered, the chat lists have been checked, and you've watched the evening news and clucked over the terrible state of the world is a recipe for disappointment. Schedule it the way you'd schedule anything else that's important to you, at a time when you're most likely to have plenty of energy for it, and stick to your schedule whenever possible.

EXERCISE *List of Dates*

Many couples in the hectic rush of things to do—children to raise, walls to paint, gardens to hoe, groceries to buy—find that it has been a long time since they spent time together for the purpose of having fun. Make a list of dates you could plan—beaches, brunch, dancing, games, sports, wrestling matches, that new restaurant—and figure out what you would need to do to make them happen. You and a partner or partners could make that list together, or you could each make a list. Try for at least five items.

Then start scheduling. When you realize how hard that is, then you are also finding out how precious time spent with your partner truly is. An afternoon on a mountain is an important investment in your relationship.

FINDING YOUR TURN-ON TOGETHER

Turn-on is not the same thing as hard-on. Turn-on is about getting into the mood, about getting ready to focus on sensual and eventually sexual sensation.

Too many of us believe that turn-on is something that happens to us like the weather. Here's an affirmation for you: "I know my turn-on is in here somewhere, and I can figure out how to find it."

Turn-ons may be visual, verbal, or sensual; they may rely on touch, sound, smell, or the sensations of muscles stretching and flexing. There are a thousand and more ways to get turned on. Make a list of your favorite turn-ons—not how you like to get off, but how you like to get started. Getting turned on is sort of like getting high, or waking up, or warming up—you are transitioning from one state of consciousness to another. This takes time, and it feels good.

Sexologists who study arousal tell us that turn-on depends on two things: safety and risk. You need to feel safe from harm, and secure that your conditions will be met and your wants and needs honored. You also need to feel a little like being at the top of a ski jump, on the threshold of something miraculous and powerful. New relationships can be very hot because there is still a lot of riskiness, but mature relationships need to seek out ways to take a little risk, to step beyond the comfortable and the familiar into something new and a little challenging.

Infinite Possibilities

Looking for your turn-on on can be a lot like looking for ways you can nourish your relationship. Here's a list of some possibilities that you might find useful.

- Dress up, clean up, wake up.

- Prepare your environment—fancy sheets, candles, music.

- Allow plenty of time—start your date three hours early, out somewhere.

- Go to the sex store.

- Talk about your fantasies (go ahead, blush).

- Play an erotic board game.

- Massage gently with favorite oils, nice and slow . . . maybe with a blindfold on one of you . . . or both of you.

- Get silly.

- Neck in the car like teenagers.

- Hold each other while you cry.

- Make a dinner and eat it with your fingers.

- Eat some very good chocolates and taste each other's lips.

- Read an erotic book together—out loud.

- Watch a movie you both find sexy.

- Go together to a strip club.

- Go to the hot tub spa and soak.

- Go anywhere in Nature and make out.

- Make your dates special any way you can.

Get Connected First

There's a reason why dates usually include dinner: dinner, whether out or in, is a great place to connect, to talk, to get caught up, and then maybe plot an adventure. Going out to dinner gives you time to dress up sexy, which is much more fun than washing dishes.

Remember when you are on a date and when you're not—some people don't like being felt up while they're washing the dishes. (Others do, of course, so you have to communicate about this too.)

EXERCISE *The Process-Free Date*

Agree to go out and do something you like together. During this date, do not talk about any problems, in your relationship, or at work, or with the kids, or in the economy, or whatever. One couple we know went out for dinner and dancing and pretended it was their first date. They danced like teenagers and came home to have lovely sex that felt, somehow, renewed.

IN BED

When you get to the bed, being equally turned on is not a requirement; you can both get there with a little time and cheerful cooperation. The more ready person can help the other person catch up. Try out what sex therapists call "nondemand pleasuring," which adds up to anything you know your partner likes, without pushing them further. Try an experiment where you agree that one partner will set out to arouse the other in the way the receptive partner chooses—with no obligations, and no blame if it doesn't work.

GETTING THERE IS HALF THE FUN

Whatever you choose to try, please try something. You have to do something different if you want a different outcome.

None of this works every time. Simply making the effort is progress, even when one particular attempt doesn't pan out. Setting aside time with the intention to hunt for your turn-on is the best way to start, and if you set out to get sexy and you don't get all the way there, you can still enjoy the journey.

Consult your "Yes" lists and scheme together for a brief encounter on a weeknight. Schedule a time when you can have a twelve-hour date—yes, twelve whole hours—without being interrupted. Go out to dinner, to a beach, hiking—whatever you like. Come home, shower the sweat off together, light the candles, and see what happens next.

PART FOUR

Sluts in Love

CHAPTER SEVENTEEN

Making Connection

ANY MEMBER OF A SEXUAL minority faces special challenges in finding partners and friends—and, as a slut or slut-wannabe, you are most assuredly a member of a sexual minority. Polyamory is not readily understood or accepted in very many social environments. If you're also gay, lesbian, bisexual, transgender, or interested in a specialized area of sexuality such as cross-dressing or S/M, you are doubly or triply challenged. And yet making the connections of your dreams is not only possible but eminently achievable, as many thousands of abundantly connected sluts can happily attest.

However, we'd be the last people to tell you that it will always be easy. We've heard, and lived, too many sad, frustrating stories about near misses: partners who are fine with an open relationship until someone falls in love, at which point they freak out and demand monogamy; or partners who rhapsodize about sexual openness and free love in principle but fall apart when faced with the reality (Janet says these remind her of the dog who chases cars all his life, then can't figure out what to do with one when he catches it). Some partners may become successfully polyamorous but come to a time when their needs, desires, and limits simply don't fit together well enough—after all, sex is not the only or the most important aspect that determines the way we relate.

Yet many people *do* succeed in finding each other, for relationships ranging from casual to lifetime. So, how do you find friends, lovers, and potential partners who not only share your values and beliefs, but are also emotionally, intellectually, and sexually compatible with you?

Who?

A good place to start is by getting an idea of *who* you're looking for. The trick in making this decision is to be neither too specific nor too vague. If your "who" list basically includes anybody who is breathing and who is willing to have sex with you, we suggest that you are perhaps broadening your field a bit too much. Even if you don't have strong preferences about gender, age, appearance, background, or intelligence, you probably do want someone who will not lie to you, steal from you, hurt you, or exploit you: basic sanity, honesty, and respectfulness are on most of our lists. It is also perfectly fine to acknowledge those preferences that are genuinely important to you: if you prefer men to women, or people your own age to people much older or younger, nobody is going to report you to the Equal Opportunity Commission.

On the other hand, if your "who" list reads like a set of technical specifications—gender, age, weight, height, coloring, mode of dress, educational background, breast size, penis size, sexual kinks—we suspect that you may be more interested in making love to your own fantasy than you are to a real, live person. Many of us, unfortunately, are conditioned to react sexually to a rather unrealistic standard of appearance and behavior: porn queens and kings are fun to watch in the movies, but they rarely appear in our living rooms. If you expect your new honey to be gorgeous, intelligent, loving, and highly sexual all the time, you are almost certainly setting yourself up for a lifetime of disappointment—few people can achieve those standards, and nobody can maintain them twenty-four hours a day.

We can't tell you the exact cutoff point at which a healthy preference becomes an unrealistic desire; only you can look inside yourself to do that. We do think that physical appearance, wealth, and social status have very little to do with the person behind them, and if any of those criteria appear high up on your "who" list, you may be a little bit stuck in your fantasy. Try getting to know some people who *don't* meet those criteria. We have a hunch that if you get to know them and like them, you will discover that they have their own unique beauties, just waiting there for someone to notice them.

EXERCISE *The Airport Game*

Next time you find yourself in a public place like an airport or mall, find a place to sit where you can look at people without drawing attention to yourself. Then, for each person you look at, imagine: What is this person's lover's favorite thing about them? Do they have a strong stride, a sweet smile, bright eyes, powerful shoulders, hair that looks soft to the touch? Pretty much everybody is, or has been, loved by someone—see if you can see what makes this particular person lovable and lustworthy, even if they're not the kind of person you're used to seeing that way.

An important note: even people who *are* gorgeous or rich or busty or whatever don't usually like to feel that their beauty, their wallet, or their breasts are their most attractive quality. Those who partner successfully with them often consider such qualities a happy bonus that has little or nothing to do with why they chose that person in the first place.

Where?

Where do sluts gather? What are your best-bet venues for finding the bedmate, playmate, or lifemate of your dreams?

In the decade since we first wrote this book, the answer to that question has changed a great deal. "Polyamory" is now listed in the *Oxford English Dictionary*. Newspapers, magazines, and websites worldwide have run detailed articles describing this strange new lifestyle. Support groups have sprung up in all major U.S. cities and many smaller ones; several larger annual conferences draw connection-minded sluts from all over the world.

It is impossible to list here the wide variety of polyamory-related venues that are available to you, because there are too many and they change too fast, but we have listed a number of them in our Resource Guide. One small caveat: there are almost as many definitions of the word "polyamory" as there are people using it. You may find yourself confronting people who insist that whatever you're doing (swinging, fuck-buddy circles, casual play, group sex, whatever) isn't really polyamory: the most conservative definition of the term encompasses only long-term committed multipartner relationships. Our strategy for dealing with this issue is to smile sweetly and agree: "OK, what I'm doing isn't polyamory by your definition."

If, for whatever reason, the online polyamory community doesn't feel like the right place for your quest, there are many options for seeking out other sluts in person. It is difficult to find sluts in dance clubs—the music is often too loud for an exchange of ideas or ambitions. Try searching the web for "ethical slut munch" or "polyamory munch" in your area, and meet some people who like to get together and talk about the lifestyle. We find a lot of ethical sluts exploring alternative realities: try your local Society for Creative Anachronism and other historical re-enactment groups, and know that many Renaissance Faires are practically sluts' trade conferences. Check out science fiction conventions or live action role-playing game groups. If your sluttery has a spiritual leaning, many groups of neopagans are far more open than traditional Judeo-Christian religions to alternative lifestyles. (Many others aren't, so don't make any untoward assumptions.)

Another good place to look can be in workshops, seminars, and gatherings that have to do with human sexuality or intimacy. While cruising is, understandably, not allowed at some of these activities (people baring their souls are doing difficult work that can be disturbed by having to be on guard against unwanted advances), graduates often go on meeting socially long after the actual session is over. There are also several regional and national conferences about sexuality and intimacy, and these are attended by many kindred slutty spirits.

When you go to events where you can expect to meet like-minded folk, you will usually need to invest a little time in becoming a member of the group you are visiting. Start out by making friends, and don't be friendly only to people you want to cruise. Make as many friends as you can, and people will start to trust you. One good initial tactic is to go find some people like yourself, not your ideal opposite number, and make friends with them. If they are like you, they probably know people you will like.

Most of these gathering places and events are made possible by a lot of hard-working volunteers, so the absolute number one best way to get to know people in a group you like is to volunteer to do something useful: greet folks at the door, help with refreshments, join the clean-up crew. You will meet a ton of people and they will be grateful to you. Both of your authors have become valued members of many communities by helping out and by offering our living rooms as meeting places to support groups and social functions. Generally, we get a friendly crew to help us set up and to clean up afterward. Then we don't even have to leave home to attend.

PERSONAL ADS

Sluts have been finding each other through personal ads for many decades, and personal-ad partner finding has expanded enormously in the last decade or two, fueled by the widespread availability of Internet access.

One couple who recently celebrated their eighth anniversary says,

> We would never have found each other if we'd met face-to-face in the first place. Anthea is tall and girly and a single mom and an agnostic; Bev is short and energetic and resolutely child-free and Jewish. Neither of us is anything like the people either of us has chosen before. But since we met through the personals, we had a chance to get to know each other at a deeper level, before we had to confront all the surface stuff that would have turned us off if we'd seen that first.

Those seeking nontraditional relationships may, however, find themselves addressing some problems of categorization. One well-known international free advertising site, for example, offers two types of relationship ads, the regular partner-seeking ones and "casual encounters"; people explicitly seeking nonmonogamous longer-term relationships sometimes find that their ads in the partner-seeking section have been removed. We don't have an answer for this, except to hope that this site will consider adding an "alternative relationships" category soon.

There are also paid sites, usually sponsored by magazines and newspapers, that cost a few dollars a month and offer a bit more flexibility in how you describe yourself and what kind of relationship you're seeking; Janet and her spouse E found each other on one of these. At this time, many online matchmaking services do not support nonmonogamous lifestyles, and some will even take down ads that mention poly, but we're sure that will change as polyfolk become more visible. However, the website PolyMatchMaker.com offers space for all sorts of poly and alternative personal ads for people of all genders and orientations. And OkCupid.com offers an ethical slut test that will help you match your values with other participants. Dossie and her partner recently took this test and are happy to report that they both qualified, although Dossie was a bit miffed to discover that her partner got a higher score than she did. On the *test*, that is.

When you meet people through a personal ad, it is customary to get to know them in stages, starting with email correspondence, then perhaps a phone conversation, and then a no-strings get-together in a public place for coffee or a meal, so that you can get to know the other person slowly and with as little pressure as possible. Be aware that you know nothing about this person beyond words on a screen, and take the same precautions you would take in meeting any other stranger.

A special case: What if you fall in love with a person who wants monogamy? This situation is going to be tough. We know that this is a valid disagreement, and also a very basic difference. In our more thoughtless moments, we have blithely assumed that once this delightful person who has won our heart discovers that ethical sluttery is possible, he or she will instantly want to join in—but that is not always the case. Please remember that nobody is right and nobody is wrong; this is about two different ways of structuring a relationship, and both, or all, choices are valid. You may choose for the present to continue exploring this relationship because it is precious to you, and you want see how things evolve, even if you may be disappointed at some time in the future. Both of you need to agree to tolerate the ambiguity of knowing that ultimately you each want something different. Entering into a relationship while planning to change your partner is not respectful to your beloved and could make big trouble in the future.

Make "for the time being" agreements about how you will live at present and seek out knowledge and experience that will help you understand each other's positions. Read this book together, read a good book on intimacy. Refrain from bad-mouthing each other's choices.

Attend some workshops together—maybe one on poly, and one on hot monogamy. Join some online support groups on relevant topics, and find time to discuss what you learn from all of these sources.

Consider the wide spectrum of relationship options available to you—perhaps the one that best fits your needs may not be what you thought you were looking for. Meanwhile, we feel sure that you entered into this potentially difficult situation because there is a great deal that you treasure in this particular relationship and that the value of your love together outweighs the differences between you. Whether the two of you wind up as friends, lovers, spouses, or something else that's unique to your pairing, we hope you'll find a way to keep on cherishing that love.

What?

What kind of relationship do you want? Do you want someone with whom you can buy a house and raise a family? Someone you can meet once a year for a hot and heavy weekend of role-playing fun? Or Ms. or Mr. Right Now? Knowing what you want up front can prevent a lot of misunderstandings and hurt feelings later.

If you're worried that nobody could possibly want what you have to offer, don't be so sure. While it may be harder to find someone who wants to be a secondary partner, or a role-play buddy, or the parent of your children, it is certainly possible—in fact, there are undoubtedly at least a few people out there who are looking for just such a situation.

Trick versus partner is not an either/or situation: there are many, many ways to relate that lie between a one-night stand and marriage. You may not know in advance what kind of relationship will develop with the person who intrigues you tonight, and that person may not fit whatever space in your life you thought you were looking to fill. Taking people as they come, how they are, here and today, can lead you to wonderful surprises that more than make up for the occasional disappointment. So watch out for your preconceptions, and be ready to approach new people with an open mind and an open heart.

Expect situations to change. Someone you thought was just an occasional playmate may evolve into a much more important figure in your personal landscape. When this happens—and it has happened to both of us—it is important to keep that person, and anyone else involved, thoroughly briefed on the emotional shifts you're experiencing. It may be that your friend is feeling the same way toward you . . . and this could be the beginning of a beautiful friendship. Or the object of your desire may just not be in a place where a deep emotional commitment feels right. In any case, treat this changed relationship as though it were a new one—in a way, it is. It may be that the two of you can go on connecting in your original, casual manner, or you may have to part for a while to maintain your original equilibrium. Full mindfulness, lots of empathy, and plenty of honest communication are strongly recommended here.

LOOK AROUND YOU

Perhaps the person you want is already in your circle of acquaintances, only you don't know it yet. Janet writes:

E and I had known each other casually for years, and with an unfortunate history: I'd once written a newspaper piece harshly criticizing one of the policies of the small business he was running at the time. So when I saw him on the street, we would say a fairly stiff "hello" and part with a slight sense of relief.

However, when I answered the personal ad from a man who described me quite precisely in his list of desired characteristics, I didn't know it was him.

It took several rounds of correspondence before we each began to figure out who the other one was, and then all our mutual friends started getting phone calls from each of us asking about the other one. E was in a relationship with one of Dossie's roommates for several years—that's how close the connection actually was, once we figured it out.

We'd already fallen half in love just through email correspondence. Our first date was for Thai food and a long walk around one of Oakland's nicest neighborhoods. We had some negotiating to do around the whole issue of poly—some of his previous partners had been pretty good at the slut part but not so good at the ethical part—but he was willing to at least try.

He moved in a year or so later, and we got married a few months after that. As of this writing, we're approaching our third wedding anniversary and our fifth anniversary as a couple.

CHAPTER EIGHTEEN

Couples

SLUTS RELATE in as many combinations and styles as you can possibly imagine, and more. Is there a typology of relationships that could possibly include every wonderful possibility? Obviously not. We believe that every relationship is unique unto itself, and thus even an attempt to think in types and forms is not going to express the essential truths of what happens when we love people.

Here is one particular and fairly unusual relationship we cherish:

Your authors have been lovers, coauthors, and best friends for sixteen years, and we have never lived together. We have both lived with other partners during those sixteen years and have both been single together for only a brief time. Our relationship is a treasure, and no other partner gets to object—we've been doing this for a long time and we do not intend to stop. Of course, if we wanted to live together we probably would have by now, so we are also no threat to any life partner. (As long as you don't get threatened by reading in extensive detail about your partner's sexual adventures with her coauthor—this is a problem only a few of you will ever face.) It is nothing short of a miracle to us that our partnering has been so fruitful and so serene and so intimate and so explorative over all this time. We both agree that to live together would run a terrible risk of spoiling a good thing.

Everybody ought to have a coauthor. But even if you don't write, you might find yourself making connections that remind you of some of the possibilities we will discuss here.

While all connections can be guided by the basic principles we've discussed in earlier chapters, new skills and concepts may get developed by brilliant sluts who want to explore the rewards and challenges of any particular lifestyle. In this chapter, we will discuss some of the many ways of exploring open sexual lifestyles and making your connections sustainable. Even if it doesn't seem like what you want has much in common with any of these ways of partnering, we suggest reading the whole chapter—there are ideas for all of us in the experiences of any one of us, and sometimes a voice from somewhere else can give us just the piece our puzzle was looking for.

We all grew up in a world in which there was assumed to be nothing between emotionless sport fucking and committed long-term marriage-type relationships, leaving the vast territory in between open to discovery by relationship pioneers of all stripes, including ourselves. What interesting ways of relating to people might we, and you, find between these two poles? When we include *all* of our connections in our picture of relationship, we expand the definition of what a relationship can be.

Each relationship seeks its own level when we let it. Operating on this principle, we can welcome each of our partners for precisely who they are: we don't need them to be anybody else or to bring us any particular resources or skills. If you don't want to play tennis with me, I'll ask somebody else, and if you don't want to play bondage games with me, again, somebody else will—our relationship will not be less for it. What we share is valuable for what we share. Period.

We like to be easygoing about sex, but what people mean by "casual sex" is perhaps too dismissive. Casual sex sounds like we are supposed to be distant: don't get too close, don't expect too much, avoid any expression of intimacy or vulnerability.

We are now hearing people refer to certain of their lovers as "friends with benefits." A euphemism, perhaps, but an interesting concept. Why shouldn't we share sex with our friends, making sex a natural part of the love and honor and faithfulness and openheartedness that we already share with friends?

We have learned the most, and had the most fun, and made the most wonderful, rich connections, when we have welcomed each new person into our lives just as they are, without trying to force them into the picture that's labeled "relationship" in our brains. This has been true whether we've been single, coupled, part of a group family, or engaged in any one of the myriad other ways of relating that creative and loving sluts can devise.

Couplings

We hear too often of folks who delight in a joyously slutty lifestyle until they "fall in love." Then, perhaps prodded by cultural messages that love must equal marriage must equal monogamy, they dive into an attempt at a conventional lifestyle, often with disastrous consequences. At least one of your authors—you can insert Janet's rueful grin here—has proven herself not immune to this kind of programming.

There is no reason why wedding bells, or the equivalent thereof, need to break up that old gang of yours. Many sluts find it possible to combine the committed stability of a life partnership with the manifold pleasures of sex and intimacy with others.

However, there is no question that being a slut within a committed relationship has some special challenges. So much of our cultural baggage tells us that commitment equals ownership—that, as the old bitter joke has it, a ring around the finger equals a ring through the nose. Even people who know better often find (sometimes to their surprise) that their expectations of a committed relationship may include the right to control many aspects of their partner's lives.

While we're going to write here about couples for the sake of clarity, all the principles apply equally to threesomes, foursomes, and more-somes. Relationships take their own shapes, but the best ones tend to share some basic principles: good boundaries, mindfulness, and a mutual desire for the well-being of everyone involved.

As you can probably guess, we don't much like the idea that a relationship commitment specifies anybody's right to anything beyond mutual respect and caring for each other. Yet once you divorce romantic love from the concept of ownership, what happens? One woman we know, who had never been in an open relationship before, was startled to find that many of her old habits have become irrelevant: "Why should

I bother to look for stray hairs on the pillow, trying to sniff out any trace of infidelity, when I know that if he has sex with someone else he'll simply tell me about it?" Yet there *are* still issues of boundaries, of responsibility, of courtesy, that complement ownership and promote sustainability, which must be dealt with.

So, how do sluts in love build a life together?

Our friends Ruth and Edward remember:

> We had a monogamous relationship for about sixteen years, then opened it up and started interacting with other people. Now we're trying to figure out what we're comfortable doing with other people and what we want to reserve for our own relationship. Sometimes, the only way to locate the boundary of our comfort zone is to cross it and feel the discomfort. We try to take small steps, so that the pain is minimal. We're definitely committed to each other and are each willing to stop doing things that the other finds threatening.

Mostly, you take care of your own stuff, recognize and protect your boundaries, and make agreements to help yourself and your partner feel safe—but we've already talked about that. Here are some special problems that may come up for partnered sluts.

We've said before that each relationship seeks its own level. For some relationships, that's a life partnership, which may include sharing living space, possessions, and so on. Others may take other forms: occasional dates, friendships, ongoing romantic commitments, and so on. Yet many folks find that they've gotten into a habit of letting their relationships slide inexorably into life partnership, without much thought or intent on their part. Well-meaning friends and acquaintances may aid in this process by assuming that you and your friend are a couple before you've ever decided to become one. In addition, many people get coupled by accident, by virtue of an unplanned pregnancy, an eviction romance where one partner loses a housing situation and moves in with the other, or simple convenience. Janet remembers:

> In my freshman year of college, I met a guy I liked a lot—quiet and shy, but when he said anything, I really liked what he had to say. Finn and I wound up going out together a couple of times and having sex a few

times. When school ended, we wrote to each other over the summer. Then fall came and I began looking around for a place to live outside the dorms. The only room I could find was a double-sized room that I could afford only if I shared it with someone. So I called Finn and proposed that we share it, putting up a partition across the middle and sleeping on separate mattresses, and he agreed.

The first night there, Finn had already gotten himself a mattress, and I hadn't yet—so I shared his. Somehow, we never did get around to getting another mattress. We wound up living together for a couple of years, then getting married. That missing mattress led to a fifteen-year marriage and a couple of kids.

While we're all for coupledom for people who choose it, we like to see folks make their choices a bit more mindfully than this. We suggest that before you let yourself slide into something that you don't really want, you do some serious thinking and talking, alone and together, about what is the best form for this particular relationship. Talk to each other about what love means to you and how you fit into each other's lives.

You may discover that while you enjoy one another's company and have fabulous sex, your habits regarding housing, money, possessions, and so on are wildly incompatible. In such a situation, you could do what generations of people have done—move in together and spend years trying to change one another, getting frustrated and resentful in the process. Or you could reconsider some of the implicit assumptions you have brought to the relationship. Do you have to live together? Why? Why not instead enjoy your friend for the things you like about him and find someone else with whom to share the other things? Slut-hood means, among other things, that you don't have to depend on any one person to fulfill all your desires.

If you know that you're a person who tends to slide into coupledom, we suggest spending some serious time trying to figure out why you've fallen into this pattern and what you hope to get out of being part of a couple. It's a very good idea for everyone to learn to live single—to figure out how to get your needs met without being partnered, so you don't find yourself seeking a partner to fill needs that you ought to fill yourself. You might also consider experimenting with some relationships unlike those you've tried in the past—instead of looking for Mr. or Ms. Right, try dating some people you like and trust but don't necessarily love, or maybe love in a quieter way than chills running up your spine.

In this, as in just about everything else we've told you in this book, the key is to build your own sense of internal security. If you like yourself, love yourself, and take care of yourself, your other relationships can arrange themselves around you, as perfectly as crystals. We hope that if and when you get coupled, you do it on purpose.

A Few Thoughts about Marriage

One of the questions facing coupled sluts is the issue of whether to enter into the special, legally sanctioned partnership called "marriage." In an increasing number of states and countries, even being in a same-sex relationship no longer exempts you from having to address this question: same-sex marriage has been legally sanctioned in several states in the United States, in Canada, and in an increasing number of countries in Europe and elsewhere, and we utterly approve. Your authors, however, think it is very important that everyone look very closely at what apples we are buying when we reach out for the marriage-rights piece of the American pie. Some of those apples have worms.

Marriage, as it now stands, is the inevitable outcome of government imposing its standards on personal relationships, legislating a one-size-fits-all prescription detailing how people in sexual or domestic relationships ought to run their lives. Here in California, for example, we have community property laws, which means that whatever income or debt either spouse creates during the marriage belongs to both spouses. We know a woman whose soon-to-be-ex-husband deliberately threw them into bankruptcy because she was planning to leave. Other states have laws just as arbitrary: in some places, if you live together for seven years you're married whether or not you want to be, by what is called, with startling narrow-mindedness, "common law."

Marriage is, we're told, a sacrament—a loving ritual where your faith and your community bless your union. Why, then, is our government, the one that says "Congress shall make no law respecting an establishment of religion, or prohibiting the free exercise thereof," requiring us to get marriage licenses?

If marriage is sacred, as we think it is, why is legal recognition of a relationship, along with privileges like health insurance and inheritance, restricted to those who are willing to shape their lives to conform to somebody else's design?

If we ran the world, we would abolish marriage as a *legal* concept, allowing people to enter into contract relationships as allowed by the perfectly adequate laws that already govern other forms of legal partnership. Sample contracts could be provided by institutions, attorneys, churches, publishers, and support networks. Those who wished to perform marriage as a sacrament could do so under the auspices of whatever religious or social institution felt like a good fit for them. Under such a system, no agreement would be taken for granted; sexual exclusivity, money sharing, inheritance, and all the other issues currently covered by inflexible marriage laws could be consciously chosen. We really like conscious choices.

There is, of course, always a need for laws about the basic responsibilities adults have for children and other dependents. Tax breaks and other support should still be available to those caring for children and dependent elders, who really need them. It's sort of like supporting public education: we have a hard time imagining a better use for our tax dollars than meeting the needs of the disabled, the aging, and our next generation.

Love is a wonderful thing, and we think it would be even more wonderful if we all acted like responsible adults and entered into thoughtful arrangements about the physical and financial foundations of our lives. If we really took care of business instead of letting a pro forma piece of paper dictate our decisions for us, we would be much freer to love in whatever ways fit for us.

Special Challenges for Couples

The commonest form of relationship in our culture, and many others, is the couple: two people who have chosen to share intimacy, time, and perhaps space and possessions for now and the foreseeable future. While couplehood has a great deal to be said for it—it's a lot of work building a life, and many hands make light work—it also offers some special challenges.

The ideas in this section are written for two-person couples for the sake of simplicity, but most of them apply to threesomes and more-somes as well.

COMPETITION

One problem that sometimes arises between partners in sluttery is competition to be the most popular, a concern most of us have carried around in the bottom of our psyches since junior high school. Some-times partners compete with each other to see who can score the most or the most attractive of conquests—an ugly picture.

We cannot reiterate often enough: this is not a contest, this is not a race, and nobody is the prize. One strategy to cut through any feel-ings of competitiveness is to play matchmaker for each other, to invest yourself in your partner's sexual happiness as you do in your own—some polyfolk use the word "compersion" to describe the feeling of joy that comes from seeing your partner sexually happy with someone else. Remember the climax of *The Big Chill*, in which a woman char-acter sets up her best friend with her husband so that her single friend could have a baby?

Janet recalls meeting a new Internet acquaintance for coffee and hearing her describe a pet sexual fantasy that was startlingly similar to Janet's then-partner's. Janet set up a first date for her new acquaintance and her partner for later that week, and the two of them (with Janet joining in later on) went on to have a long and intense relationship.

Dossie was once out on a date with a longtime lover of hers when she noticed an attractive person trying to catch her eye behind her date's back. She explained the situation to her date, who had a stroke of genius. He strode over to the young man in question and with great dignity announced, "My lady would like you to have her phone num-ber." The young man looked terrified at the time, but he called the next morning. Dossie has made use of this strategy repeatedly since then and recommends it highly: they always call!

CRUSHES

We have pointed out before that it is impossible for anyone to predict what depth of feeling may potentially exist in any sexual relationship.

Many people new to open relationships try to limit outside sexual encounters to a casual, recreational level to avoid the terrifying specter of seeing your partner in love with, or at least crushed out on, another. It is true that sometimes an outside relationship will threaten to become primary and supplant the existing partner. When this happens everyone involved will feel horrible, especially the partner left behind: it really sucks to spend months or years struggling to own your jealousy and working hard on your fears of abandonment, only to be actually abandoned.

But it is not possible to predict when or with whom a crush, or any other deepening of feelings, might happen, and most crushes pass in time and do not need to lead to breaking up. We certainly do not want to draw the boundaries of our agreements so tightly that we exclude everybody we like. There is no rule that will protect us from our own emotions, so we need to look beyond rules for solutions and for a sense of security.

It can help to do a reality check on your fantasies and expectations. New relationships are often exciting because they *are* new, glowing with sexual arousal, and too untested to have uncovered the inevitable conflicts and disturbances that come with true intimacy over time. Every relationship has a honeymoon phase, and honeymoons do not last forever. Some people get addicted to the honeymoon (which you may hear called "limerence" or "new relationship energy" or NRE) and wind up flying from partner to partner, always imagining that the next partner will be the perfect one. Such unfortunates may never stay with anyone long enough to discover the deeper intimacy and profound security that comes with confronting, struggling with, and conquering the hard parts of intimacy together.

Our friend Carol wisely notes:

Sexual time is connected with intimate time for most of us; we come to depend on our partners for various kinds of emotional support. So we get into this pattern where we share all our hard emotional unsexy needs—all the work of living together, the sickness and health, richer and poorer stuff—with our life partner, and we're on our best behavior with our other partners. However, while being in a long-term relationship may involve trading away some of the juicy excitement of a brand-new unknown partner, the intimacy you get in return is valuable too, and you can't have that with a person you met two weeks ago. The trick is to find a way to manifest both possibilities—the intimacy of sharing and the heat of novelty—in your own life.

Remember, please, that fantasy is not reality, and enjoy your fantasies while you maintain your commitments. When your expectation is that a crush is a brief, if wonderful, experience, you and your partner can live through one with relative equanimity and without destroying your long-term stability and love with each other.

The Two-House Couple

Not all couples live together. In recent years it has become more common that couple-style partnerships, with all the closeness and longevity of couplehood, may nonetheless span two or more households. Dossie has extensive experience living this way. Sometimes this situation comes about by happenstance: school or career commitments, for example, may create geographical distance. Other couples have made a conscious choice, like one duo of our acquaintance who have maintained a ten-year bond by deciding about three years ago that they should live in separate dwellings. According to them, this saved their relationship.

This life choice, we think, may well become even more common in the future. In times of financial security, sharing a house is no longer an economic necessity. Individuals in these couples may well be sharing a home with housemates, not necessarily wasting resources living alone. While some of them are polyamorous, others may be more or less monogamous. Arguments about who sleeps where become unnecessary when everybody has their own beds, but that's not the main reason these couples cite for living separately: most of them simply feel that their relationships work better that way. Your authors, for instance, have been coauthors and lovers for sixteen years and have never chosen to cohabit: we understand our relationship to be a magical gift that daily living might well destroy (if Dossie's inexplicable need for clean dishes didn't do the trick, Janet's devil-may-care attitude toward past-due bills certainly would).

We should not assume that such relationships represent a failure of intimacy or commitment. Rather than look for what is wrong, we might want to examine what is uniquely adaptive about these partnerings and what special skills or wisdom have developed from these new, assumption-challenging partnerships.

Often such partners create rituals that maintain their connection when apart—agreements about phone calls, ways of reaffirming love at comings-together and leave-takings, keeping caught up with the news in each other's lives, marking one space or time as "theirs" and another space or time as belonging to one or the other of them.

Making this arrangement work requires some skills in scheduling and keeping time commitments, so differences between individuals in how they handle time and punctuality must be worked out. Differences in patterns of sexual desire can become problematic when opportunities don't happen every night.

How do you respect your partner's space in this arrangement and feel secure in your own? Do you have to go home when you want a little distance, or can you figure out a way to maintain your own space in a house that belongs to one of you? How much stuff do you get to keep there?

People often have differences about how much staying-in-touch they are comfortable with when they are apart—some people chat on the phone or text or instant message two or three times a day, while others would find that too distracting.

All of the differences that all couples need to manage still need to be managed when they live apart: differences in gregariousness, tidiness, work patterns, focus on careers, how money gets handled, how often you have your mother over for dinner—no two people have identical patterns in any, much less all, of these items. And, sorry, living apart is not automatic protection against couple bed death. Nor is every time together automatically an occasion for sex, even though we often wish it were.

We suspect that couples living separately will not be that different in their sexual lifestyles from those who live together. It can, however, make being together much more of a special occasion, so people tend to respect these times and be willing to invest a little effort into making them special.

Many couples date for some period of time, perhaps even years, before moving in together. Are they then to be considered couples who lived separately by choice, or were they merely getting ready for the "real" stuff? Some couples, after dating for a very long time, may look at what living together would look like and decide that it would be a bad idea—maybe all those differences would work out better in separate spaces. This decision can be hard to make in a society where living together is practically the definition of relationship.

One question people often ask such couples is: "Then how do you know you're a couple?" They know by how they feel about each other and, by extension, how much of their lives they are sharing. We'd like to see a world where all of our relationships are honored and valued and where it is understood that a couple's love and their journey together is in no way less important just because it occurs in two houses rather than one.

Relating to Third Parties

Your relationship with your lover's lovers brings up points of etiquette that Emily Post never dreamed of. One couple we talked to noted, "It's important that we not be totally grossed out or disgusted by one another's lovers—especially if it's going to be long-term, it helps if we can all be friends."

Dossie notes,

I was once in a relationship with a man who had a primary partner whom I had not met. I had asked to meet her, and she was considering whether she felt safe enough to do that. Their arrangement was that when Patrick had a date with me, Louisa would make a date with her other lover, and everybody would, hopefully, feel safe and taken care of. Unfortunately, Louisa's other lover frequently stood her up, and then Patrick would stand me up, which I began to find unacceptable. This was the first time I had asserted any right to consideration of me as the outside lover—we are so used to seeing the outsider as the home wrecker that we rarely think to protect that person's feelings. With much back and forth, and after the promised meeting, Louisa finally agreed that Patrick could see me whether or not she had a date, and we would make sure that she got plenty of advance notice, that he got home on time, and that she got lots of support from both of us. As we worked through this, Louisa and I got closer and closer—I particularly remember one night when we were worried about Patrick and sat up late talking about him while he slept in the next room. Louisa and I became best friends and went into business together, putting on workshops and theater presentations. We all three traveled together and had a wonderful time. Patrick and I wound up growing apart as lovers, but the friendship between Louisa and me carried on.

Should you meet the third party? We vote yes: if you don't, you'll almost certainly wind up imagining someone cuter, sexier, more predatory, and more threatening than anyone could be outside a Hollywood erotic thriller. Besides, who knows?—you might wind up liking him or her.

Do your best to fall in like. If you take against one of your partner's lovers, things can get very messy, and happy balances can get hard to find. We sometimes regard lovers whom we do not instantly adore the way we do in-laws. We may not exactly love our brother's wife, or our mother's new husband, but we recognize that this person has joined our family and has rights and feelings just like everybody else, so we find ways to be cordial at the various gatherings that we all attend.

Some of our best friends are people we met because someone we were fucking was fucking them too. You may even find yourself considering forming a liaison with this person yourself—we talked to one woman whose first experience with open relationships took place when her girlfriend was sleeping with another woman and our friend wound up falling in love with the other woman. "My girlfriend got kind of cranky about this," she remembers wryly. "We're all tight family now, but it took a decade to get here." We suggest a few moments of soul-searching to make sure your motivation is loving or lustful rather than vengeful or competitive—then, if you "test clean," go for it. It's really not too surprising that you like the same people your partner likes, and mutual attractions like these can form the nucleus of a long-lasting and very rewarding little tribe.

On the other hand, we sometimes see sluts who feel that they *have* to be sexual with their lover's lovers. In some cases, both parties in a partnership have an agreement to play with a third party only together. Such agreements require that both partners have veto power over potential thirds—being sexual with someone you find unattractive or unpleasant is a very bad idea for you and for them. On the other hand, basic slut ethics should not allow you to abuse this power to prevent your partner from having sex with anyone at all by veto-ing everybody: a strategy that may seem tempting, because until you unlearn jealousy, all outside engagements can look very threatening. Sometimes you need to gather up your strength, face down your fears, and unlearn by doing.

You may simply feel that since your partner likes and lusts after this person so much, you should too—to assuage your partner's guilt or to satisfy some obscure sense of fairness. Please don't. If you simply don't feel hot for your squeeze's squeeze, don't let yourself be driven into a position where you feel you have to fuck out of politeness: there are many other excellent ways for people to relate to one another. Cook a nice dinner, go to the movies together, play cards together, or find some other way to help this person feel accepted into your life.

Which brings up an important question: how much responsibility do you have for helping your lover's lovers feel secure and welcome? We've both spent many long telephone conversations reassuring our lovers' lovers that, yes, it's *really* okay, and have a great time, honey. We think that your own needs should be of primary importance to you, and if you really just can't be welcoming and supportive then simple civility can suffice. On the other hand, we also think it's gracious to be as friendly as you can without having to grit your teeth and force a smile. At minimum, we suggest that you try to provide some reas-surance that this is not a competition, that you are not being harmed by anything that's going on, and that you are able to take care of your own emotions—in other words, a promise to own your own stuff and not blame the third party. After all, such people come into your life because you share something very important: the belief that your part-ner is the hottest thing on legs. They presumably have better things to do with their time and energy than sitting around plotting how to destroy your happiness.

Some couples take meeting and interviewing prospective partners very seriously, and we suggest this strategy when your model of polyamory requires that you include any new partner in your family. People with children, for instance, care a lot about who comes home to the house and could wind up as an uncle or an auntie to your kids. Some poly people will not consummate sex with a lover until all these issues have been dealt with, and those are fine decisions to make if they fit your lifestyle: long engagements can be a very good idea.

After the crush is over, some people will find a long-term place in your life, often unexpected, like the lover who has become your kid's favorite uncle or your partner's business partner. Others may leave, and when they leave with warm feelings, they may come back again in the future, when once again there is a place for them in your life or for you in theirs. Thus the infinitely connected polyamorous slut builds his web of extended families and tribes.

Two of our favorite sluts have been together nearly twenty years, loving each other and a lot of other wonderful people. One year, for Tina's birthday, Trace bought her what we think is the ultimate birthday present: *three* season tickets to an excellent performance series . . . one for Tina, one for Trace, and one for whichever of Tina's lovers she chose to invite to each event. (Dossie got to see Ravi Shankar!)

Primary and Primary and . . .

Some very capable sluts maintain more than one primary relationship. Dossie has known one such couple, Robert and Celia, for almost four decades. They together raised two children from previous relationships, and subsequently some grandchildren. Each has another primary partner, both usually women, and family relationships with all their exes. Robert's outside partner May was originally lover to Celia's lover Judy back in 1985, then became lovers with Celia, and finally with Robert from 1988 to the present and, they intend, on into the future. Some years ago Miranda and Celia lived upstairs, and Robert and May lived downstairs. Currently Cheryl, another of Celia's previous girlfriends, lives upstairs and helps with the grandchildren; Miranda, another of Celia's exes, visits two days a week since she lives out of town but attends school nearby. Are you dizzy yet? All of these people, plus many other friends and lovers of various degrees of intimacy, both present and historical, and most of *their* friends and lovers, form a very long-term extended family that has lived, loved, and raised children together for nearly forty years and plans to care for one another in their old age. We are impressed.

CHAPTER NINETEEN

The Single Slut

TO LIVE SINGLE is unusual in most cultures. Most people look on their periods of singlehood as temporary, often accidental, and to be ended as quickly as possible. You are recovering from your last relationship, mourning a breakup, or too busy working on a career to handle hunting for romance. Perhaps there aren't any good candidates around right now. Something better will surely come along soon . . . so you wait, not even thinking of making a lifestyle out of how you are living today. Your authors hasten to assure you that there there are more positive approaches to the lifestyle of the single slut.

What would it be like to be *intentionally* single, to choose for some period of time to live by yourself? Potential partners can pop up when you least expect them—and in a culture that is built in twos, any relationship that has any life in it is generally regarded as an express train to couplehood. How, then, to stay single?

What would your social support network look like? Would everybody regard you as an outlaw? Might it be possible to get your needs met and feel loved and secure through a community of friends, lovers, family, mentors—your personal human resources?

Building your network by yourself can be hard at first—no one but you to make the phone calls, schedule dates for lunch or the movies, make sure to stay connected. It's up to you to build yourself a family, and it's up to you to take care of yourself gently and with an open heart.

Your relationship with yourself is a lifelong commitment. When you are single, you have unique opportunities to live out that relationship with yourself, to find out who you are, and to celebrate your journey in whatever relationships you may move through as you travel through your life. To live single and in love with many is a voyage of self-discovery, an opportunity to get to know yourself intimately and to work on any changes you want to make in your life. Dossie was single when she first struggled with her jealousy, and having it all to herself made it easier to see inside herself rather than blame someone else, and to make conscious decisions about how she wanted to deal with her feelings.

We are not here to advocate being single over being partnered—this is not an either/or choice. But our culture tends to discount singlehood as a lifestyle, and thus very few people choose to remain single, which means there are relatively few resources and little social status available to the single person. Perhaps if being single were an acceptable, even valued, lifestyle, partnerships might develop more out of choice and less out of a sense of necessity or a desperate grab for salvation.

Partnered people get to share the basics of their lives—working together on shared goals, pooling finances, splitting the hard work of child rearing. Partners also get to share with each other when things are less than pretty—and we all need somebody to let us know that we are still lovable when we are not at our shiniest. The challenge for the single slut is to find ways to deepen the intimacy in relationships that may not be life partnerships.

Being single, on the other hand, offers the opportunity to spend time being purely who you are. Singles enjoy more freedom to explore, fewer obligations, and the ability to lounge around the house in a holey T-shirt playing video games with nobody the wiser. Perhaps you are single for negative, and valid, reasons. The last relationship was a disaster, and you are terrified to try again. You only feel safe controlling your own finances, or your own kitchen, or your own life. The only way you know how to be in a relationship is to try to be the perfect wife, or husband, or lover, or provider, and you're exhausted from trying to be someone you are not. You are recovering from a breakup, you want to avoid rebound romance, you need time to grieve. You just haven't found anyone that you really want to live with.

Perhaps you are actively choosing to live single at this time in your life. Living alone, you're free to explore any kind of relationship that crosses your path. You can love someone who wouldn't make a good partner. You can love someone who already has a partner and who doesn't need you to help with the mortgage or taking the kids to the orthodontist. You might choose singlehood because you love the joy of the hunt, the magic of flirtation, all the mystery and excitement of newness. Or you might be choosing to develop sexual connections with your friends, or without possessiveness, or any other relationship that is possible without coupling. Each utterly unique person you meet offers a new mirror in which you can see a new view of yourself: each new lover increases your knowledge of the world and your self-knowledge as well.

Some Thoughts about Love

As our relationships blossom all over the rainbow of possibility, each one may inspire different feelings of love. When we learn to recognize and welcome love as we find it in our hearts in all of its many and marvelous manifestations—sexual love, familial love, friendly love, passionate love, gentle love, overwhelming love, caretaking love, and millions of others—we discover a river of rich and nourishing love that can flow through our lives in a constantly replenishing stream.

The way to feel solid enough to swim in that ever-changing river is to learn to love yourself. Some people believe that to love yourself is selfish, in a negative way, and that to spend some part of your life focusing on yourself is not only selfish but also narcissistic. How do you draw a line between healthy self-esteem and pathological narcissism? How much self are you allowed to have?

Practice self-nurturing, not only to get you through hard times but to guide you into a loving relationship with yourself. When you follow through with a simple act like comforting yourself with homemade soup, bringing home a fragrant flower for your night table, or taking a sweet solitary walk in a beautiful place, then you get an experience of being kind to yourself that can answer all those questions about "what do they mean, love myself?" This question is more easily answered by doing than by thinking.

If you have a hard time feeling valuable when no one is around to tell you that you are, why not do something that is valuable to others? Many unhappy sluts with no date this weekend have gone off to serve dinner to the homeless at a local church and come back filled to the brim with good feeling about all the pleasure they were able to give to others.

Once you have a handle on loving yourself, you can practice sharing that love with others. You've probably been taught to reserve the language of love for when you're feeling overwhelmingly tender and passionate, and only for those who have made huge commitments to you. We recommend instead learning to recognize and acknowledge all the sweet feelings that make life worthwhile even when they don't knock you over—and, moreover, learning to communicate those feelings to the people who inspire them.

EXERCISE *Words of Love*

1. Write one or more letters you are not going to send to one or more of your lovers telling them how you feel about them: what you love about them, how much you love them.

2. Freewrite for ten minutes: what's embarrassing about telling people you love them?

You can decide later if you want to share any part of what you've written with anyone you love.

Ethics for the Single Slut

What are the rights and responsibilities of the single sexual partner? Start with rights; you have them, and you will need to assert them. Too often our culture sees the single partner as "secondary," "outside," "an affair," a "home wrecker," and your place in the ecology of any life or relationship or community is dismissed as inconsequential at best. What does a single person have to do to get taken seriously, in this community or any other? If you're in this position, a good place to start thinking about rights and responsibilities would be with some respect, honor, and consideration for each person's feelings—including your own.

THE RIGHTS OF THE SINGLE SLUT

- You have the right to be treated with respect—you are not half a person just because you are single.

- You have the right to have your feelings heard and respected and responded to.

- You have the right to ask for anything you want—the person you ask may not have to give it to you, but you are definitely allowed to ask.

- You have the right to have dates and plans honored, not changed by a third party simply because that person has seniority.

- You have the right to chicken soup when you are sick, and whatever other emergency support you may need—rides to the emergency room, help when your car breaks down. Your lovers are your friends, and friends help each other when things go wrong.

- You have the right to negotiate family holidays like Thanksgiving and weekends involving your own and your lovers' children: you are a member of any family you are in relationship with. How this works may look different depending on the values of the family you're connecting to, but you definitely have the right to ask for more than just being somebody's dirty little secret.

- You have the right to have limits and to set limits: what you will and will not do, what is and is not negotiable for your emotional well-being and personal ecology.

- You have the right to not be blamed for problems in other people's relationships.

- You have the right to refuse to be a dumping ground for someone's marital woes—you may not want to listen to how much your lover wants a divorce, and you shouldn't have to.

- You have the right to count. Everybody counts, including you.

- You have the right to be valued and welcomed and respected as the wonderful human being that you are.

THE RESPONSIBILITIES OF THE SINGLE SLUT

- You are responsible for developing and maintaining good solid boundaries. Boundaries, are, quite simply, how you can tell where you end and the next guy begins. Good boundaries are strong, clear, and flexible; bad boundaries are weak, foggy, and brittle.

- You are responsible for making clear agreements. Make and keep agreements about time, about public and private behavior, and about courtesies in shared spaces. Always do what you say you are going to do.

- You are responsible for being clear when what you want to say is "no." Don't waffle, and don't make promises you can't or won't keep.

- You are responsible for carefully choosing who you confide in about your relationships. Gossip can be a destructive force, and yet most of us need to be able to talk out our stuff with someone. Be clear about who those people are.

- You are responsible for respecting the other relationships of your lovers, especially their life partners, and for treating these people with respect, empathy, and openheartedness.

- You are responsible for safer sex: opening discussion with potential partners, making your own decisions about your level of acceptable risk, respecting other people's decisions, and learning to be adept with barriers and little bits of essential rubber.

- You are responsible for owning your feelings, as is everyone else. Learn to handle your own crises and get support when you need it from others who are free to be there for you at that particular time.

- You are responsible for being straightforward about your intentions. When you practice being openly affectionate with your lovers, they may expect more from you than you are offering, and you must be willing to speak out and make yourself and your desires clear to all concerned.

- You are responsible for finding ways to say what another person might not want to hear. Single sluts may need to state uncomfortable truths in relationships that might not have the customary intimacy for such vulnerable discussions.

- You are responsible for promoting intimacy in all your relationships. If being single means that you are committed to being coolly invulnerable in all situations, you'll be living in a cold and distant world.

- You must value and welcome all of your lovers as the wonderful, brilliant, unique human beings that they surely are.

Rainbow of Connections

If you're single and slutty, you may find yourself interacting with a lot of different people in a lot of different patterns. Here are a few that we've encountered and that you may too.

SINGLES WITH SINGLES

Isn't it funny how we call single people "available?" Available for what? When you are single, your lovers might be other singles, but that doesn't mean that each of those relationships is anything like any other. With one person you may love to go dancing, with another it's hiking.

With any individual, you might be dating frequently, regularly, irregularly, or rarely. That rare time might be a very special thing—quantity doesn't always equal quality. When everyone is single and no one is auditioning for partners, then each relationship is free to seek its own level, and there may be fewer obstacles to flowing into exactly the relationship that fits for the two of you.

Just because you are single and not planning on changing that right now, please don't take your lovers for granted. Let them know how precious and valuable they are to you. Convention says we should be more reserved: we say let's change that convention. We love hot dates, and we also love warmth.

PARTNER TO A PARTNER

You may be dating someone who has a long-term, life-sharing partner—married or living together. When you are dating that person, there is someone else whose feelings must be taken into account.

Perhaps you find yourself in the position of sleeping with someone who's cheating. Whatever you think about the ethics involved—different sluts make different choices on this one—it is certain that difficulties can arise when your lover's partner doesn't know about your connection. Contortions may be required to keep the partner from finding out—and even with all the cleverness and forethought in the world, there is no sure way to keep such a big secret forever. This kind of secrecy imposes pretty severe limits: if the relationship consists of weekly trysts at the no-tell motel, how much connection can really take place? If the relationship goes well, someone may very well wind up wanting more. It's the "outside" lover in a secret affair who will most likely get abandoned if anybody gets caught.

Perhaps your sweetie is in a "don't ask, don't tell" agreement; many couples new to nonmonogamy try this one in an attempt to feel safer. In our experience, this can create problems for all concerned. First, most people find their lovers in their social networks, so keeping them all separate can be difficult or impossible. Or lies must be told to protect the agreement—and then it's back to the cheating paradigm we just discussed. Maintaining untruths, even when you're asked to do so, will create distance in any relationship and is particularly damaging to live-in partnerships, where secrets are a lot harder to keep.

On the other hand, when everybody involved is informed about your involvement, things are often easier. Even if things start out uneasy, being out of the closet offers the possibility of working toward learning to be more comfortable for everyone involved. If your lover is part of an experienced poly couple, both of them will know their boundaries and be able to let you know what their limits are, which can make for a lot more clarity. If they're new to this kind of relating, good faith and a willingness to talk through problems can get you through most if not all difficulties.

Your authors have found that we are happiest when everybody knows and acknowledges everybody. Common courtesy is essential, as is scrupulous avoidance of anything that smacks of competition or one-upmanship. Catfights are only fun in porn.

Both of us much prefer to meet our partners' partners and make friends with them when at all possible. Sometimes they are not entirely sure that they want to be friends with us, and occasionally they're pretty sure they'd rather not, but with patience and good will, most of them come around. After all, we have at least one thing in common: we both love the same person.

There is no reason why our interests need be opposed to our lover's partner's interests. We all want to collaborate on creating a happy outcome where everybody gets respected and everybody gets their needs met and their desires fulfilled. In the long run, we are all on the same side.

The experienced slut can take some initiative in reaching out to frightened partners in a gentle and openhearted way. Some of our best friends over the years were first met in these circumstances. The vulnerability of feeling jealous or nervous about each other is its own form of intimacy, and friendly feelings may be the most useful response.

Taking care of a partner's partner by sharing sex with them is optional for both of you. It's rarely a good idea to get intimate with someone just because they might feel left out, and it is not often sustainable to enter into a relationship that doesn't interest you in and of itself. Occasionally, you will discover a sweet fit and become lover to a couple, as we will discuss soon. But avoid committing yourself to an interaction that you don't like very much or don't want at all. Giving in to someone to assuage jealousy just about never makes the jealousy go away. You can respect your own limits while offering support, warmth, and welcome to your lover's lover.

A special case: you may find yourself in a relationship with someone whose life partnership is no longer very sexual, whether from the normal cooling of passion as relationships mature, or through illness or disability. When you are dating such a person, do remember to approach their partner with an added measure of care and respect. Such people may be happy that you are keeping their partner happy but still somewhat sorrowful at not being able to fulfill that role themselves. It helps to discover what valuable contributions that person *does* make, and recognize and honor them.

ROLE-CONSTRAINED RELATIONSHIP

Sometimes your relationship may be defined by the roles you play together, roles that a person's life partner may not want or enjoy. Your connection could be as simple as a love of watching football on TV or, perhaps more complicated, being the same-sex partner to someone in an opposite-sex marriage. Your shared roles might be about S/M power exchange, erotic roleplaying, exploration of gender, spiritual journeying, or any other sexual sharing that the partnership doesn't provide. Your shared role makes you part of a family's ecology, part of what makes it run smoothly, and is both a joy and a responsibility not to be taken lightly.

LOVER TO A COUPLE

Sometimes sexual connection comes together quite beautifully between multiple people—a threesome, a quad, or whatever. The very riskiness is exhilarating, and the adventure can be very new and exciting. If you are fortunate enough to have this experience, you can expect to honor the relationship that you are privileged to share in and to be honored as a very special member of that relationship. The sex can be very luxurious—think of all that can be done with those extra pairs of hands!—and feature various configurations of two on one. How delicious to have two people spoiling you, how fascinating to share the active lovemaking with another, a virtuoso trio when you get practiced at it.

There may be times when someone has little to do and could feel left out. When that happens to you, think about how an extra pair of hands might be useful in whatever the other two are doing and gently join in. One time in such a moment, Dossie was temporarily left out while the couple who were her lovers were having intercourse with each other. She felt a little shy, thought about joining in, and then noticed that these two people, who had been together for quite a few years, were amazingly graceful in their deep connection with each other, so Dossie settled in to watch for a while and was quite happy and content just to witness such beauty. When they were through, they welcomed Dossie into their embrace, and further delights occurred that were well worth waiting for.

Do remember that there is privilege in being an outside partner: you can, if you choose, get to be all about fun and leave the heavy stuff to the partners who will go home with one another afterward. Or maybe you'd rather be there to help out when the kids all come down with chicken pox. Whatever fits for you, remember that there is privilege in being the play partner. As one friend of ours puts it, "I get to be dessert!"

GROUPS

When your lover has a whole bunch of partners, making agreements can look like major treaty negotiations and might require some diplomacy. Some groupings have boundaries around who a member may connect with. Perhaps the other members want to meet and approve—that's an easy one. Some will want outside partners to clearly understand the group's limits and boundaries, especially about safer sex, which is great. And we are very happy to see that some poly groups are very thoughtful about how they make connection to a new person and are willing to take the time to get things right.

Some groups might want you to join in one way or another—having sex with the group, moving in with the group, becoming part of a group marriage—that may or may not fit for you. You, of course, get to look at what's being asked and decide if that is what you want, and to define your own desires and limits.

Many initial disagreements can eventually be negotiated if all the parties involved are open-minded and operating in good faith. And if they aren't, you might be better off learning that right at the start. One friend of ours connected with a person who had two primary partners and wanted our friend as a secondary. But when our friend asked what would happen if he were to acquire a primary partner himself, they said, "Oh, no, that wouldn't be acceptable." So our friend opted out.

Most group marriages and circles that we have encountered are much more lightly held and flow easily with new partners who may someday join the group at large, over time and one step at a time. Dossie belonged to one such family when her daughter was a baby. There were no formal membership requirements, and everyone fit together and grew together as they went along, with partnerships forming and separating and reforming on their own timetables, and everyone responsible for the whole gang of children. This adaptive arrangement worked very well for quite a few years—not forever, but for a good, happy, memorable long time.

Single Soliloquy

Dossie writes:

Someone at a workshop once asked me: "Don't you get lonely, living alone?" I was startled, and it took me a second to understand that he wasn't trying to make me feel bad. What an ache he innocently opened in me. I had to say: "Yes, of course I get lonely." And yet . . .

I have lived about half my adult life single. Some things are hard to do by yourself. I recently bought my first house. How I yearned for a partner in that scary endeavor! But I managed, somehow. I dealt with my fears, and with realtors and mortgage brokers and roofers and inspectors, and now I have a sweet little home in the woods: like me, mine to share with others, when and how I choose.

Nothing lasts forever. Someone asked me if I feared being alone in my old age. I am now in my sixties, and you bet I'm afraid of that. I saw my mother live to be ninety-three in the house she shared with my father during their thirty-seven-year marriage: only he died of cancer when they were sixty-five.

Nothing lasts forever. I still crave the thrill of falling in love, the dream of a romance so magical it could never fade. And I know better. When I have fallen in love in the past, the long-term outcome has been a crapshoot: sometimes great, sometimes disastrous. After eight such relationships, I must admit I have no idea how to predict the future of any passion: whether we will grow into a solid and sustaining kind of love, or whether we will grow to hate each other.

Now I am a person who prefers burning passion to sweet reason. And I don't consider myself very good at compromise. But my compromise for my own survival is to learn to live single and to make a very good life of it: a lifelong commitment to myself.

Long ago, I thought of singlehood as being "between old men": some condition of waiting for the next one-and-only to show up. It was like being on hold, waiting for one-and-only number four to pick up the phone, not like living a real life.

In 1969, when I was first a slut on purpose and a baby feminist, I decided to live single for five years so I could discover who I might be when I'm not trying to be somebody's wife. But how was I going to make this work? I didn't want to live and raise my child in a cold world with no affection or intimacy, so I devised a scheme for sharing love with lovers I had no intention of living with.

Back then, there was very little precedent for sharing sex with someone you were not auditioning for a long-term partnership. So I invented ways that I could take the risky steps of sharing affection openly with people I had not "secured," if I can call it that. I told them what I liked about them. I good-mouthed. I sought out opportunities to be demonstrative. I used the L-word and insisted on calling the feelings I had for each of my lovers by their true name: love. And when I had the courage to be loving, the result was that I got a lot of love back.

It is true that I first learned to love this way as a survival technique for living single. But it has become something far more valuable: an open affection for who and what I love around me has become my foundation and my way of life, whether or not I am living with a partner.

I am confident that this approach can work for everyone, whatever their lifestyle, and even when they are not sharing sex: wouldn't it make a fine world if we all made it a point to honor and cherish and openly value every person we make a connection with?

I raised my child with this sense of community. Being a mother taught me to respect limits and boundaries and certainly to refuse to welcome in my home or in my heart anyone or anything that threatened the well-being of my child or me. By extension, I learned to better protect my own vulnerabilities, which made me even more capable of expressing my love for others.

I live in the country, and I feel this same kind of heart-opening love when I walk on a beach, or look at the world from the top of a small mountain, or discover, around some bend in a trail, a two-thousand-year-old tree standing in majesty. I feel no desperation, nor any desire to cling. I just feel happy.

Do I sometimes feel lonely? Sure. Do I love my life? Immensely. Sometimes I think I am the luckiest person in the world.

217

CHAPTER TWENTY

The Ebb and Flow of Relationships

WE OBSERVE, with much delight, the number of our old lovers we count among our present friends, and we marvel at how sexual relationships can develop into family memberships. There is a reality limit here: You have only twenty-four hours a day to devote to your love life, and presumably you need some of those hours for work and sleep and so on, so you have a finite amount of time to devote to each of your lovers. You can fit only a certain number of people in your life and expect to do any of them justice.

We find that most people do okay letting their partners come and go as it feels right for each of them. Extended family sexual relationships are more likely to grow apart than to break up. One of the very wonderful things about building sexual friendships is that, while past relationships and smaller affairs may come and go over the years, each pairing has its own characteristic and unique intimacy. You create this intimacy the way you learn to ride a bike—by trial and error, slipping and falling, and ultimately zooming along together. Just like riding a bike, you'll never forget this particular intimacy or your own role in it. Even after the most bitter of separations, when conflict is cleared and time has healed the wounds, you may find that you can slip that connection right back on, like a comfortable old glove.

On the other hand, sometimes conflict in an intimate relationship goes on so long, or seems so impossible to resolve, that it threatens the very foundation of that relationship. We hope you bring the same high level of ethics and concern to a conflicted relationship that you brought to a happy one.

It is always tempting to respond to a major relationship conflict by assigning blame. In childhood we learn that pain, in the form of punishment from our all-powerful parents, is the consequence of doing something wrong. So when we hurt, we try to make sense of it by finding somebody doing something wrong, preferably somebody else. We have discussed the problems that come from blaming and projection before.

What is important to remember is that most relationships break up because the partners are unhappy with each other, and no one is to blame: not you, not your partner, and not your partner's lover. Even if someone acted badly, or was dishonest, your primary relationship probably isn't falling apart for that reason—relationships tend to end due to their own internal stresses. Even your authors have trouble remembering this when we are in the middle of a bitter breakup.

When you find yourself wanting to blame, it may help to remember a truism of relationship counseling: the client is the relationship itself, not either of the people in it. During a breakup it is supremely useless to try to ascertain who is "right" and who is "wrong": the question is, what needs to happen next? If you start looking at conflicts as problems to be solved instead of trying to decide whose fault they are, you have taken an important first step in solving them.

Some people habitually bear the burden of being responsible for everybody's emotional well-being and feel that they're somehow at fault because they're unable to magically make everyone's pain and trouble disappear. Instead of refusing to own their stuff, one partner takes too much responsibility for the problem at hand. Such people need to learn to own their own bit and let everybody else own theirs.

It's also common for one partner to take too little responsibility. People who have a lot of their self-esteem connected to their ability to maintain a relationship may feel the need to make their partner into the villain in order to justify their own desire to leave. This strategy is unfair to both of you: it gives the "villain" all the power in the relationship and disempowers the "victim." Deciding that you have no choice but to leave because your partner is so horrible is denying the fact that there are always choices. Our experience is that relationship troubles are almost always two-sided: if you can acknowledge your own contribution to the problem, you can work toward solving it.

If your relationship problems include anybody being physically violent, or emotionally or verbally abusive, it's not time to waffle over whose fault it is—it's time to get professional help in learning to resolve conflict in a nondestructive manner. The Resource Guide in the back of this book will tell you how to get in touch with groups in your area that help both battered and battering partners. Similarly, professional support is often a good idea to deal with substance abuse—no partner, no matter how wonderful, can resolve something like alcoholism with love alone. If a child is being abused in any way, safety becomes the first priority, and you need to leave right now. You can work on resolving these issues from a safe distance.

Breaking Up

It happens. Good relationship skills and high ethics don't mean you get to be with the same partner or partners forever and ever. It is our experience that relationships change, people grow out of them, people change. They may acquire new desires, new dreams. Some breakups in our own lives, as we look back with 20/20 hindsight, were actually constructive moves toward personal growth and a healthier life for each of us. At the time, however, we just felt awful.

It helps to remember that in the contemporary world, a breakup doesn't have to mean that you and your ex did something dreadful. Most of us can count on going through a breakup at some time in our lives, possibly quite a few times. Rather than hide in denial, or torture ourselves with wondering what we did wrong, what would happen if we thought, in advance, about how we would like breaking up to be in our lives?

When a traditional marriage breaks up, nobody takes that as evidence that monogamy doesn't work—so why do people feel compelled to take a slut's breakup as evidence that free love is impossible? Your breakup may be for reasons entirely unrelated to the openness of your relationship. At any rate, it probably isn't evidence that you aren't meant to be a slut: we suspect you wouldn't have done all the hard work it takes to live this way if you hadn't had a strong desire for sluthood in the first place.

When a relationship shifts dramatically, it's great if everybody feels calm enough to separate with affection and equanimity. But all too often, partnerships break up in a harsh way, with painful, angry, hurt, and bitter feelings. Grief at losing a relationship that we had counted on cuts deep, and while we are going through the hurtful process of an unwelcome separation, none of us are at our best.

A typical grief process takes about three months to get past the acute phase. It helps to look at grieving as productive work. Loss has left a hole in your life, and you need to pore over what you valued as you figure out how you want to fill the empty space and knit the wound together. You probably will need to do this work on your own—your ex can't really do it for you. Feelings of grief, loss, abandonment, anger, resentment, and such that are overwhelming or intolerable today will probably seem sad but manageable three months from now as you move through this process. As the most intense feelings die down, you can find a good time to get back into communication with your ex—have some coffee or go to a movie or some such. It would be a shame not to come out of this breakup with at least a friendship, after all you've shared.

BREAKUP ETIQUETTE IN THE TWENTY-FIRST CENTURY

Sadly, many people approach the ending of a relationship as if they have been given a license for drama, and furthermore, some people just can't leave in a good way. They need someone to blame (other than themselves), a villain, a perpetrator, the bad guy, to feel okay about themselves or to clear their consciences.

The Internet has provided us with fabulous new technology for accomplishing drama—friending and unfriending, publishing your wise and wicked judgments about your recently beloved, spreading your indignation like lava over everything.

So while surfing the web has brought new opportunities, tons of information, and a great many joys into the lives of contemporary sluts, it also offers unprecedented opportunities for acting out, especially during the sensitive period surrounding a breakup.

All the rules that tell us who it's safe to confide in go triple when electronic communication is involved. If you're in the habit of using your blog or social-networking page as your personal journal, please consider keeping a separate page—if it's online, lock it so you're the only one who can see it, but we actually prefer paper for this—on which you can pour out anger, blaming, grief, and all the other emotions that are important to feel but inappropriate to share with your entire online community.

As for junior-high-school behavior like making a big drama about unfriending someone on your MySpace page—well, just don't. If it's no longer appropriate for an individual to have access to your personal information, consider posting less personal information for a while . . . or, if you absolutely must, simply remove that person from your friends list, without comment to them or to anyone else. Unfriending someone so you can badmouth them behind their back is silly and rude, and they'll probably hear about it from some mutual friend anyway. Look for safer and more constructive ways to vent your feelings.

If you look at advice columns from the early twentieth century, there is considerable judgment about the rudeness of using a typewriter (horrors!) to write a personal letter: new technologies often seem very impersonal at first, and email is no exception. The advantages and disadvantages of email are the same thing: on a computer screen you can't use your face or body to communicate, and little smiley and frowny faces don't really help much. Email can be very helpful in clarifying a point that feels too emotional or dangerous to communicate with your voice, but it can also come off sounding a lot harsher than you meant it, since your sympathetic smile gets lost somewhere in the ether.

WHO GETS THE FRIENDS?

One of the joyous consequences of open sexual lifestyles is that everybody tends to get interconnected in an extended family, sexual circle, or tribe. When a couple breaks up with lots of pain, then the whole circle is affected. For the people in pain, it can feel like there is no privacy. Your friends and other lovers may be full of their own ideas about who's in the wrong. It hurts them when they feel your pain, so the entire circle may start looking for someone to blame.

Ethically speaking, the separating couple has some responsibility toward their intimate circle, and the circle has some responsibility toward the erstwhile couple. The members of the couple should refrain from trying to split the community. In other words, you don't demand that all your friends sever whatever friendships they may have with your ex and you don't divide your community up into those who are on your side and those who are against you by virtue of who continues to speak to your unspeakable ex.

Privacy is a touchy issue here, because no one likes the consequences of gossip run amok—but we all need a confidant to tell our troubles to, especially in hard times. Sometimes separating couples can make agreements about who it's okay to talk about private matters with, and who we would rather not have familiarized with our dirty linen. Other times, no agreement is reached, and the chips fall where they may.

If you feel that you and your ex should not be at the same parties for a while, you need to work that out with each other and not wind up screaming at your host for having invited both of you to the same event. It is particularly unethical to call up the host of a certain party and demand that your ex be disinvited, or to threaten not to come if your ex *is* invited. This adds up to foisting your work off on your friends. It is your task to set your boundaries, to make agreements with your ex, and, if you find yourself feeling bad in any place where your ex is also socializing, then it is your decision whether to stay or leave. If you wind up deciding that you want to attend this event so much that you will just have to deal with your ex's presence, good for you: you will get some practice at sharing social space with your ex, which you are going to need to do eventually unless one of you moves to Timbuktu. Eventually, with practice, you *will* get good at dealing with your feelings about your ex, and all of this will hurt less, and you will be closer to achieving resolution and even possibly friendship after a bitter breakup.

Your circle of friends and family is responsible for not getting split, for listening without judging, and for understanding that all of us think harsh thoughts while we are breaking up. Validate how bad your friend feels and take any condemnations with a grain of salt. The exception to this rule occurs when a breakup is based on the revelation of serious issues, like domestic violence or destructive substance abuse: there are no easy answers here, because a circle of sexual partners really does need to make judgments about these things. But most of the time, the accusations are about what a thoughtless, selfish, insensitive, needy, bitchy, dishonest, manipulative, passive-aggressive, rude, and stupid oaf that ex-partner is; we have all been all of these at some time or another, so we should be able to understand and forgive.

Happy Endings Are Possible

While breakups are very hard for all concerned, and while we understand that you may feel very angry, sad, abandoned, or ill-treated for a while, we implore you to remember that your soon-to-be-ex-partner is still the same terrific person you used to love, and to burn no bridges. Janet says:

> After our divorce, Finn was very angry with me and pretty depressed, and I felt very guilty. Still, for the sake of the kids of whom we had joint custody, we made a point of staying on civil terms. Now, twenty years later, I count him among my best friends and wound up being one of his support people during his serious illness a couple of years back. If we'd been awful to one another back when things were raw and difficult, I don't think we'd be able to be on such good terms today, and we'd both have missed out on a very important and rewarding friendship.

Smart sluts know, even if they sometimes forget in the heat of conflict, that a breakup need not mean the end of a relationship—it may be, instead, a shift to a different kind of relationship, possibly a relationship between courteous acquaintances, or friends, or maybe even lovers.

Dossie relates:

> I dated Bill for two years, during which our connection on all levels was wonderful to me, especially an intense sexual connection: we explored a whole lot of famous firsts together. So we moved in together, and that lasted for all of six months before we blew up in a massive fight and separated. We really did have very different life goals. It was about a year before we could be around each other much, but then we

started dating again, and the sex was even hotter and more profound than before. We wound up getting together once a month or so for the following nine years, as good friends and lovers, continuing the lovely steamy sex that had brought us together in the first place.

EXERCISE *A Healthy Breakup*

Make up a story about a healthy constructive breakup. Include details about how each person could work through difficult feelings. Invent agreements for right after the breakup, for six weeks later, for six months later.

One of the nice things about being an ethical slut is that your relationships don't have to be either/or: you may have as many ways of relating to your friends and lovers as you have friends and lovers. Once you have survived a breakup, there's not a lot worse that can go down. A relationship with an ex is real security, a friendship with someone who has seen you at your utter worst. When we know someone with their complete complement of flaws and failings—as we do our exes— we have the foundation of a truly intimate and important relationship that can continue to change, grow, and provide support for many years to come. As Edna St. Vincent Millay wrote:

After all, my erstwhile dear,
My no longer cherished,
Need we say it wasn't love
Just because it perished?

CHAPTER TWENTY-ONE

Sex and Pleasure

SEX IS NICE and pleasure is good for you. We've said this before, and it bears repeating. In our present lives, your authors enjoy sex for its own sake, and it feels natural and comfortable, but we want you to know that it wasn't always this easy for us. In a culture that teaches that sex is sleazy, nasty, dirty, and dangerous, a path to a free sexuality can be hard to find and fraught with perils while you walk it. If you choose to walk this path, we congratulate you and offer you support, encouragement, and—most important of all—information. Start with the knowledge that we, and just about everybody else who enjoys sex without strictures, learned how to be this way in spite of the society we grew up in—and that means you can learn too.

What Is Sex, Anyway?

The word "sex" gets used as though everyone agrees on what it means, but if you ask people what they actually do when they have sex, you'll hear about a huge range of behaviors and interactions.

We have talked before about sex being part of everything and about everything being part of sex. Now let's talk about the parts that most people call sex—the parts that involve lips and nipples and clits and cocks and orgasms. Sex may *involve* these parts, but we don't think it's *about* them; the genitals and other erogenous zones are the "how," not the "what."

The "what"—what sex actually is—is a journey into an extraordinary state of consciousness, where we tune out everything extraneous to our emotions and our senses in this very moment, travel into a realm of delicious sensation, and soak in the deep connection that we share in sex. This journey is a voyage of awakening, as if the nerves whose job it is to transmit feelings of delight had been lying asleep but have suddenly leaped to attention, aflame, in response to a nibble or a caress.

Perhaps what we call foreplay is a way of seeing just how awake we can get—all excited attention from our earlobes and ankles out to the ends of our hair—the prickling of the scalp, the tingling in the arch of the foot. The glorious miracle of sexual anatomy is that any of these awakenings can set off the swelling in the loins, lips, nipples, cocks, and cunts, which awakens lots more intense nervous networks buried inside us, till we are all lit up like fireworks.

Sex is anything you do or think or imagine that sets the train in motion: a scene in a movie, a person on the street you think is hot, swelling buds of wildflowers bursting in a meadow, a fragrance that opens your nose, the warm sun on the back of your head. Then, if you want to pursue these gorgeously sexy feelings, you can increase the swelling tension, and your sensual focus, with any kind of thinking or touching or talking that humans can devise: stroking, kissing, biting, pinching, licking, vibrating, not to mention erotic art and dance and hot music and silky stuff next to our skin.

So sex covers a much larger territory than genital stimulation leading to orgasm. Sex that's limited to perfunctory foreplay and then a race down the express track to orgasm is an insult to the human capacity for pleasure.

Here's a happy way to answer the question of what is sex: if you or your partner is wondering whether you're having sex at any given moment, you probably are. We like to use an expanded definition of sex, including more than genitals, more than intercourse, more than penetration, and, while we definitely wouldn't leave them out, much more than the stimulations that lead to orgasm. We like to think that all sensual stimulation is sexual, from a shared emotion to a shared orgasm. One friend of ours, a professional sex worker, remembers:

> I'd had a regular session with this guy once before, but one day he showed up, put $400 on the table, and said that he just wanted to talk. So we lay down together on the futon and talked all evening. It was one of the most intensely sexual experiences of my life; it felt like being in love. We were in this profound heart chakra communication, a space of pure communion that felt luscious and sweet, as thick as honey. We were close enough that we could feel the heat of each other's bodies, almost but not quite touching—we tried touching a couple of times, and it diminished the energy. We were so turned on I felt nauseous. It was mind-boggling.

When we expand our concept of what sex is, and let that be whatever pleases us today, we free ourselves from the tyranny of his hydraulics, the chore of getting her off, perhaps even birth control and barriers, if we decide that outercourse is perfectly good sex in and of itself.

Pleasure is good for you. So do what pleases you, and don't let anybody else tell you what you ought to like, and you can't go wrong.

Bringing Clean Love to Sex

Remember the clean love, in the moment and without expectations, that we talked about earlier in this book? It's a skill you can bring to your sex life, and it's based on getting present and accepting yourself.

Cast your mind back to your childhood, some time you remember being happy. Children are naturally adept at being in the moment. To recover that consciousness, take yourself to a park and investigate that interesting twig you've found in the interesting dirt. Go to a beach and take your shoes off. Wade at the water's edge; how do your toes feel, in the grass, the sand, the surf? Dig a hole in the sand while the tide is coming in. Pay attention to your surroundings; pay attention to your experience.

Then pay that same rapt, joyous attention to your beloved; this will probably feel good. So do it some more—you are a nice person, so is your beloved, you both deserve to feel good.

Hands on skin is a great way to get into the present, into connection, and into love. Wash each other's feet, find some lotion, and massage your lover's feet. Take turns. Put aside future tripping: will this lead to sex? Who cares? The two of you are in the moment, feeling your feet.

Your authors are in no way opposed to the intense beauty of genital sex. But all of us need to work on paying attention to what we feel in the moment and to how that connects us to the people we love. We are not in the moment while we are planning the future. Too much wonderful sensual joy gets lost in projecting what will happen next. Learn to enjoy mystery, that little frisson up the spine when you realize that you're on a path to something interesting. Follow that path and find out where it meanders; appreciate the miracle. Don't miss the glories of the moment in your zeal to zoom up to the crotch like a superhighway, fast as ever you can. Efficiency is not what we're looking for here and now.

The feet are relaxing, you hear a groan of ecstasy: should you slide your hand up that gorgeous leg? Oops! Let go of that and get back to those tender, sensitive feet. Nobody can relax and feel their feet if they're worrying about what you are going to do next. When you bring your full attention to making those feet feel better than they have ever felt before, you're in the moment and so is your partner, lost in the bliss of a tingling, creamy instep. And when you are through, reconnect in a lovely hug or a sweet cuddle, and *then* figure out what you two would like to do next.

Whatever that may be, vow to stay present with that too. Perfect presence and acceptance is an ideal, perhaps never to be perfectly achieved but transcendent even in the trying. It's a joyous practice of letting go of what's not needed right now, washing away all the grit and dust of your histories and expectations and opening yourself as completely as possible to meeting another person in the fullness of your open, waiting heart.

What Obstacles Do You Face?

Good sex seems as though it ought to be easy—but often, in our experience, it is not. Everything from ignorance to distraction can get in the way of responsible, enjoyable sex. Here's our A-list of fun-spoilers:

SEX-NEGATIVE CULTURAL MESSAGES

At the top of the list, many of us start out paralyzed by shame and embarrassment, even after we figure out that we don't want to be embarrassed by sex. Shame, and the beliefs we were taught that our bodies, our desires, and sex are dirty and wrong, make it very hard to develop healthy sexual self-esteem. Many of us spent our adolescences consumed with guilt for our sexual desires, our fantasies, and our masturbation, long before we managed to pull anything off with another human. When we did connect with others, many of us spent those encounters obsessing about our performance, often so busy worrying if we were doing it wrong that we forgot to notice how good it felt.

When our desires and fantasies stretch further than a monogamous marriage with a member of the opposite sex, we suffer additional attacks on our self-acceptance—to some, we are sex-crazed perverts, deserving objects of scorn to others and, all too often, ourselves. According to some people, even God hates us. It's hard to feel good about an expansive sexuality when you feel so bad about yourself that you just want to hide.

BODY IMAGE

None of us look sexy enough. The advertising and fashion industries see fit to line their coffers by making us all feel bad about our bodies so that we will buy more clothes, makeup, cosmetic surgery, or whatever in a desperate attempt to feel okay about how we look to others. The perfume industry floods us with images designed to convince us that we smell bad (and if we smell worse than these highly synthesized scents, we must smell very bad indeed). Even those lucky souls who are young and thin and cute suffer from constant worry about how they look: why else do you think they throng to gyms and aerobic classes?

The more people you want to share sex with, the more people you are going to have to expose your naked body to, so there you are. To enjoy a free sexuality, you need to come to terms with the body you are living in, unless you want to wait till you lose twenty pounds, which could take forever, or until you look younger—don't hold your breath. Do remember: your sexiness is about how you feel, not how you look.

EXERCISE *Buy Something Sexy*

Go to a store, any store—a discount clothing store, a thrift store, a lingerie store, a sex toy store—and buy yourself something sexy. Something that feels sexy to your body today. Sensual is a good place to start—anything from silk to soft new flannel or really fine cotton. Loose-fitting or tight, it doesn't matter what it looks like as long as you feel good in it. What colors are sexy to you? Rich deep shades, delicate hues? What expresses your inner slut? Close your eyes and feel your way through the racks. Leather and velvet are divine to the touch, so invite the touch you dream of. Even some denims are startlingly sensual, so try buying your jeans by feel. Let go of what anything is supposed to be, and let your skin choose what it wants. Go home and parade around in it.

AGE AND DISABILITY

It is foolish and rude to assume that people with physical disabilities don't enjoy sex. Differently abled people may indeed engage in differently organized forms of sexuality, but that doesn't mean no sex at all. People with spinal cord injuries who have lost all sensation below the neck report orgasms: there is a lesson here for all of us about how sensitive our ears and lips can actually get.

Sex for a person with physical disabilities is not that different from any other form of sex. Focus on what you can do, what you can feel, what feels good, and how to go about experiencing the most intense feelings that this particular body can feel. Learn about your body just as any other person does. What supports you in moving or reaching? How can you deal with any medical appliances? What safety precautions must you keep in mind?

Most important of all, what do you like? People who have lost physical abilities in accidents may spend a long time rediscovering what this new body can do and feel—finding what feels good is the joyful part of the journey. People disabled from birth or childhood often get treated as nonsexual beings; they may need to go to work when they grow up to discover what their sexuality can be.

Don't forget the advantages of using tools—vibrators tap into the entire electrical grid for their strength and endurance and never get repetitive stress injuries. Implements can reach where arms may not, and pillows can prop up any limbs that need propping. Medications—hormones that keep vaginas flexible and moist, pills that help sustain erections—can help with some of the sexual changes that relate to aging or health issues.

Investigate possibilities. Whether disabilities are visible, or invisible like asthma or diabetes, you get to explore what works for you and get cooperation from your partners to work around anything your body can't do.

If the prospect of being a lover to a physically challenged person seems utterly strange to you, don't forget that one day *you* will be old—at what age do you plan to give up enjoying sex? Will you just give up at the first obstacle, the first bit of arthritis that interrupts a nice thrash with a painful twinge? We do hope this book supports you in grasping your sexuality in any way that works for you. Remember, whatever the physical possibilities of the body you or your friend inhabits, the most important sexual organ is always found between the ears.

SEX DISINFORMATION

Another obstacle on our course is inaccurate or just plain bad information we may have learned about sex. For many years, information about sexual behavior and basic functioning was censored, along with most other discussions of sexual pleasure. Depending on where you live in the culture now, you may or may not have access to good information. We need to politicize to protect our right to accurate and positive information about sex.

To acquire a basic knowledge of sexual functioning and how the sexual response cycle works in men and women, we recommend strongly that you read one or several good books. Books about sex provide a lot of information—more than we can give you in a chapter—about how sex works and what you can do about it when it isn't working as well as you'd like. Self-help exercises are usually provided for concerns about erections or orgasms, timing, coming too soon or too slowly, and what to do when you can't find your turn-on. You can learn more strategies for safer sex and birth control and more language so you can more easily talk with your partners about all of this good stuff. Some clever sluts read a chapter a week of a good book with a partner and perhaps talk about it on Friday over dinner—a nice way to prepare for the weekend.

These days there is also a lot of information and discussion on the Internet. We applaud this freedom of information, and we also want you to be careful, because much of the information you read and hear about sex will be inaccurate. Because sexology is such a new science, and because research into what people actually do in sex is difficult and often inconclusive, and because we as a culture have not talked explicitly about sex for a very long time, fairy tales abound, and reality can be hard to come by. Collect all the information you can, use what works for you, and take it all with a grain of salt. Fortunately, there's lots of sex information available these days in books, magazines, podcasts, websites, and more—plenty to choose from. The best part of learning about sex is that you'll love the homework.

SPEECHLESSNESS

If you can't talk about sex, how can you think about it? The historical censorship of discussion about sex has left us with another disability: the act of talking about sex, of putting words to what we do in bed, has become difficult and embarrassing. Although most of us have had the experience of failed sexual functioning in one way or another, most of us never get the chance to get support from our friends and lovers about it—sexual dysfunction becomes our secret shame, a position from which it is virtually impossible to figure out a way to function better.

What little language we can use to talk about sex is riddled with negative judgments. Either you speak in medical language of vulvas and penile intromission—which sounds like you need to be a doctor to talk about sex, so it must be a disease—or you have gutter language (fucking cunt, hard dick) that makes everything sound like an insult. What you can't talk about, you can hardly think about—a crippling disability. People who can't use words often resort to trying to communicate without words: pressing their partner's head downward, moving their hips to try to get that tongue in just the right place, feigning ecstasy when a hand strays in vaguely the right direction . . . while hoping desperately that the bewildered partner will figure out what they're trying to ask for. Wouldn't it be easier if we could just say, "I would really love it if you ran your finger around my clit in a circle instead of up and down" or "I need you to grab my dick much harder"?

GOAL ORIENTATION

The tyranny of hydraulics is a tremendous obstacle to terrific sex, and not in the way that the manufacturers of Viagra would have you believe. Many people believe that if there is no penis with an erection, nothing sexy is happening. (Lesbians, of course, disagree most vehemently.) Many men feel they can't even engage in foreplay while they are soft, and many women are insulted if they discover a soft penis while they are getting aroused. And still more people are completely nonplussed if the penis in question decides to release at a time that is inconvenient for the rest of the activity, as if there were no sex after ejaculation. We want to encourage you to think beyond the hydraulics of erection and allow your playful explorations to go wherever they want to go, no matter where the participants may be in the sexual response cycle.

When sex becomes goal oriented, we may race to orgasm with such single-minded focus that we never even notice all the lovely sensations that come before (and, for that matter, after). When we concentrate our attention on genital sex to the exclusion of the rest of our bodies, we are excluding most of ourselves from the transaction. When we ignore most of the good parts, we increase our chance of developing sexual dysfunction, and we miss out on all the good feelings.

GENDER ROLES

To be truly free to explore our sexual potential to the fullest, most of us need to examine how we have been taught that a man or a woman is supposed to enjoy sex. Many of us were taught that it is natural for men to be sexually aggressive and for women to be passive responders. Your authors like both of these roles and many others too. When it comes to what feels good, we are all highly individual human beings—and, despite what you may have heard, we all come from the same planet.

When men are forbidden to be receptive, then a man is not allowed foreplay or to ask for any sensory input at all. He's not supposed to need it, much less want it. So then if a man is not automatically turned on when his partner is, he may wind up thinking he's impotent when all he needs is a little nibbling on the ears.

Women consigned to passivity can fall into the Sleeping Beauty trap—some day my prince will come, and so will I (because people in fairy tales always have simultaneous orgasms, right?). In the real world, however, a woman who is allowed to take her turn at being the active partner is well on the way toward figuring out for herself and her lover what works for her to get really, really hot.

Active and receptive are both great roles when they're not dependent on gender. Think of oral sex—is sixty-nine the only way to enjoy it? Or is there a particular delight in taking turns? When we focus on the active role, we can all be great lovers and get off on our partner's pleasure. When it's our turn to receive, we can truly appreciate the gift we are being given, not to mention feeling free to thrash and shriek and otherwise express our appreciation.

We'd love to see a world where everybody knew how much lovely sex they have to give in the active role and how much they give their partner when they receive.

How Can We Learn Good Sex?

The mythology has it that once you start having sex, it will all come naturally—and if it doesn't, then you must have some deep-seated psychological problem, right? We're not sure why sex stands alone in this regard. If you want to get good at anything else, from cooking to tennis to astrophysics, you're going to have to put some effort and time into learning how. If you want to enjoy sex and to make sure your partners enjoy it too, you're going to have to do the same thing.

One friend of ours had her first orgasm at the age of thirty-four, after reading for the first time in one of the sex manuals that became popular in the early 1970s that it was okay for her to masturbate—she'd grown up in the generation that was told masturbation would make you sick or crazy. This is a horrible story—how many years of orgasms did this woman miss because of bad information?

Whatever you do now you learned somewhere, somehow, so you can learn new or different sexual skills and habits if you choose. Learning requires some effort, but the rewards are great, and we know you will be brave and persistent. Many of the books we recommend include exercises you can use to expand your sexual skills and your repertoire—try them.

TALK DIRTY

Talk to people about sex. Ask them about their experience, and share yours. Janet remembers seeing her first porno movies and feeling confounded because the women in them all masturbated face-up, and she wasn't sure if she'd been doing it wrong all those years. She started asking her women friends and found that she was far from alone—not only in her face-down preference but also in her sense of uncertainty. Talk to your intimates and any friends or people you respect who are accessible to you. Breaking the ice can be scary at first, but establishing discussion about sex with your friends and lovers will be a valuable resource for all of you, well worth risking a few minutes of embarrassment as you get started. A friend of ours used to believe that she was the only person in the whole world whose cheeks got sore from sucking a big cock. Talking to a few friends let her know that she was in the majority. If you find you can't talk intimately and explicitly about sex with your lovers, then how can you deal with a problem or try something new?

GOOD SEX STARTS WITH YOU

We mean this quite literally. When Masters and Johnson began their research into sexual functioning in the late 1950s, they wanted to start by learning about good sex before researching sexual dysfunction— so they started by selecting 382 men and 312 women, including 276 heterosexual couples, all of whom had satisfactory sex lives. One surprising fact they uncovered was that virtually all these sexually satisfied people masturbated—regardless of whether or not they were also having partnered sex.

Write this on your mirror: sexually successful people masturbate. You are not jerking or buzzing off because you are a loser, because you can't find anyone to play with you, or because you are desperate to get your rocks off. You're making love to yourself because you deserve pleasure, and playing with yourself makes you feel good.

EXERCISE *A Hot Date with Yourself*

Set aside a couple of hours for this. Turn off the telephone, lock the front door, and get rid of any distractions. Then prepare as though you were preparing for a date with someone you were very excited about: put clean, soft sheets on the bed and place all your favorite sex toys near to hand. Next, take a steamy bubble bath with candles, or a luxurious shower and close shave, accompanied by soft, sexy music. Style your hair, perfume yourself, trim your nails, rub in lotion so your skin is soft and touchable all over. Slip into silk boxers or a sexy nightie. Have a glass of wine, if you like.

When you're ready, turn the lights down flatteringly low and lie down. Tease yourself with soft, gentle touch all over, feeling your soft hands as though they were the touch of your perfect lover. Take your time. Tantalize yourself with lots of foreplay, using your hands, maybe your mouth, and maybe a toy or two.

Only when you absolutely can't stand it any more—when you would be begging for release if there were anyone there to beg—may you bring yourself to climax, as many times as you like.

Lie there and soak up the warm, rich feeling of loving yourself enough to give yourself slow, mindful pleasure. Your perfect lover is waiting for you anytime you want . . . right there in your own skin.

We have never met a person who suffers from low self-esteem at the moment of orgasm. Your relationship with yourself is what you bring to a relationship with another person: it is what you have to share, personally, emotionally, and sexually. The sexier you are to yourself, the sexier you will be to your lovers.

People who play with themselves are good lovers for two reasons. First is that sex with yourself is a really good time to explore new sources of stimulation, like touching yourself in different places, or vibrators, or new positions. Because you will never fail to notice what doesn't feel good, you will always do it the way that feels best, and there will be no one to get embarrassed in front of. So masturbation offers you an opportunity to practice all sorts of interesting things: for instance, if one of your goals is to be able to enjoy more sex before you come, you can practice relaxation exercises with yourself and learn to slow down and speed up your response however you like. If your concern is that sometimes you are not able to come when you would like to, you can pay attention to what works for you when you have sex with yourself and teach your partner your particular preferences in sexual stimulation. Try different rhythms and stimulations so that you don't get into a rut of being able to get off on only one sensation. Practice makes perfect, so masturbate a lot.

Start by putting some energy into supporting your own self-esteem and developing a positive feeling about your body—no, not the body you plan to have next year after you work out every day and live on lettuce. What have you done recently that helps you feel good about the body you are inhabiting today? It's hard to have a good relationship with your body when all you do is yell at it. Try giving your body treats: a bubble bath, a trip to the hot tubs, a massage, silk underwear, anything that feels good. Be nice to your body, and then go find somebody else's body to be nice to, and somebody will be nice to your body too.

Love yourself as you would your lover. Masturbation is a good way to nourish and develop our relationships with ourselves. We can improve our self-esteem by the simple act of pleasuring our bodies.

TOYS FOR EVERYBODY

Don't forget: grown-ups play with toys. A huge variety of excellent sex toys is available. While these can be purchased online if you're shy, we strongly recommend a visit to one of the hundreds of excellent erotic boutiques—modeled on San Francisco's classic Good Vibrations—that have sprung up in large and small cities all over the United States. Such stores allow you to shop in a welcoming, safe, and remarkably unsleazy environment, with helpful staff who are knowledgeable about the mysterious devices on the shelves. Dossie used to sell toys at pleasure parties, which are Tupperware parties for sex toys, usually run by a sex educator invited in for the occasion—a great idea for a bachelorette party.

If you've never tried a vibrator, it's never too late. Battery-operated vibrators are less powerful than the plug-in and rechargeable kinds, so try to find an opportunity to check out all kinds—they work through clothes, so it's not really that hard to find a way to experiment. (They're not just for women, either—many a man has had his life changed by a vibrator against the perineum.) You will find insertables in a huge variety of sizes and shapes to meet every need, texture toys in fake fur or spiky gels, satin blindfolds and velvet restraints—and usually a thoughtful selection of good books and erotica. There is no reason why a sex store has to be hidden in a basement.

Toys can add to your pleasure and make some things possible that never were before—for instance, if you're curious about anal play, it helps to start small. Vibrators have given many women an assurance about orgasm that was never before possible: many women share sex however they want to, and if they have not had an orgasm by the time they are getting tired, curl up with their good friend and their vibrator—a surefire solution. Not having to worry about how orgasms are going to happen can take a lot of the worry out of getting close for both women and men.

If you really want to be the world's greatest lover, and you want to know exactly what pleases your partner the most, try masturbating in the same room. Who knows, you might like to watch—we find it a tremendous turn-on. Watching or showing, you will teach and learn each other's individual pattern of pleasure and become the most perfect, and the most perfectly satisfied, lovers that ever could be.

GET YOUR CONDITIONS MET

It's hard to focus on pleasure when you're worrying about whether the baby is asleep, the door is locked, the shades are drawn, or whatever bothers you. Figure out what your conditions are, what you need to feel safe and free of worry, so you can enjoy your sex completely. Deal with your needs beforehand.

Establish agreements with your partner about safer sex and/or birth control. It is not appropriate to argue with anyone's limits regarding pregnancy and disease risk reduction: respect the limits of the most conservative person, because sex is a lot more fun when we all feel safe. Personal limits may be idiosyncratic, and that's okay too. Dossie has a minor obsession about being clean and likes to set up clean sheets and have a shower so she feels all fresh and sparkly. Someone else might not care as much—so what? There is no one right way to get ready to have sex. Give yourself permission to take care of your own needs; it will free you.

Sometimes you discover that your conditions aren't what you thought they were and that the new ones might offer some special fun. Janet remembers:

> I'd been to a concert that night with two friends, who were lovers with each other and with me. One of us had recently acquired a treasure: a '64 Lincoln Continental the size of a studio apartment. On the way back, we decided to stop by the river to admire the moonlight, and before we knew it we were throwing a full-scale orgy in the front seat of the Lincoln. I'd always thought I wouldn't like sex in a car, but when I found myself stretched out in the front seat with my head in one partner's lap as I masturbated him over my shoulder, and my other partner kneeling in the passenger footwell with her head buried between my legs, I began to change my mind. The scene ended in hysterical giggles: the one I was masturbating began to come, his body went into an orgasmic spasm, and he hit the horn—the car emitted an enormous blast of sound from its mid-'60s Detroit horn that must have awakened everybody for miles around and made us all practically fall out of our seat!

COMMUNICATE

Most of us have been struck dumb by the scariest communication task of all—asking for what we want. Is there any one of us who has never failed to tell our partner when we want our clit or cock stimulated harder or softer, slower or faster, more on the shaft or more on the tip, on the side, on both sides, up and down or round about, or whatever it is that would work for us? Take it from us, the way to get what you want in sex is to ask for it. And the way to get a good reputation as an excellent lover is to ask each partner what he or she likes and let them show you how to do it exactly right: Janet makes a point of having her lovers masturbate for her early on in the relationship, so she can watch how they do it and make mental notes about what kinds of stimulation they like to feel. Once you get past the initial embarrassment, this is actually easy and will make you a very popular lover indeed.

If you find this impossibly difficult, here's a good way to start:

EXERCISE *Yes, No, Maybe*

Try this exercise with yourself or with a lover with whom you are very familiar, and as you get comfortable, repeat it with each new lover.

First, make a list of all the sexual activities you can think of that anyone, not just you, might like to do. You will immediately discover that this is also an exercise in developing language, so pay attention as you name these things. Are you more comfortable with intercourse or fucking, oral sex or going down, cock sucking or eating out? What do you call your own sex organs: penis, dick, cock, prick . . . pussy, cunt, vagina, clitoris? If you get stuck, put a little effort into finding any name that describes the activity, take a deep breath, and repeat those words five times, and breathe again. Make your list as complete as possible, and include activities that you don't like as well as those you do. You can get prefab lists online, but then you miss the experience of naming all these unspeakable delights.

Then each of you take a separate, smaller piece of paper and make three columns: YES, MAYBE, and NO. YES means I already know I like this. NO means this act is outside my limits and I don't want to try it in the foreseeable future. MAYBE means you would try it if the conditions were right. The conditions might be:

- if I feel safe enough

- if I'm turned on enough

- if I know it's okay to stop if it feels bad

- if we go slow enough

- if we have a backup plan

and so forth.

Decide where every act on the big sheet fits into your limits today.

Share the lists with a partner. Discuss where you fit together well and where you have differences. There are no rights and wrongs here. Think of your likes and dislikes as if they were flavors of ice cream.

Notice the wealth of what you both like on your YES lists.

This exercise will need to be done more than once, as your limits will change over time. You can do it to look at what you can share with any particular partner when you are sharing sex.

These are ideas about how you can start communicating explicitly about sex and negotiate consensuality. Remember, we define consent as an active collaboration for the pleasure, benefit, and well-being of all persons concerned. Consent means that everybody involved must agree to whatever activity is proposed and must also feel safe enough that they could decline if they wished. We believe that if you are not free to say "no," you can't really say "yes." We also think it is essential that everyone involved understands the consequences of both responses, which is another way of saying that it's not acceptable to take advantage of someone's naïveté.

We cannot say this often enough: You have a right to your limits, and it is totally okay to say no to any form of sex you don't like or are not comfortable with. Having a limit does not mean that you are inhibited, uptight, no fun, or a permanent victim of American puritanism—it just means you don't like something. When you want to learn to like it, we think there are better ways to do that than to succumb to guilt tripping, shaming, or outright bullying. Say no to what you don't want, and when you decide to try something new, arrange for lots of support from your partner, get your conditions met, and be kind to yourself. Positive reinforcement is really the best way to learn.

In many areas, workshops and groups about sex are available, put on by dedicated sex educators and counselors, sometimes at birth control clinics or organizations supporting sexual health. All of these workshops are designed to be safe, to respect everyone's boundaries, and to give you an opportunity to learn new information, increase your comfort level, and speak for yourself about your own feelings and experience. What we are advocating here is communication by, with, and for everybody.

EXCERCISE *More Fun with Your "Yes, No, Maybe" List*

Once you've made a list, there are lots of further activities you can do with it:

- Put your lists up on the fridge or in the bathroom where you can see them every day.

- Write a possible script for your next date based entirely on items found on both of your YES lists.

- Write a script from the YES lists for a satisfying half-hour date you could do on a weeknight—a quickie plan.

- Choose an item from your MAYBE list and figure out what you would need to try that and how your partner could help you. What are your conditions?

- Choose an item from your partner's MAYBE list and create a fantasy of how you could seduce him into it. Tell him about the fantasy—this is not a time for pouncing and yelling "Surprise!"

FIND YOUR TURN-ON

Have you ever set out to make love and discovered that you couldn't find your turn-on? There you are, hunting for that elusive state of excitement and wondering what's wrong with you when your lover does the things you usually love and your response is just plain nothing, or, worse yet, irritation or ticklishness. Women wonder why they aren't getting wet, men agonize over absent erections, everybody either fakes it or gets embarrassed. It happens to everybody. Really. It's not just you.

For some people, losing their turn-on happens when they are nervous, maybe with a new partner or in a new situation. For others, familiarity reduces arousal, and they have a hard time grasping their desire in their relationships with the people they know the best and love the most.

Getting turned on requires a physical and mental transition into a different state of consciousness. Every night, when you go to sleep, you make such a transition: you turn the lights down, get into loose clothing, lie down, perhaps read quietly or watch a little TV, deliberately changing your state of consciousness from wide awake to sleepy. Some people do this automatically, while others have to work at figuring out what helps them get to sleep.

Similarly, we all need to know how we get turned on, what works for us when arousal doesn't just come of its own accord. Our mythology tells us that we are not supposed to have to do this on purpose, that we are supposed to be swept away with desire, or else something is wrong: we don't really want to make love to this person, we've made a terrible mistake and now what are we going to do with the kids? Men are told that they are supposed to be so turned on by the mere availability of a partner that their erection should stand up and salute without any actual sensory stimulation. Women are taught that they ought to be turned on in response to any stimulus from a partner they care about and, if they aren't, they are frigid or perhaps feeling hostile. These are only some of the very destructive lessons you may have learned.

The first thing you need to do when desire doesn't come up like thunder is to remember that lots of serious sluts have dealt with this problem successfully, and so can you. Let's look at how we could go about deliberately getting turned on.

Some people just charge on, start sexual stimulation, and keep on with it until their turn-on catches up with them, and this works for many people much of the time: Dossie once had a partner who liked to leap into cold mountain lakes when they were camping, insisting that you'd get warm eventually if you just thrashed around. Other people like to get in the water one toe at a time, warming up gradually and sensually, allowing time to appreciate the changes in sensitivity that occur as they move slowly into their sexual response cycle. For many people, simply slowing down gives them the chance to get in synch with their turn-on, and once you find your turn-on it makes it easier to speed up.

Many people experience hypersensitivity, which means feeling ticklish or jumpy or irritated, when they attempt to take in sensations that are too focused or too intense in the early part of their journey to arousal. Such ticklishness usually disappears once the person is thoroughly excited and may reappear right after orgasm. The only way to deal with hypersensitivity is to remember that very few people can get turned on while they are being tickled or irritated, so take your time. (Dossie's partner who loved to leap into cold lakes also really loved to be tickled—that's why you gotta ask.) Feel free to tell your lover about hypersensitivity, and what sensations you enjoy early on, and how that may be different later. Most hypersensitivity can be cured with a firm touch and a gradual approach. Start with caressing backs and shoulders and less sensitive parts of the body, making sure of serious arousal before touching the more exquisitely sensitive areas.

Talk with your lover about what turns you on—a fantasy? A story? Having your fingers or toes gently bitten and sucked? Ask your lover what turns him on—chewing on her neck? Brushing his hair? You could prepare for this talk by writing down a list of all the things that you know excite you, each of you on your own, and then sharing your lists. Talking can be a little risky, and risk can be exciting in and of itself.

Get into your body: sensual delights like hot tubs, bubble baths, naked skin by the warm fire, massage. These are the slower delights that give us time to focus our attention on physical pleasure and allow our busy brains to slow down or drift off into fantasy. This kind of pleasure should not be demanding; this is not the time to worry about heavy breathing or undulating hips—it is the time for entrancement.

Fantasy is a big turn-on for many people, and yes, it is perfectly normal to fantasize when your partner is doing sexy things to you. Many people also like to fantasize on their own before their erotic encounters, building up a nice head of steam before any touching actually takes place. Perhaps you would both enjoy watching an erotic video or reading each other grown-up bedtime stories. Maybe it would be hot to tell each other your favorite fantasies.

Although lust for one person is seldom satisfied by sex with another, experienced sluts know that turn-on is transferable. The excitement you feel about the sex you're planning with Bill next weekend can easily set a fire under your session with Jane tonight, because arousal is a physical experience that can be used for anything you want. The lust in the mind persists and will still be there for you when you get around to Bill—we promise.

Excitement begins with a slow, sensual warmth, and when the warm-up has begun, the door is open for more intense excitement, exploring the sensitivities of ears, necks, wrists, and toes, or tongues in mouths. Breathing becomes deeper, and hips start to move of their own accord.

So does this excitement mean it's time to leap on that express train to orgasmic release? Just because your body is physically ready to enjoy sex doesn't mean you need to rush to fulfillment! Why don't you take a little more time? This feels good, right? So what about feeling good a little more, getting a little more turned on: remember when you were in high school and you could kiss for hours?

SLOW DOWN

Don't we all want a lover with a slow hand? The most common mistake people make when they get nervous about sex is to rush things. Tension does tend to speed us up, and it is also true that both men and women develop a lot of muscle tension as they approach orgasm, which adds to the furor. Now when we are truly ready, there is nothing we like more than to grunt and gasp and heave and shout and make fists with our toes on the speeding express train to orgasm. But there is more to sex than orgasm, so let's not leave out sensuality, seduction, the oh-so-gradual turn-on, the building of suspense, the exploration of every part of the body that can arouse the senses—we want to do it all. To explore the entire range of sensual and sexual intimacy, we need to learn techniques for slowing down.

The first technique for slowing down is very simple. Take a deep breath and hold it. Put your hand on your abdomen and feel the hardness of your muscles. Then breathe out, slowly, and you will feel the muscles in your torso relax. When we are tense, we tend to breathe in gasps, gulping air in and exhaling very little; that's how we maintain tension in our muscles and in our minds. When we breathe out, we relax. So anytime you are tense, in any situation, you can relax a little by taking three long, slow, deep breaths, making sure to breathe out as thoroughly as you breathe in.

You can learn more about relaxation and slowing down by taking a class in any form of yoga, practicing sensual massage, trying tantric techniques, or just slowing down long enough to discover what fun it is to focus on what you're feeling when you're feeling good.

You can reduce your nervousness when you talk about sex, and you can slow yourself down during sex, just by breathing. When you slow your breathing while you are turned on, let your awareness go down into your body. Scan your whole body with your mind, starting from your toes, and let yourself notice how each part of you feels. Chances are you will discover a lot of good feelings you haven't even felt before. Sex therapists call this "sensate focus" and advocate it in particular for those who want to slow down their response and enjoy more sex before they come. You can slow down your physical sexual response by breathing, relaxing, and focusing your attention to reduce your physical tension, because, you see, not only do we all tense our muscles before we come, but most of us cannot come when our muscles are relaxed. So orgasmic control is not achieved by grunting and bearing down, but rather by relaxing and enjoying yourself.

Slowing down is also useful when you are trying out new activities or feeling nervous for any reason. Our friend Mandy relates one of her early learning experiences with condoms:

Rob and I had been occasional lovers for many years, and we were getting together for the first time after a long hiatus. We had very little experience of safer sex at the time but decided, due to our various experiences, that if we wanted to fuck we should use a condom. This was all fine in theory, but when the time came to put it on after a suitable and exciting round or two of outercourse, Rob picked up that difficult little piece of rubber and promptly lost his erection. I'm sure this has never happened to any of you.

We fooled around for a little while and tried again, with the same response—Rob's mind and his cock were not in agreement, and his cock was not cooperating. I dragged myself up into a more active consciousness and decided to put what I had learned in adult sex education to use.

I got him to lie back and agree to be done to, and I set up the environment: candles for light carefully placed where we wouldn't knock them over, lubricant and towels handy, two or three rubbers in case we

247

broke one, plus slow sensual music on a very long disc. I got myself in a comfortable position between his legs—comfortable because I wanted to take all the time in the world, and I did not want to be interrupted by an aching back or a cramped shoulder.

I started by stroking his body—thighs, tummy, legs—very gently, in a soothing way, for a long time, till he first relaxed and then responded with an erection. I waited a little longer so he could enjoy that erection without any responsibility for taking things further: in sex therapy, this is called "non-demand pleasuring." Then I moved the stroking to his genitals, around but not on his penis. His erection went down again, so I moved further back and continued sensual stroking on his skin until he got hard again. I continued again a little longer and then moved to touching closer to his cock. This time his erection fell only a little and got hard again after only a few seconds. By now he was breathing hard, and so was I. For me, the experience was very sensual and kind of trance-like, warm, and pleasurable: a major turn-on, too.

I spent a very long time stroking around, but not on, his cock, until he was very hard indeed. He reached for me, but I slapped his hand—no distractions, please. I am doing this to you, get it? When the suspense was virtually unbearable, I ran my hand lightly over his dick—he shuddered. Stroking his cock and pulling gently on his balls aroused him even more, and he was beginning to moan and sweat. I picked up the condom, checking to make sure I was unrolling it in the right direction, and he lost his erection almost instantly. I went back to stroking around, not on, his cock, and he sprang up again, getting impatient . . . but I made him wait, played with his dick for a long time but gently enough that I knew he couldn't come.

The next time I approached with the rubber, he only wilted a tiny bit, so I rubbed a bit more, and we went round a few times until he was so turned on he couldn't think any more and his cock stood up nice and straight while I rolled the rubber over it. I continued playing with him while he got used to the new sensation.

By this time I was seriously turned on and more than a little impatient, so when I gave the word, he attacked and did the raging bull thing, and we both finally got to fuck fast and hard. It was well worth the waiting—I'm sure they heard the explosion in the next town!

To sum up, and maybe catch our breath a little ourselves, a basic skill for good sex is knowing how to relax, and slow down, and then knowing how to tense and speed up. And once you know how, you can go round and round as many times as you can bear to hold off, enjoying every minute and building up excitement for the grand finale. Relaxing your breathing, and relaxing your body, can help you get centered, grounded in your body and in the pleasure you are feeling, and give you more choices about your sex life.

AFTERGLOW

Sometimes we get so fixated on the challenges of successfully steering our course through the tortuous rapids of getting there that we forget to pay attention to where we have gotten. Afterglow, that dreamy, relaxed, exhausted, sweet state that follows the thrashing and shouting, is a delicious time. Enjoy it. Rest in it, curled up with your partner. Forget the mess, and drift in the profound relaxation. Feel the connection to your partner as you float together in a warm pool of your conjoined energy, swirling around in the comfort of satisfied love. Feel good.

EXERCISE *Get Loud*

Why have you never heard your neighbors having sex? Why have they never heard you?

Do you believe that your partner should make a lot of noise but you should not? Why is that?

Masturbate as loud as you can. Pump your hips to the rhythm of your breath. Open your mouth and throat as wide as you can. Breathe hard, moan, yell, scream.

See how much noise you and your partner can make the next time you make love.

Smile when you see your neighbors.

CHAPTER TWENTY-TWO

Public Sex, Group Sex, and Orgies

DO YOU WANT to be an orgy slut? This is a choice. No matter what you might have heard, group sex is not obligatory for open relationships, and we know many fine outrageous sluts who don't attend orgies or promote three-ways and four-ways in their homes. We also know monogamous couples who frequent public sex environments for the sheer pleasure of playing with each other in a special and sexy place, complete with an appreciative audience.

If you have ever had a fantasy of being made love to by five people, or having an extra pair of hands to make love with, or having lots of hot people to get impulsive with right now, or performing before an audience that will thrill to your thrashing and screaming in delight . . . in other words, if you are attracted to the idea of sex parties, this chapter is for you. Here we will tell you what you need to know to have a good time and deal with any difficulties that might come up.

We believe that it is a fundamentally radical political act to deprivatize sex. So much oppression in our culture is based on shame about sex: the oppression of women, cultural minorities, and sexual minorities. All these kinds of oppression are instituted in the name of the (presumably asexual) family. We are all oppressed. We have all been taught, one way or another, that our desires, our bodies, our sexualities are shameful. What better way to defeat oppression than to get together in communities and celebrate the wonders of sex?

Going to a sex party presents an exciting challenge. It's an opportunity to stretch and grow as you deal with stage fright, performance anxiety, and the wonderful and scary tension of planning and getting ready for elaborate sex in an intensely sexual environment. Everyone is nervous, and the shared vulnerability adds to the arousal. We love the giddy feeling of conquest when we succeed in overcoming all these obstacles and creating a hot sexual encounter. There's not a lot of room for prudery and shame at an orgy, and when we play in a group of people, we get powerful reinforcement that sex is good and beautiful and that we are hot and sexy people.

Why Public Sex?

Your authors both enjoy public sex and regularly attend what we call play parties, environments in which people gather to enjoy a wide variety of sex with each other. In a highly charged sexual atmosphere we feel a synergistic kind of arousal when everybody else's excitement feeds our own, and we feel connected to and turned on by all this happy sex that is going on around us.

Group sex offers the chance to try out new partners in a safe environment, surrounded by our friends—we even get the opportunity to check out a person we might be turned on to while they make love with someone else (an audition or advertising, depending on your point of view). Group sex offers the opportunity to challenge ourselves, move our sexuality out into the open, banners flying, with lots of support in getting past the fears and bashfulness and lots of friendly people to applaud your ecstasies.

In a group sex environment we can learn new sex acts with lots of support: we can watch someone else actually doing a form of sex that we had previously only seen in our fantasies, and we can ask them, when they're through, how they do that. We learned many of our safer-sex skills at orgies, where rubber barriers are de rigueur and there is plenty of support for dealing with awkward bits of latex and maintaining everybody's safety and well-being. Most public sex spaces provide condoms, rubber gloves, and whatever else you may need to play safe.

Play parties can help you get over bad body image. As we have pointed out before, people enjoy sex at all ages and in all kinds of bodies, and at any orgy you will see them doing it. One good way to prepare for your first adventure at an orgy is to visit a nude beach or hot spring, if you never have before, to see what real people look like without clothes and to experience being naked in public yourself. You'll start to see beauty in a lot of bodies that don't look anything like the ones in *Playboy* or *Playgirl*—this may be a good time to repeat the "Airport Game" exercise you learned in chapter 17, "Making Connection"—and there's a lot of sensual delight to the feeling of warm sun and gentle breezes on all the parts of your body.

It is amazing to us to think, after many years of practicing sex in public, that most people in our culture have never had a chance to watch another person enjoy sex. We worry about them—it seems like a terrible deprivation. We remember what it was like when we wondered and worried about whether we looked foolish with our legs up in the air and our faces screwed up in an ecstatic scream. Group sex is a great antidote to bad body image. You will feel much better about how you look, how you perform, and who you are when you have a chance to see real people having real sex. Look around you—every single person is gorgeous when they come. Which is why the orgy can be a perfect stage for the consensual exhibitionist: at the sex party, we all get to be stars and shine our brightest.

Party Spaces

Sex clubs are very special environments. San Francisco, where we live, has a delightfully wide choice of orgiastic environments to choose from. There are party spaces for women only, men only, couples, S/M enthusiasts, and lovers of drag and costumery, and parties that specialize in just about every sexual practice you can think of—and some that have to be seen to be believed. You may want to check out the website for Cuddle Parties (see our Resource Guide) for some new ideas about getting together and perhaps a safer introduction to connecting in groups: at Cuddle Parties, everyone wears pajamas and snuggles to explore intense closeness, without taking it on into actual sex.

Parties may be openly advertised to the public, advertised only in newsletters or at support groups, or private and by invitation only. There are public clubs, like the gay men's baths, that are open twenty-four hours a day, seven days a week, and smaller spaces, perhaps an adapted basement recreation room, whose owners host parties once or twice a month. Other congenial groups sponsor small private gatherings in their members' living rooms.

San Francisco and many other major cities boast a fair number of party houses, where one or two stories of a building have been dedicated to social areas and play rooms for partying. Party houses may rent space to private groups, who might host a party once a month or so for their particular guest list.

The first group sex parties that Dossie attended were held in a communal flat in San Francisco, under the presiding genius of Betty Dodson. Those who lived there were all dedicated to feminism, gay liberation, and sexual liberation, and their commune was a conscious experiment to radically change the conditions in which we can enjoy sex. They took out all the doors and made the loft space upstairs into one unbroken room by getting rid of the furniture. On a typical day, you could find several people on the deck sunbathing nude, some others organizing dinner, two more playing chess, a couple fucking, and another person across the room vibrating her way to her own orgasm. There were larger parties three or four times a year, full of people making love in groups, in twos, or singly, with lots of massage, and tantric practitioners chanting "Ommmm" in tune with the ever-present hum of vibrators. This space and what happened in it were private, available to the friends and lovers of the six or seven people who lived there.

Public sex environments, whether they're large public clubs or small party houses, have the common function of providing an agreeable space in which you can be sexual. Although the decor and furnishings of group sex environments vary as widely as the human sexual imagination, there are basics that you will find in most party spaces. There will be a door person to check you in, and you may be asked to sign a waiver of liability. There will be a social area, with places to sit and talk and meet people, usually with a small buffet of snacks and beverages. Sex does not usually take place in the social area, so if you're feeling shy you can hang out there until you work up your courage.

There will be lockers or coat racks or shelves or some place to put your street clothes, then either change into party costume or simply disrobe. Some parties are mostly naked, others feature a dazzling array of costumes for every sexual fantasy. There will be provisions for cleanliness, including bathrooms and showers. Then there will be the play room or rooms.

Play rooms vary from tiny cubicles, often set up in mazes, with a small bed just big enough to fuck on, to large rooms with mirrored walls and upholstered floors for puppy piles, group gropes, and other orgiastic activities. There may be hot tubs, steam rooms, and gardens for you to cruise and relax in. There may be an area for dancing. There is almost always music with a very strong beat, to wake up your natural rhythm and to give a sense of aural privacy so you won't be distracted by your neighbor's heavy breathing or squeals of delight. The lights will be low, and often red or orange, so we all can look a little tan and perhaps a little sexier. There may be rooms with furniture imaginatively designed to have sex on, like medical examining tables or slings, mirrored beds or dungeons for S/M fantasies, or perhaps a giant waterbed for those who like to make waves.

In recent years, hotels that host conferences for various groups cel-ebrating their lifestyles have been allowing party spaces, even dungeons, to be built in their ballrooms for the guests to enjoy. These parties are run by the conference and usually staffed by helpful conference volun-teers, with cooperation from the hotel staff to keep the space private. Hotels tend to like our conferences—we don't drink too much, we are polite to the staff, and we wear great outfits. Talk about the radical political act of deprivatizing sex! Major hotel chains now have policies about play parties, policies that support us. Yay.

Play party spaces tend to form communities. People try out the various parties in their area and usually return to one or two groups that they find congenial. As people get to know each other and share the special intimacy of sexual connection, they often become friends and form extended families. It is not unusual at all to find a sex party club hosting a benefit for a member who has had an accident or a major illness. These are communities, and communities take care of their own.

Group Sex Etiquette

We know they didn't teach you in school how to behave at an orgy, and we bet your mother didn't teach you either.

There is a particular etiquette needed for public sex environments, since everyone in them has let down some of their customary boundaries in order to get closer to each other. Social boundaries usually serve the purpose of keeping people at a predictable distance, so we all feel safe in our own personal space. Group sex poses the challenge of figuring out how to feel safe and comfortable while getting up close and very intimate with a whole bunch of presumably nice, sexy people—so new boundaries must be developed, learned, and respected so that everyone can feel safe enough to play.

Many party houses show you a list of rules as you come in or post them on the wall. Read them. They will make sense. Most places specify the level of safer-sex precautions they require, and provide condoms, rubber gloves, lubricants, dental dams, and so on. Even if you and your partner are fluid-bonded, you may be asked, or feel it is polite, to use latex barriers in a public environment. Ethical sluts obey the rules of the parties they choose to attend.

Responsibility in voyeurism is a must. You may watch what people do in public places, but always from a respectful distance. If the participants are aware of your presence, you are too close. Whether or not it is okay to masturbate while watching varies from place to place, but it's always polite to keep your own excitement discreet enough that you don't distract the good folks who are putting on such a nice show—they are probably not doing it for you, anyway. Also be aware that when you are close to people who are playing, they can hear you—this is not an appropriate place to tell your friend all about how awful your boss is or about your recent experiences at the proctologist.

The boundary between social/talk space and play space is very important—when you enter play space, you enter into a different state of consciousness that tends to get you out of your intellect and into your body very quickly. Too much talking in play space can yank you back into everyday, verbal, nonsexual awareness.

Cruising is active but must not be intrusive. Ideally, a respectful request receives a respectful response, which means it's okay to ask, and if the answer is "no, thank you," that is okay too. Remember, people who come to orgies are pretty sophisticated, and they are here because they know what they want. If that person you found attractive doesn't want to play with you right now, take it easy and find someone else. Pestering anyone at a sex party is unspeakably rude and will quickly earn you an invitation to the outside world.

Cruising at group sex parties is not that different from elsewhere, although perhaps more honest and to the point. Usually, you start with introducing yourself as a person: "Hi, I'm Dick, what's your name?" is way preferable to "Hi, do you like my big dick?" People will talk for a bit, flirt a little, and then ask quite directly, "Would you like to play with me?" When the answer is yes, negotiation follows: "What do you like to do? Is there anything you don't like? Let's check that we both mean the same thing by safer sex, and by the way, I have this fantasy . . ."

Nonverbal Communication

Cruising by body language also can work, as long as you are willing to be relaxed about any misunderstandings that may arise. We believe that it is important to learn how to put what you want into words, so you have an option for absolutely clear communication. Then you can pursue nonverbal cruising if you like it, knowing your good communication skills will back you up if you need them.

Body language is about catching someone's eye, exchanging a smile, moving your body closer—always checking the response. If you catch someone's eye and they turn away, well, there's your answer. Don't take it personally; maybe they have another commitment, maybe they're just not in the mood—people have as many reasons for *not* wanting to play as they do for wanting to play. If you move into someone's personal space and they move closer, there's another answer. It helps to initiate touch on a relatively neutral part of the body—a shoulder, a hand— and again, does the person move away, or closer? If they freeze, it's probably a good idea to communicate with words.

Gender Differences

We live in a society where people learn some pretty warped ideas about sex. Women learn that they are not supposed to be sexual without falling in love, men learn that sex is a commodity that you get from a woman, men may even learn that women themselves are commodities. Group sex only works when everybody is acknowledged as a person. Nobody likes being treated like a thing. To avoid such problems, most group sex environments that include both men and women restrict the number of single men who are invited or insist that no man is welcome without a female escort. These requirements are a sad last resort for dealing with an unpleasant reality, and we quite agree that it is unfair that men of good will get penalized for the intrusive behavior of men who evidently don't know any better. But that's how it is, and the only way we are going to change it is to work on our own behavior and teach our brothers and sisters what we learn. Pansexual environments that make a point of including a variety of people—gay, straight, bi, transgendered—tend to inspire more respect for all, and in such environments we get to learn from a lot of people whose lives and sexualities may be different from our own.

Cruising is different by gender, and those differences become very visible when you compare gay men's environments to lesbian orgies and see how they are similar to and different from hetero or bisexual groups. Gay men seem to feel safer with anonymous sex, and gay male cruising at baths or clubs is often nonverbal. One man might catch another's eye, smile, walk across the room, touch a shoulder, and then embrace, with little or no verbal communication. Lesbians are often more cautious and tend to talk for a while before moving into the play room and getting down.

Women in all group sex environments tend to be less open than men to anonymous sex and to prefer some communication and personal connection first. When a woman seeks to realize a fantasy of anonymous sex with a number of people, often one of her friends or lovers will act as emcee, doing traffic control and whispering into a stranger's ear, "She doesn't like anything that tickles" or "I think she'd like it if you fucked harder." The emcee takes the responsibility for safety and limit setting so the star can feel utterly free. This respect for caution is probably because women have had serious reasons to feel less than safe around sex with strangers and need some support to feel safe enough to let down their guard. There are no rights and wrongs to this situation—or what wrong there is exists in our history, which we can't very well change. What is important is that everyone—male, female, or transgendered; straight, bi, or gay—has a right to feel safe in order to get free to enjoy sex.

Establishing Consent

Consent is an absolute requirement. Naive people sometimes assume that when two or three or four people are already having sex, it is okay to just join in and start fondling somebody. Well, it isn't, because you didn't ask and because you don't know what these people want or what their limits are. So you might do the wrong thing, and the people you tried to join will have to stop whatever they are having so much fun doing to deal with you, and they will be justifiably angry. At you.

How are you going to get consent from people in the middle of a hot fuck? Tap them on the shoulder and say, "Will you please stop a moment so I can ask if I can join you?" There is just about no way to join a sexual scene that has already started unless you are already lovers with all the people involved, and even then you should be careful. When we wonder if it's okay to join friends of ours who have already begun to play, we usually watch from a respectful distance till somebody catches our eye and either beckons us over or doesn't. Respect for boundaries, as we have said before, is mandatory if everyone is going to feel safe enough to play freely and without constraint. Don't be the person who makes the environment unsafe.

If you are playing at a party and someone invades your space, you are quite right to tell that person to move away. It is also appropriate to let your host know about intrusive people and pushy come-ons—party hosts develop skills to talk with people about appropriate behavior and explain why the etiquette is as it is, and if the person will not learn, the host has the power to remove that person from the guest list.

Watch Your Expectations

Most people approach their first group sex party in a mental maelstrom of fears, fantasies, and wild expectations about what might or, worse yet, might not happen. We strongly recommend that you get a grip on yourself, acknowledge that you actually don't know what is going to happen, and go to the party with the expectation that you will be proud of yourself if you manage to walk in the door. If you stay for an hour and watch, you get a gold star. If you manage to introduce yourself to someone and hold a conversation, give yourself a medal of honor.

Going to an orgy is very challenging. Expect to be nervous. Expect to worry. Expect a fashion crisis, and allow at least two hours to get dressed. Helpful hint: build your outfit from fabrics that feel sensual—silk, leather, latex—so you feel sensuous too. Avoid fragile antiques or pricey designer clothes if you want to fuck in them. Dress to feel hot, look good, and be comfortable—it's bad enough to have your stomach churning, you don't need your shoes pinching.

Many parties specify when doors are open and when they're closed, because otherwise all these nervous people will arrive late after spending hours working up their courage and their outfits, and the party hosts will never get any time to play.

If this is your first party, take it easy on yourself. Promise yourself, and each other, that you will leave if either one of you gets too uncomfortable. Establish a signal, perhaps a hand on the elbow, to let your partner know that you need a private place to talk or that you need support. Use another signal—Janet uses "Calgon," from the old TV commercials that said "Calgon, take me away"—to communicate to your partner that you'd like to leave soon, with the understanding that a partner who's happily cruising or flirting or fooling around may need some time to wrap up whatever's going on so that you can leave.

Go with the goal of making a few acquaintances and getting familiar with the scene and your reactions to it. If you do get inspired to play and find someone who wants to play with you, that's fine, and if you don't, that's fine too. Just walking into a play environment for the first time requires a lot of courage, so be proud of yourself. Always remember that this is your first party, potentially the first of many. You don't need to accomplish a lifetime of fantasies tonight. You have the rest of your life to do that. You just need to take your first steps.

Couples at the Orgy

Deal with your relationship before you go to the party. This is important. Are you going as a couple, to show off your incredible sexiness? Are you cruising for thirds and fourths? Or are you going as two separate individuals, to meet people and share sex with them? If one of you connects with a hot number, is the other welcome to join in? Do you need your partner's agreement before you play with anyone? If you need to pause in a flirtation to check in with your partner, experienced sluts will admire your thoughtfulness and integrity. Are you committed to going home together, or is it okay for one or the other of you to sleep out, and if both want to, what about the babysitter? The reason you decide all this in advance is that it is way too ugly to have a disagreement about this sort of thing in public, where if you do disagree, you are likely to feel embarrassed and angry and make a big unhappy mess.

Two friends of ours got locked in a disagreement about going to sex parties. They both wanted to go, but one wanted to go and play with the other, and the other wanted to play the field. What to do? Well, there are parties at least once a month around here, so they decided to go one month as a couple to do things together, and the next to support each other in separate cruising.

We like to watch couples make love with each other at parties—you can see the intimacy, and how well they know each other's ways, how beautifully they fit together, how exquisitely orchestrated lovemaking can become with years of practice. We like it as a fine experience for the voyeur and because we can learn a lot from watching people who are experts on each other. We like to point out that showing off your wondrous beauty together is excellent advertising for the next time when you come to the party ready to welcome new partners.

Play parties can also offer you the opportunity to process fears and jealousies about your partner. How does it feel to watch your partner make love with another person? Is it really awful? You might be surprised to find yourself feeling pretty neutral, like "Gee, I thought that would bother me but actually it doesn't!" You might like the chance to observe your lover, how powerful she looks when she thrusts, how sweet he looks when he comes. It might even turn you on. There is definitely arousal to be found in taking risks. Some couples find that group sex can rev up their sex life at home by providing a lot of stimulus, new ideas to try out, and the motivation and energy to make their home life as hot as an orgy.

Buttons and Biases

Expect to get your buttons pushed. Expect to discover your biases. At a group sex party you will share unprecedented intimacy with a bunch of strangers, and sometimes that will be difficult. You might start into a three-way with your girlfriend and another man, which seems like a hot idea but might turn out to push some buttons. Yeah, we know, you set out to both make love to her, but there you are, with this man, being sexual, and probably in physical contact, and how does that feel?

We like to attend pansexual group sex parties, which means that attendees may identify as gay or lesbian or bisexual or hetero or transgendered but are generally comfortable and happy to play side by side with people whose desires and identities may be entirely different from their own. We are always running into issues about the unfamiliar: the lesbian who has never been naked in the presence of men; the gay man who fears judgment from women or violence from straight men; the transgendered woman who gets to wonder if that person who is so attracted to her knows what she's got under her skirt, and does she care, and if she cares what is she going to do?

Whatever your prejudices are—the people at this party are too old, too young, too male, too female, too queer, too straight, too fat, too thin, too white, too ethnic, whatever—it really is good for you to learn to get bigger than your biases. Sexy, too.

Everything Embarrassing You
Never Thought of Doing in Public

In our fantasies, we all come together as smoothly as Fred and Ginger, carried away by the music on a rising tide of passion—and sometimes it will be like that. But you probably will need to practice first, just like Fred and Ginger. Your erection might refuse to cooperate as you near the moment of truth, especially when you suddenly remember you need to put a condom on it. Orgasm might be more difficult to focus on in a noisy environment with an unfamiliar partner. What if you set out to play with someone and you can't find your turn-on?

If you find yourself internally panicking, we encourage you to breathe. Slow down. Remember that you are not in a race, and you are not in a hurry. This is not the Olympics. You have nothing to prove—you and your new friend are setting out to do things that feel good with your bodies. Touch feels good. Stroking feels good. Taking time feels good. Slow down enough so that you can truly feel what you are doing. Worrying about the future will not help you get there: focus on what you are feeling in the present. Erections and orgasms might come, might go, but you can never go wrong by doing what feels good.

The noise and hectic energy of a party can lead people to rush, when slowing down is the best way to connect with your turn-on. People don't get turned on by magic, at least not very often, or very reliably. And different people are turned on in very different ways. A very important kind of self-knowledge will come in handy at these times: know what turns you on. Whether it's biting on the neck or sucking on the backs of knees, when you know what gets your juices flowing you can ask for it, and then your play partner will know what turns you on and feel freer to tell you what turns her on, and before you know it there you all are, completely turned on and floating down the river of unbridled lust.

We'll end this chapter with a true story of love discovered during public sex, just to give you some inspiration to explore.

June had never been to a play party before. That's evidently what they call orgies in California, she mused. Well, at least it's a lesbian orgy. How on earth, she wondered, did I come to be the guest of honor at an orgy?

Actually, she knew how it came about. She was visiting her dear friend Flash in San Francisco, and Flash announced that she had the use of a house in the country for the weekend, and she wanted to throw a party and introduce June to her friends. Sounds like fun, thought June . . . and then Flash began to talk about having a Chick Rite to celebrate the advent of spring by setting up mattresses and safer-sex supplies in the middle of the living room.

June had argued and at first had refused to attend. But Flash talked her into it, pointing out that she didn't have to actually have sex with anybody if she didn't want to. June finally said okay, adding that if she couldn't stand it she would hike down to the local coffeehouse with a book. So Flash went on setting up the house for the convenience of sexual pleasure, and June hid in the kitchen making dip, one party function that she at least understood.

As the guests began to arrive, June began to wonder whether she'd be able to stay at this event. She was introduced to a parade of the most outrageous dykes she'd ever seen, femmes and butches like birds in bright plumage, sporting exotic garments designed to display a gallery of tattoos, gleaming here and there with jewelry set in body parts that June did not want to think about. And they were all so young! June felt the full weight of her forty-eight years. She figured you can't go wrong being polite, so she said the same how-do-you-dos she would anywhere else, wondering how she'd respond if one of these enthusiastic orgiasts actually told her how she *did* do.

In, at last, came a couple of women of unabashed middle age. One of them, Carol, was a dead ringer for June's Great-Aunt Mary, if Great-Aunt Mary had ever chosen to dress in high butch gear complete with boots and cowboy hat. June felt relieved to have found one woman she could relate to. Then Carol smiled a dazzling smile and announced that she would like to put her hand in June's cunt.

June, swallowing a gasp but resolutely polite, said that she didn't really feel quite ready for that, and Carol replied cheerily, "Okay, then, I'll check in with you later." Great Goddess, thought June, there's no escape. June knew about fisting, had learned to do it with a lover who liked it, knew it was safe when done properly—but it seemed an odd way to get acquainted with someone whose name she'd only learned in the last half hour.

Then Lottie came in—close to June's age, but not dressed like it. Lottie's obviously dyed, flaming red curls set off a black chiffon dress through which could be clearly seen long black stockings, a black leather corset, and a great deal of voluptuous pale flesh. How does she balance on those heels, June wondered, as Lottie hugged, kissed, and chatted her way through the progressively less clothed mass of partygoers. June overheard Lottie thanking various women for their participation in a previous orgy held in celebration of Lottie's fiftieth birthday. Do these people ever get together and *not* have sex, wondered June.

Puppy piles began to form on the floor in front of the couch where June was sitting—untidy heaps of women necking and petting, smiling and laughing, Lottie and Carol conspicuously among them. June decided to retreat to the deck, where she could perhaps soak out her terror in the hot tub.

The hot tub was quieter, and June managed to chat with a few women and began feeling marginally more comfortable. Then Lottie reappeared. Off came the dress, the stockings, the shoes—June found herself wondering what it would feel like if she could see Lottie's pussy and instantly wondered if anyone else had noticed her looking. Lottie slipped into the warm water and immediately asked June if she would rub her neck, because it felt stiff. "Sure," June heard herself say, "I'd be happy to." Oh, no, she thought, what have I let myself in for?

Lottie's skin felt warm and silky under her fingers, and June rubbed and soothed. June felt relaxed by the rhythm of massage and reassured as Lottie conversed about perfectly normal things: her work and June's, their philosophies of life, June's Buddhism, Lottie's paganism. Eventually, Lottie's neck relaxed, and the hot tub began to feel too warm, and Lottie brightly suggested they find out what was going on inside. She climbed out of the tub, pulled on her stockings and heels, and darted inside. Holy Minerva, thought June, can I follow her in there? No, she decided firmly, I can't. June found a table in a corner on the patio and determinedly admired the stars.

Lottie, meanwhile, was finding she had a thing or two to think about as well. In the living room, her friends were happily disporting themselves on couches, in armchairs, and in front of the fire, but Lottie was thinking about June. What is it about her that turns me on so much? Does she like me? Will she play with me? Doesn't look like she's used to playing at parties—ah, well, there's always a first time. Now where did that girl go?

Lottie scanned the living room, but there was no June to be found. The living room was actually pretty interesting, and Lottie contemplated giving up the chase and finding a friend to play with, but intrigue triumphed. She made her way toward the kitchen, stepping over various happy people and lingering here and there to appreciate some particularly exciting activity. Pausing to check out the dip and replenish her blood sugar, Lottie looked out the window and there was June, hiding out on the patio.

Ah, here's the opportunity, thought Lottie as she arranged a few goodies on a plate and trotted outside to share them with June. But, although they were chatting quite amiably, Lottie felt she wasn't connecting. Her most flirtatious sallies were met with no response whatsoever: June, petrified, would only breathe deep and consciously hold as still as she could. Lottie, frustrated, decided on the direct approach. "I think you're really attractive. Would you like to play with me? What sort of things do you like to do?" June, cornered again, stammered, "I don't think I'm ready to have sex in public, so sorry."

Just then, Carol, sans cowboy hat but still wearing her boots although she seemed to have lost her shirt somewhere, sauntered up to the table and sat down. While June wondered how she could disappear into the bushes without appearing gauche, Lottie greeted Carol by placing her thigh—which Carol, being a woman who knew how to act, promptly stroked and admired—in Carol's lap. Lottie, not out of revenge but simply from a desire not to waste a perfectly good party, asked Carol: "How's your dance card tonight? Got room for me?"

Carol asked what was her fancy, and Lottie suggested that she had a yen for a sensitive fist, and Carol said she would be happy to oblige but first needed to check with Susie about a plan they had for later. Both happily trotted off, and June was left to herself. Was she relieved, she wondered? Well . . . not exactly.

Returning to the living room, Lottie was surprised to see Carol and June both sitting in the window seat, backs to the sides, feet in the middle. Lottie, never slow to leap on opportunity, sashayed across the room, climbed up on both pairs of feet, and proclaimed, "Here I am!" Carol, well versed in the ways of femmes, called for gloves and lube and firmly pushed Lottie into June's lap: "Will you hold her for me, please?" June opened her mouth, but nobody waited for her answer— and next thing, there she was, holding Lottie's gently squirming body. Amazing, thought June, just amazing. She got a good grip on Lottie, took a deep breath, and off she went on the ride.

June concentrated on keeping up a good front and trying not to notice several smiling women who had settled down to watch the action on the window seat, while Carol competently went to work to turn Lottie on, lube her up, and get her off. Omigod, thought June, how am I going to get through this? I'm touching this woman's breast and I hardly know her. Maybe, she thought, I can pretend this is someone I've already made love with.

Lottie had braced her foot over Carol's shoulder against the window frame and was energetically pushing herself down on Carol's hand. She let out a big groan as the hand slipped in, and they both started fucking hard and loud. June had all she could do to prevent Lottie from writhing out of her grip and falling onto the floor. Lottie finally came—loudly, noticed June, very loudly—and June noticed she hadn't breathed for a while and took a big gasping breath. All three let their bodies go limp on the window seat and invested a few moments in just feeling good.

Reality eventually asserted itself. Lottie sat up and politely offered to fuck Carol in return. Carol said no, thanks, I already promised Susie, and Lottie and Carol went off in different directions, leaving June alone on the window seat and feeling a bit thunderstruck. I must have fallen into some other universe, marveled June. Who *are* these women, anyway? Although it was kind of fun, and I think I did okay. But it was still too much. I think I'd better go to sleep.

A day passed. Back at home, Lottie found she could not stop thinking about June. She called Flash and discovered that June had flown out of San Francisco that morning. Two days later, June received this letter:

Dear June,

It's a beautiful morning up here on my mountain, the sun is stream-ing through the redwood trees, the sky is very blue with little cloud puffs—yesterday, walking up on the ridge, I saw a huge jackrabbit. The irises are finished, and it's time for morning glories, rhododendrons, and lots of tiny bright exquisite flowers to whom I have not been properly introduced. Do you live in the city? If I make your mouth water for the mountains, will you come visit me?

Who are you anyway? Write me and tell me about yourself. I am particularly interested in how, as a Buddhist, you deal with desire and passion. I've been thinking some about this since we met and realized that I am not a Buddhist because, although I have gotten a great deal from my connections to Zen, including learning a lot about letting go of desire, my spiritual path is about grasping desire (passion might be a more appropriate word here) as if it were the ox and riding it as a vehicle to communion with the Tao. I worry that this might not be an acceptable practice to you: although I am used to being various people's version of anathema, I would rather that not be the case with you.

I really like you. I really like the connection we made at Flash's, and I hope we get the chance to explore it further. So write and reveal yourself to me. What are your thoughts about sex, connection, art, nature? What are your fantasies? I really want to know. I bet you dream up some great bedtime stories.

I wish you were here—writing to you is making me nervous and I would like a cuddle. As I read over this letter trying to decide how far to go, I realize I have probably already gone too far—oh well, I always do.

Love,

Lottie

Eight months and approximately three thousand dollars' worth of phone bills later, not to mention a few impulsive airfares, June put all her worldly goods in her truck, Lottie flew out to meet her, and they drove across the Great Divide to a sweet little house in the country, where they lived together for many happy years.

A Slut Utopia

WELL, HERE WE ARE, at the end of our book. But before we launch you back out into the world, we want to leave you with one final concept that may help you shape your thinking as you design your own life full of whatever kinds of sex and love you want.

From Two to Many

The world is very fond of twos: black and white, male and female, mind and body, good and bad. These pairs, we all learn, are opposed: there's the right way and the wrong way, and our task is to do battle to defend the right and destroy the wrong. This kind of thinking dominates our courts, our politics, and our talk shows, with some crazy results: for instance, some people believe that anyone who enjoys sex outside of marriage, or a kind of marriage that's different from theirs, must be attacking *their* marriage. Anything that is different must be opposed, must be the enemy.

When right and wrong are your only options, you may believe that you can't love more than one person, or that you can't love in different ways, or that you have a finite capacity for love—that "many" must somehow be opposed to "one," or that your only options are in love and out of love, with no allowance for different degrees or kinds of love.

We would like to propose something different. Instead of these simpleminded either/or arguments, consider the possibility of seeing, and valuing, everything that there is, without viewing them as in opposition to one another. We think that if you can do this, you will discover that there are as many ways to be sexual as there are to be human, and all of them are valid. There are lots of ways to relate, to love, to express gender, to share sex, to form families, to be in the world, to be human . . . and none of them in any way reduces or invalidates any of the others.

When we open our mind to a world beyond opposites, we become able to see beyond unrealistic perfection and unachievable goals. We can free ourselves to be fully conscious of all the wonderful variety and diversity that there is right now in the world, right here, in the present, available to us.

Thus sluthood can become a path to transcendence, a freeing of the mind and spirit as well as the body, a way of being in the world that allows expanded awareness, spiritual growth, and love beyond imagining.

A Slut Manifesto

We believe that when we examine the issues that limit our relationships and our understanding of how we might be, we are essentially planning for a society that is appropriate to the way many people live today—that meets our need for change and growth while it feeds our fundamental desire for belonging and family.

We believe that monogamy will continue to thrive as it always has, a perfectly valid choice for those who truly choose it. (We don't think it's much of a choice when you are forbidden to choose anything else.) We want to open our vision to accommodate monogamy as well as a plethora of other options—to plan for family and social structures that have growing room, that will continue to stretch and adapt, that we can fit to our needs in the future. We believe that new forms of families are evolving now and will continue to evolve, not to supplant the nuclear family but to supplement it with an amazing abundance, a whole world of choices about sharing family and sex and love. We want to set you free to invent the society you want to live in.

Our vision of utopia has free love, in all its forms, as the foundation of our beliefs about reality, about possibility, about staying in the moment and planning the future. We believe that sexual freedom helps us to see our lives as they really are, with the honesty to perceive ourselves clearly and the fluidity to let us move onward as our needs alter, as a changing and growing self with changing and growing partners in a changing and growing world.

We see ethical sluthood leading us to a world where we respect and honor each individual's boundaries more than we honor any preconceived set of rules about what their boundaries ought to be.

And in expanding our sexual lives, we foresee the development of an advanced sexuality, where we can become both more natural and more human. Sex really is a physical expression of a whole lot of stuff that has no physical existence: love and joy, deep emotion, intense closeness, profound connection, spiritual awareness, incredibly good feelings, sometimes even transcendent ecstasy. In our utopia, intellect is not a trap that we get stuck in, but an honored tool we use to discover and access all the parts of ourselves and give form to our experience. We free our natural selves by opening our intellects to sensual awareness of our bodies, and when we are no longer stuck in our intellects we become more like spirit: intuitive, experiencing the joy of life for the simple sake of experiencing, in communion with ourselves, with each other, and beyond.

Our Favorite Sex Fantasy: Abundance

We want everyone to be free to express love in every possible way. We want to create a world where everyone has plenty of what they need: of community, of connection, of touch and sex and love. We want our children to be raised in an expanded family, a connected village within urban alienation, where there are enough adults who love them and each other, so there is plenty of love and attention and nurturance, more than enough to go around. We want a world where the sick and aging are cared for by people who love them, where resources are shared by people who care about each other.

We dream of a world where no one is driven by desires they have no hope of fulfilling, where no one suffers from shame for their desires, or embarrassment about their dreams, where no one is starving from lack of sex. We dream of a world where no one is limited by rules that dictate that they must be less of a person, and less of a sexual person, than they have the capacity to be.

We dream of a world where nobody gets to vote on your life choices, or who you choose to love, or how you choose to express that love, except yourself and your lovers. We dream of a time and a place where we will all be free to publicly declare our love, for whoever we love, however we love them.

And may we all look forward to a lifetime of dreams come true.

A Slut's Glossary

Most of the language available for us to talk about sex has built-in value judgments, just like the word "slut"—the legacy of our sex-negative history. Without language, how are we to communicate with each other and share our thoughts and feelings? Without language, we can hardly even think about sex.

New words and terminologies are coined constantly, which is a challenge for writers and sluts alike. Thus, many of the terms in this book may be unfamiliar to you and may be defined differently in different regions and communities. In this glossary we'll define these words, and some others you may encounter in openly sexual communities, as we understand them.

BDSM: Activities in which one person controls the behavior of another, and/or puts them in bondage, and/or gives them intense sensations. BDSM derives from B/D for bondage and discipline, D/S for dominance and submission, and S/M (or SM or S&M) for sadomasochism. You may also hear it called "erotic power exchange" or just plain "SM."

Centrist: We use terms like "heterocentrist," "eurocentrist," "male-centrist," "female-centrist," "queer-centrist," and "couple-centrist" to draw attention to unspoken expectations about the way things "should" be. Couple-centrist beliefs, for example, are those that treat the couple as the primary unit of our culture, thus placing anyone who isn't part of a couple outside the mainstream.

Commitment: In common usage, this word seems to mean lifetime monogamy. Obviously, we don't use it that way in this book. To us, "commitment" means making a promise for the future and following through on that promise—whether it's a promise to "cleave unto you only" or to meet for a hot weekend once a year.

Drama: Those of us who have chosen to avoid the well-paved road of social expectations regarding relationships must hack our way through some fairly dense shrubbery to blaze our own pathways. This process sometimes involves misunderstandings, hurt feelings, and so on. "Drama" is a slightly pejorative term for the struggles that often accompany this process.

Faithful: *See* Fidelity.

Fidelity: Outside these pages, this term is generally used to mean having sex only with one person. However, the dictionary says fidelity is "demonstrated by continuing loyalty and support," and that sounds about right to us.

Free love: The idea that it is possible to love and have sex with more than one person as a means of interpersonal connection as well as an idealistic sociopolitical statement—a movement that has spanned centuries, although it was most widely accepted during the 1960s.

Friend with benefits: Current parlance for someone with whom you can have sex (the "benefits" part) without the need to commit to a lifelong romantic relationship (the "friend") part. Also known in some circles as a "fuck buddy."

Fuck: Still the four-letter word that gets the strongest reaction (with the possible exception of "cunt"), but it seems a shame to us that such a nice activity gets used as a curse. Can mean genital sex in general, or specifically penetrative sex such as penis/vagina, penis/anus, or fisting.

Gender: The catchphrase used in gender-explorative circles is, "Your sex is what's between your legs, your gender is what's between your ears." Someone who was born with female genitals and chromosomes, but prefers to interact with the world as a man (possibly using surgery and/or hormones to further that goal), is thus of the male gender. Those who prefer to occupy a place somewhere between the extremes of binary gender, or who like to be playful with their gender presentation, are called "gender-queer," "gender-fluid," or "gender-bent."

Kink: Any form of sex outside the mainstream. Often used specifically for BDSM, leather, and/or fetish play.

Leather: Another way of talking about BDSM and related behaviors. Generally in wider use in gay, lesbian, and queer circles.

Munch: A social get-together of polyfolk in a restaurant or similar location. Munches started as a way for Internet-based polyfolk to meet face to face. Munches have been established for many online communities.

Nonjudgmental: An attitude that is free of irrational or unjustifiable moralizing. "Nonjudgmental" does not mean all-accepting; it means being willing to judge an activity or relationship on the basis of how well it works for the participants and not on some external standard of absolute rightness or wrongness.

Nonmonogamy: We don't generally use this term, because it implies that monogamy is the norm and that any other way of relating is somehow a deviation from that norm (i.e., it's "monogamy-centrist"—see our definition of "Centrist" above).

Nymphomania: *See* Promiscuity.

Openheartedness: Greeting the world with compassion and without defensiveness; opening yourself to whatever love or connection life offers you.

Open relationship: A relationship in which the people involved have some degree of freedom to fuck and/or love people outside the relationship. Hence, an eight-person group marriage may still be either "open" or "closed."

Orientation: Usually used to mean gay, lesbian, bisexual, or heterosexual. Many people engage in sex, romance, and/or intimacy outside the boundaries of their chosen orientation, without feeling the need to change that orientation—it is quite possible that "orientation" has at least as much to do with culture as it does with sex.

Outercourse: Non-penetrative sex, including sex toys, mutual masturbation, phone sex, roleplaying, and such . . . just for fun, or as a safer-sex strategy, or both.

Pansexual: Inclusive of all genders and orientations.

Pathologize: To treat a functional sexual or relationship pattern as a disease, usually because it's unfamiliar.

Polyamory (often shortened to "poly"): A new word that has gained a great deal of currency in recent years. We like it because, unlike "nonmonogamy," it does not assume monogamy as a norm. On the other hand, its meaning is still a bit vague—some feel that polyamory includes all forms of sexual relationships other than monogamy, while others restrict it to committed love relationships (thereby excluding swinging, casual sexual contact, and other forms of intimacy).

Polyfidelity: A subset of polyamory in which more than two people, possibly two or more couples, form a sexually exclusive group. Sometimes used as a safer-sex strategy.

Promiscuity: One of several words used to pathologize those who like to have a lot of sex. Mainstream culture tips its hand about its underlying paradigm of sex-as-commodity when it refers to such people as "cheap."

Public sex: Sex in an environment containing many consenting people, such as a sex party.

Queer: A recently reclaimed word, originally an insult aimed at homosexual people. In some communities this word means specifically "gay or lesbian." However, it is used increasingly as a political/sexual self-definition by anyone who doesn't fit neatly into mainstream sexual expectations. Often combined with a description of what makes you queer, as in "genderqueer" or "leatherqueer."

Reclaiming: If someone uses a word about you in an attempt to insult or offend you, you can either get angry, or you can defuse the word by using it yourself so it's no longer an insult. Words that have been reclaimed in this way include "queer," "dyke," "fag," and, yes, "slut."

Sex: Frankly, it doesn't matter what definition *we* use; sex is whatever you and your partners think it is. Whatever you think sex is, we approve of it—because all forms of consensual sex are wonderful.

Sex addiction: The subject of heated debate in sex therapy communities, this phrase refers to compulsive sexual behavior that takes over a person's life to the extent that it interferes with healthy functioning in relationships, work, or other aspects of life. Far too often used as a way of pathologizing happy sluts.

Sex-negative: Sex is dangerous. Sexual desire is wrong. Female sexuality is destructive and evil. Male sexuality is predatory and uncontrollable. It is the task of every civilized human being to confine sexuality within very narrow limits. Sex is the work of the devil. God hates sex. Got the picture?

Sex-positive: The belief that sex is a healthy force in our lives. This phrase was created by sex educators at the National Sex Forum in the late 1960s. It describes a person or group that maintains an optimistic, open-minded, nonjudgmental attitude toward all forms of consensual sexuality.

Slut: A person who celebrates sexuality with an open mind and an open heart.

Transsexual ("transman," "transwoman," etc.): Someone who identifies as a gender different from the one that their chromosomes and/or genitals dictate. Transfolk may or may not decide to take hormones and/or have surgery to change their physical appearance. Some transfolk are *reclaiming* the formerly derogatory term "tranny."

Resource Guide

The following is a list of books, websites, networks, and other resources for polyamory and other sexually adventurous lifestyles. New books and resources about polyamory and open relationships are proliferating like bunnies in the springtime, and we can't keep up with all of them—so our apologies if we've omitted your favorite.

The books we're most familiar with are all terrific, and each one offers viewpoints that others don't, but as of the latest count we know of dozens more, each with lots to offer. Read them all, but if you can only afford a few, we suggest that you check out the ones we list here.

GENERAL POLYAMORY

Opening Up: A Guide to Creating and Sustaining Open Relationships, Tristan Taormino (Cleis Press, 2008). Offers a taxonomy of all the many kinds of open relationships and includes interviews with hundreds of people who are succeeding at nontraditional lifestyles.

Polyamory: The New Love without Limits, Dr. Deborah Anapol (Intinet Resource Center, 1997). The classic text for those seeking group marriages and other long-term multipartner committed relationships.

Redefining Our Relationships: Guidelines for Responsible Open Relationships, Wendy-O Matik (Defiant Times Press, 2002). Targeted to younger alternative relationship–seekers, this book frames open relationships as a radical choice that is political as well as personal.

Alt.polyamory (www.polyamory.org). Start your search for poly-friendly information and resources here. Support groups, communities, mailing lists, and such come and go more quickly than we can keep up with in a printed book, but you can find up-to-date information and links to groups all over the world here, as well as relevant articles, glossaries, book reviews, and much more.

Society for Human Sexuality (www.sexuality.org). This remarkably comprehensive website links to hundreds if not thousands of articles, reviews, and other resources about all forms of human sexuality.

Poly in the Media (polyinthemedia.blogspot.com). If you're curious about news coverage of goings-on in polyland, check out this blog.

DATING AND RELATIONSHIPS

If the Buddha Dated, Charlotte Kasl (Penguin, 1999). How to navigate the world of dating openheartedly, without hauling along all your expectations.

Human Awareness Institute (www.hai.org). These folks put on excellent weekend-long workshops on intimacy, sex, and love, all over the world.

Tribe (www.tribe.net). "Tribes" of like-minded individuals include ethical sluts, as well as general polyamory tribes and some regional polyamory tribes.

Adult Friend Finder (www.adultfriendfinder.com). If you're seeking a relationship that is primarily sexual and/or kinky in nature, check out this website.

Cuddle Party (www.cuddleparty.com). Cuddle parties are fun, friendly social events in which participants can explore touch and cuddling without sexual expectations.

Lifestyles (www.lifestyles.org). Information, ideas, and events for folks who are specifically interested in swinging.

PolyMatchMaker (www.polymatchmaker.com). Most dating services assume that you're seeking a monogamous relationship; some will refuse to do business with you if you're looking for something else. A happy exception is PolyMatchMaker. Their website also offers links to useful articles and websites.

SEX

The Erotic Mind, Jack Morin (Harper, 1996). A brilliant untangling of the eternal conflict between the comfortable ease of long-term relationships and the passionate tension required for hot sex.

The Good Vibrations Guide to Sex, Cathy Winks and Anne Semans (Cleis Press, 2002). A thorough, inclusive guide to how sex actually works.

Hot Monogamy, Patricia Love and Jo Robinson (Plume, 1995). Who better to teach you how to keep your relationship sexy than the folks who have committed to having sex with only one person for the rest of their lives?

Urban Tantra, Barbara Carrellas (Celestial Arts, 2007). How to use the techniques of tantra—breath, gaze, motion, and so on—to bring greater intensity and connection to your sex play. Inclusive of all genders and orientations, including BDSM/leather.

San Francisco Sex Information (www.sfsi.org). Our friends at this website maintain a useful and accessible information line. They can answer your questions one-on-one, by telephone (415-989-SFSI) or online.

American Social Health Association (www.ashastd.org). For the latest information about safer sex and sexually transmitted diseases, check out this website.

MANAGING CONFLICT

The Intimate Enemy: How to Fight Fair in Love and Marriage, George R. Bach and Peter Wyden (Morrow, 1968). The concept of "fair fighting" was first expounded by Dr. Bach in this wonderful book. Published forty years ago, the book is somewhat outdated, but the material on communication, and detailed descriptions of constructive ways to share your anger with a partner, is priceless—this book is a classic.

Difficult Conversations, Douglas Stone, Bruce Patton, Sheila Heen, and Roger Fisher (Penguin, 2000). How to discuss the uncomfortable—not just with your lover(s) but with anyone.

Nonviolent Communication: A Language of Life, Marshall B. Rosenberg and Arun Gandhi (Puddledancer Press, 2003). One of the best contemporary books for dealing with communications skills in conflict of all sorts.

Poly-Friendly Professionals (www.polychromatic.com/pfp). Provides lists of counselors, attorneys, therapists, physicians, and other professionals who are familiar and nonjudgmental about alternative relationship structures.

Kink-Aware Professionals (www.ncsfreedom.org/kap). Lists professionals (doctors, attorneys, therapists, bodyworkers, and more) who are nonjudgmental about BDSM, leather, kink, fetish, and other alternative modes of sexual expression.

LEGAL AND SOCIAL ISSUES

A Legal Guide for Lesbian and Gay Couples (Nolo, 2007). A useful book with a CD-ROM that can help you set up whatever legal underpinnings your relationships require.

Living Together: A Legal Guide for Unmarried Couples (Nolo, 2008). Another useful resource with an accompanying CD-ROM.

The National Coalition for Sexual Freedom (www.ncsfreedom.org) and the Woodhull Foundation (www.woodhullfoundation.org). Information about protecting your legal and political rights as a practitioner of a nontraditional sexual lifestyle. Please support them with your charitable donations.

Index

About the Authors

DOSSIE EASTON is a licensed marriage and family therapist specializing in alternative sexualities and relationships, with twenty years of experience counseling open relationships. She is the author of four other books. She has been an ethical slut since 1969.

Visit www.dossieeaston.com.

JANET W. HARDY is the author of more than 10 books and founder of Greenery Press, a San Francisco Bay Area book publisher specializing in sexually adventurous books. She has an MFA in creative writing from St. Mary's College. She swore off monogamy in 1987.

Visit www.janetwhardy.com.

Dossie and Janet have authored several other books, available from Greenery Press.

When Someone You Love Is Kinky is for the friends, family, coworkers, and partners of anyone who's involved in an alternative sexuality like S/M, D/S, leather, crossdressing, or fetish. (Note: Janet wrote this book under her former pen name, "Catherine A. Liszt.")

The New Bottoming Book and *The New Topping Book* show how to bring all your power, sexiness, and smarts to your role as a BDSM bottom or top.

Radical Ecstasy: SM Journeys to Transcendence chronicles Dossie's and Janet's individual and mutual experiences with altered states of consciousness during BDSM play and offers some ideas drawn from tantra and other practices about how to journey there yourself.

Janet is also the author of several other books: *The Sexually Dominant Woman* and *The Compleat Spanker* (both written as "Lady Green"), *The Toybag Guide to Canes and Caning, Twenty-First Century Kinky-Crafts,* and (with Dr. Charles Moser) *Sex Disasters . . . And How to Survive Them.*